Research on Technology in Social Studies Education

A volume in
Research Methods for Educational Technology
Walt Heinecke, *Series Editor*

Research on Technology in Social Studies Education

John Lee
North Carolina State University

Adam M. Friedman
Wake Forest University

INFORMATION AGE PUBLISHING, INC.
Charlotte, NC • www.infoagepub.com

Library of Congress Cataloging-in-Publication Data

Lee, John (John K.)
  Research on technology in social studies education / John Lee, Adam M.
Friedman.
      p. cm. – (Research methods in educational technology)
  Includes bibliographical references.
  ISBN 978-1-60752-278-2 (pbk.) – ISBN 978-1-60752-279-9 (hardcover)
  1. Social sciences–Study and teaching (Elementary)–United States. 2.
Educational technology–United States. I. Friedman, Adam M. II. Title.
  LB1584.L396 2009
  372.83–dc22

                                                    2009035539

Printed in the United States of America

CONTENTS

SECTION 1
RESEARCH CONSTRUCTS AND CONTEXTS

1 More to Follow: The Untapped Research Agenda
in Social Studies and Technology 3
John K. Lee and Adam M. Friedman

2 Using the Affordances of Technology to Develop Teacher
Expertise in Historical Inquiry 19
John W. Saye and Thomas Brush

3 Student-Created Digital Documentaries in the History
Classroom: Outcomes, Assessment, and Research Design 39
Thomas Hammond and Bill Ferster

4 Conceptual Change and the Process of Becoming a Digital
History Teacher 67
Philip E. Molebash, Rosemary Capps, and Kelly Glassett

SECTION 2
RESEARCH ON STUDENTS' LEARNING IN SOCIAL STUDIES WITH TECHNOLOGY

5 Student and Teacher Perceptions of the WebQuest Model in
Social Studies: A Preliminary Study.. 101
Phillip J. VanFossen

6 Multimedia-Based Historical Inquiry Strategy Instruction:
Do Size and Form Really Matter? 127
David Hicks and Peter E. Doolittle

SECTION 3

RESEARCH ON TEACHERS USING TECHNOLOGY
IN SOCIAL STUDIES

7 If You Build It, Should I Run?: A Teacher's Perspective
on Implementing a Student-Centered, Digital Technology
Project in His Ninth-Grade Geography Classroom 155
Sonja Heer Yow and Kathleen Owings Swan

8 Technology Integration: The Trojan Horse for School Reform.... 173
Cheryl Mason Bolick

9 The Effect of Teachers' Conceptions of Student Abilities
and Historical Thinking on Digital Primary Source Use 189
Adam M. Friedman

SECTION 4

RESEARCH REVIEWS

10 Utilizing the Power of Technology for Teaching with
Geography.. 207
Tina L. Heafner

11 Artificial Intelligence in the Social Studies.................................... 231
Daniel W. Stuckart and Michael J. Berson

12 Digital History: Researching, Presenting, and Teaching
History in a Digital Age 253
Fred Koehl and John K. Lee

SECTION 1

RESEARCH CONSTRUCTS AND CONTEXTS

CHAPTER 1

MORE TO FOLLOW

The Untapped Research Agenda in Social Studies and Technology

John K. Lee and Adam M. Friedman

In 2001 at the height of a long period of enthusiasm about technology use in seemingly all aspects of life in the United States, Larry Cuban issued a scathing critique of the impact of computer technology in the public schools. In his 2001 book, *Underused and Oversold: Computers in the Classroom,* Cuban argued that the use of computers in the classroom has not transformed teaching and learning in the ways that some claimed it would. At the same time educational technology enthusiasts continue to trumpet the potential of new technologies to transform teaching and learning (see Levin, 2008 for one particularly wide reaching example). These claims and counterclaims fit neatly within what has emerged as a superficial and common debate pitting supporters and detractors of classroom computer technology (see also Oppenheimer, 1997). While these two sides are essentially split on the question of whether technology has or will transform education, it seems as if the disagreements have emerged because we are asking the wrong questions about technology use in education. In commenting about the lack of

Research on Technology in Social Studies Education, pages 3–17
Copyright © 2009 by Information Age Publishing
All rights of reproduction in any form reserved.

effectiveness of large scale technology integration efforts in education, Harris (2005) noted that "perhaps a new approach is warranted at this point in time—one that genuinely respects pedagogical plurality and honors teachers' academic freedom" (p. 121). In this book, we aim to extend Harris's critique to suggest that a more reasoned and well-informed consideration of technology use in education can emerge from research and scholarship focused on discovering the educational technology applications that have deep and consistent academic and pedagogical potential.

Unfortunately, a considerable amount of technology use within social studies to date has proceeded without supporting research findings. Despite limited research in the past twenty years, technology tools have emerged as central to teaching and learning in social studies, and recent surveys of students and teachers reveal this trend. The 2006 Project Tomorrow Net Day Speak Up survey, which reached more than 230,000 K–12 students, teachers, and parents across the United States, provides a snapshot of technology use in schools. The survey results paint a picture of increasingly refined and wide-ranging technology uses. The survey showed that 77% of teachers believe technology makes a difference in learning and that an equally large number use technology in their everyday teaching. These findings support survey findings from other research that suggest technology is increasingly being used in all school subjects including social studies. In a survey of 158 social studies teachers, Hicks, Doolittle, and Lee (2004) found that more than 60% of the teachers used web-based primary historical resources at least two to three times a month (see Lee, Doolittle, & Hicks, 2006 for similar findings from a survey of a single school system). The same patterns can be seen in technology use among social studies teacher educators and members of the College and University Faculty Assembly (CUFA). In three separate studies (1999, 2001, 2005–2006), technology use among CUFA members has markedly increased (Berson, Mason, Heinecke, & Coutts, 2001; Bolick, Berson, Coutts, & Heinecke, 2003; Bolick, Berson, Friedman, & Porfeli, 2007).

However, what we know much less about is the quality of these uses of technology. Recent research has suggested that even with increases in technology utilization within the social studies classroom, much of this use has been unsophisticated. In addition to finding that social studies teachers used technological resources with some regularity, Hicks et al. (2004) found that teachers' uses of technology were limited with regard to the disciplinary nature of that work. Similarly, in a study of Indiana social studies teachers, VanFossen (1999–2000) reported that although the majority of respondents felt comfortable using the Internet and almost every respondent (95.8%) had access, nearly half (48.7%) were "low-frequency users," and of those that did use the Internet, many did so in an unsophisticated manner (p. 99). In a similar study of social studies teachers in North Carolina, Friedman (2008) found that almost all respondents (97.2%) used the Internet regularly, however many did so for their own edification, and when using technology tended to assign students low-level tasks.

Surveys on technology use in social studies only paint a partial picture of the extent to which technology, particularly computer technology, has been effectively and meaningfully integrated into social studies education. To better understand how technology is being used in social studies, we need to look at the broader literature, which suggests that technology is being used, but that use is not particularly advanced, sophisticated, or effective. These shallow uses of technology, or what Cuban refers to as "underuse," may be a consequence of a lack of a research-based understanding of what works and does not work. For the past 20 plus years, the National Council for the Social Studies publication *Social Education* has published reports on technology use in social studies. Bolick, McGlinn, and Siko (2006) recently reported on the history of these publications, identifying 87 articles from 1983 to 2006 on social studies and technology. These articles spanned topics from reviews of technology tools to descriptions of practice in the social studies classroom using technology. Bolick, McGlinn, and Siko (2006) did not find many reports on research. While, in all fairness, *Social Education* does not publish research reports on a regular basis, the lack of research reports in the journal is reflective of a larger trend in social studies. Illustrative of this trend, VanFossen and Shiveley (2003) found in a review of technology presentations at the National Council for the Social Studies that the vast majority of presentations were non-research, with less that 5% of the presentations being research-oriented.

Other reviews of more research-oriented outlets have resulted in similar findings. *Theory and Research in Social Education* (TRSE), the flagship research journal of CUFA and the social studies teacher education community, has published two themed issues focused on technology (2001 and 2007) in addition to numerous other reports of research on social studies and technology. The sum total of these publications is less than twenty over the last ten years, representing less than 10% of all the publications in TRSE over that time period. Counter to this overall trend, there is one publication, *CITE Journal Social Studies* (also endorsed by CUFA and available online at http://www.citejournal.org/socialstudies/) that is exclusively focused on social studies and technology; the only publication with such a mission. The mission of the journal notwithstanding, *CITE Journal Social Studies* has only published 17 data-based research reports since 2000 (out of a total of 31 articles published). There are other technology-related journals that have published special issues with reports on social studies and technology, such as the *Journal of Computing in Teacher Education* Volume 20 Issue 4, which included six articles on technology use in social studies teacher education, two of which were reports on research. Likewise, the *International Journal of*

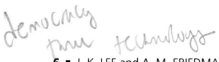

Social Education Volume 21, Issue 1 which was a themed issue focusing on citizenship education entitled "Enhancing Democracy through Technology." Of the 10 articles published in this edition, two were research-based. Overall the research and theoretical reports that have been reported represent an initial corpus of evidence on topics such as how social studies teachers are prepared and how students in social studies are learning through the use of technology. But even with this emerging record of research, much more needs to be known before we can act with confidence on specific uses of technology in social studies.

Research on social studies and technology is situated within a larger framework of research on education in general. Recently, efforts to expand educational research have occupied a front and center position in the journals *Educational Researcher* and *American Educational Research Journal*. For example, Slavin (2002) presented an argument for evidence-based research, randomized trials, and research replication in educational research. This call echoed a more general call from the United States Department of Education for educational researchers to conduct 'scientific' research, as they are encouraged to report upon empirical research that aims to collect evidence-based measures of the impact of various teaching methodologies and tools on student learning gains and achievement. The United States Department of Education advocates using "randomized control trials" to evaluate the effectiveness of an educational policy or practice (U.S. Department of Education, 2003, p. 1), and has created the 'What Works Clearinghouse' as a method of "provid[ing] educators, policymakers, researchers, and the public with a central and trusted source of scientific evidence of what works in education" (Institute of Education Sciences, n.d., online). In a critique of educational research on technology, Roblyer (2005) laid out an argument for four distinct types of research all built on foundational methodological pillars related to significance, rationale, design, reporting results, and place of a given study in a larger body of research. The four types of research Roblyer (2005) described include (1) Research to Establish Relative Advantage, (2) Research to Improve Implementation Strategies, (3) Research to Monitor Impact on Important Societal Goals, and (4) Studies That Monitor and Report on Common Uses and Shape Desired Directions.

Given these contexts, the educational research we need to be conducting will not be easy. Berliner (2002) has noted that educational researchers "face particular problems and must deal with local conditions that limit generalizations and theory-building" (p. 18). In other words, because schools, teachers, and students were not designed for experiments, evidence-based research can be exceptionally difficult. Further, because teaching is central to economic and social well-being, educational researchers need to make a special effort to design and implement meaningful research in the complex environments that schools present. This was reflected in a recent commentary in *Educational Researcher* that called for educational research to be rooted in "serv[ing] people's well being" (Hostetler, 2005, p. 16). We agree with this sentiment and hope to see such an ethos extended into research on social studies and technology.

The need for data-based research is particularly acute within the field of social studies and technology; not only is it a nascent field necessitating new conceptualizations, but it has been characterized as both in its "adolescence" (Berson & Balyta, 2004, p. 148) and "research light" (Friedman & Hicks, 2006, p. 251). While there is a current dearth of research reports in social studies and technology, this is not reason enough for a call to research. Instead, as the primary purpose of social studies is to prepare the young people of today to be the citizens of tomorrow, it is necessary to examine how technology tools impact, improve, and otherwise affect teaching and learning in social studies. Ultimately, the effectiveness of technology is tied to the purpose of education within the specific content area. Such connections between educational aims, content, and technology form a context for the evaluation of the effectiveness of particular instructional approaches. In social studies, this might result in the evaluation of specific historical thinking tools that would support the development of the critical literacy needed by young people to actively contribute in a democratic life. Given these circumstances, we have prepared this collection of research conceptualizations, reports, and reviews to achieve three goals.

1. Put forward reports on how research is being conducted in the field.
2. Present findings from well-designed research studies that provide evidence of how specific applications of technology are affecting teaching and learning in social studies given the purposes of social studies.
3. Showcase reviews of research in social studies.

It is with this framework that we edited this volume, *Research on Technology and Social Studies Education*, as an effort to address emerging concerns related to theorizing about the field and reporting research in social studies and technology. The book is divided into four sections. The first section of the book includes three descriptions of research constructs and contexts in social studies and technology. The second section is focused on research reports from studies of student learning in social studies with technology. The third section contains research reports on teachers' pedagogical considerations for using technology in social studies. In the fourth and final section, we present work that broadly reviews and critiques research in focused areas of social studies and technology.

We have made an effort in this book to present deeply contextualized ideas about how researchers' approach their work. In Chapter 2, John Saye and Tom Brush theorize about their research, which is informed by nearly a decade of focused work on how best to utilize technology to create a professional development community that describes teaching social studies through problem-based historical inquiry. Their work is centered on professional development as a means of demonstrating and exemplifying to teachers how problem-based historical inquiry can be implemented. Through their Persistent Issues in History (PIH) project, Saye and Brush seek for students to engage in higher order thinking in a technology-rich environment as they consider overarching questions on historical problems and ideas. Saye and Brush have designed open-ended learning environment (OELE) technologies to support the PIH project. The OELE allows for video clips to be uploaded and displayed, as well as enabling communication and interaction between and among teachers and researchers. This professional development is undertaken with the understanding that the end goal is for students to engage in inquiry, and accordingly, scaffolding techniques are included.

Saye and Brush as well as Hammond and Ferster propose work that may very well result in teachers fundamentally altering the way they think about teaching social studies. In Chapter 4, Philip Molebash, Rosemary Capps, and Kelly Glassett pick up this line of theoretical thinking by proposing a model for conceptual change related to using technology in social studies. Similar to Saye and Brush, Molebash, Capps, and Glassett note the importance of students engaging in social studies instruction that is rooted in inquiry and constructivism, and facilitated by the transparent use of technology tools. Molebash, Capps, and Glassett argue that in order for this type of instruction to take place on a wide scale, a conceptual change must occur within teacher education. They present five factors related to teacher educators' beliefs that influence the degree to which this conceptual change occurs including; types of assignments given in class, practice and feedback, time allowed, use of technology, and teacher educator beliefs and presentation. Molebash, Capps, and Glassett's research methodology also involves the study of actual classrooms, as they followed twelve pre-service teachers into the first two years of their in-service teaching. They utilized analytic induction in order to obtain descriptive data on whether pre-service teachers' exposure to inquiry learning during a methods course translated into practice in their classroom.

Tom Hammond and Bill Ferster's approach to assessment and research on student uses of a specific technology tools in social studies exemplifies this contextualized approach. Hammond and Ferster's chapter is presented in the context of a results-driven school and classroom-based research. They lay the framework for using digital documentaries in social studies and advocate for assessment and research strategies that focuses on student learning outcomes. While Hammond and Ferster argue for the use of experimental or quasi-experimental design studies in order to determine digital documentaries' impact on student learning, they simultaneously outline several issues that may limit this type of research. For example, they point out that if a digital documentary is created as a group project with teacher input, it is difficult to determine individual knowledge. To alleviate this concern, they suggest evaluations that are distinct from the digital documentary project work and instead focused on content knowledge, disciplinary knowledge, and writing skills.

This book includes a number of research reports of technology use within various contexts of social studies: from the secondary social studies classroom to university graduate courses and from a specific focus on students learning social studies using technology in high school to more general attention to the culture and community of technology use among master teachers. In the first of these research-based chapters, Phillip VanFossen reports on a study in which he looked at the impact of WebQuest use on teaching and learning between 32 teachers and 796 students from grades 3–11. The teachers had participated in an intensive summer in-service workshop over the course of several days on the design and development of WebQuests, and used these WebQuests as part of their instruction during the following school year. VanFossen surveyed teachers and students around a series of research questions related to perceptions and attitudes about using WebQuests. Beyond specific findings that suggest students and teachers tended to enjoy WebQuests more than traditional teacher-centered activities, the strength VanFossen's work rests in the manner in which he investigated a specific application of technology in social studies. WebQuests, in particular, are a widely utilized, yet under-researched technology application, and VanFossen's work, in concert with other recent research (see Lipscomb, 2002; Milson, 2002; Strickland & Nazzal, 2005), can aid social studies educators as they attempt to make rational and research-informed decisions about technology use.

David Hicks and Peter Doolittle likewise present research findings on student uses of technology from a study of a multimedia scaffold designed to support inquiry learning in history. Their work is based on the assumption, rooted in literature, that children as early as the elementary grades are able to engage in historical inquiry. This inquiry work involves processes in which students analyze historical sources and work toward developing personalized interpretations. Unlike VanFossen who researched a widely used, but lightly theorized technological application in WebQuests, Hicks and Doolittle designed a highly theorized and narrowly focused multimedia scaffold to support specific historical processes known as SCIM-C (Summarizing, Contextualizing, Inferring, Monitoring, and Corroborating). In their chapter, Hicks and Doolittle look at how the multimedia scaffold supports students' SCIM-C work and how it impacts their learning in history. The chapter examines the extent to which the level of strategic engagement with the SCIM-C multimedia scaffold and the nature of the multimedia presentation (animation, narration, and onscreen text) impact students' understandings of historical inquiry and the strategic knowledge required to engage in source analysis. Hicks and Doolittle found that both recall and application of the SCIM-C strategy were greater when students' strategic engagement was more comprehensive, but found no effect for the nature of the multimedia presentation. Their work advances our understanding of how social studies educators might best use SCIM-C as a specific and generalizable instructional tool for supporting students' historical thinking—and advances our understanding of the value-added when manipulating the technological design of the SCIM-C tool.

In their work with a ninth grade geography teacher, Sonja Heer Yow and Kathy Swan look broadly at how the introduction of specific technology tools affect a teacher's efforts to facilitate his students' geographic inquiries. Using a narrative interpretative approach, Yow and Swan report on the story of Henry as he wrestled with the complexities of new technologies in his class. The authors provide rich detail including data from interviews with Henry's students about the progress of the class's work with technology. As with all stories, this one includes a twist and a resolution. Suffice it to say Henry experienced challenges with the new technology. In this work, Yow and Swan demonstrate the importance of technology integration following from a reasoned and deep consideration of content and pedagogy.

Cheryl Mason Bolick applied an equally useful technique in her research by investigating the extent to which teachers in a graduate teacher education program integrate technologies they learned about in their graduate courses into their social studies teaching experiences. She found a disconnect between these teachers' uses of technology as graduate students and their uses as teachers. In her analysis of these findings, Bolick unpacks one of the most persistent claims of technology enthusiasts, namely that technology integration in teacher education can transform teachers' school-based teaching. Like Molebash and Glassett in their theoretical work presented in Chapter 4, Bolick's work provides a valuable research-based example of how social studies educators negotiate through the claims and counter claims of those who advocate for technology in education as transformational.

Adam Friedman's chapter continues the focus on how social studies teachers use technology, this time given specific contexts. Friedman's work is a qualitative study of six world history teachers and the factors that impact their instructional uses of digital primary sources. The goal of this study was to examine the extent to which world history teachers' conceptions of historical thinking as well as student achievement level influenced the frequency and type of digital primary source use. Each of the teachers in this study desired to use digital primary sources and none felt obliged to integrate the use of digital primary sources into their curriculum. The teachers integrated digital primary sources at differing rates with the major determining factor being their beliefs about student abilities. This study illustrates the importance of knowing and understanding the contextual barriers that influence (either positively or negatively) the use of content-specific technology in the secondary classroom. Friedman's study demonstrates that although new technologies have made a wide range of new instructional resources available, this availability in and of itself does not necessarily mean teachers will use the materials.

In the remaining chapters, authors present research framed toward addressing three specific areas of concern in social studies and technology. Tina Heafner's chapter looks at geography by focusing on the use of technology to engage students in higher order thinking. Arguing that technology and geography are a "good fit," Heafner describes how the teaching of geography can be strengthened by the integration of technology resources. Heafner contributes to our understanding of research on technology integration in geography by situating a review of research and theory in a mini-case study of a teacher's uses of specific geography-related technology tools. She notes that in this era of standards and high stakes testing, it is increasingly necessary to incorporate the teaching of geography into other social studies courses. Heafner's chapter presents an overview of a wide variety of studies in both higher education and K–12 schools in which technology was integrated into geography, using tools such as Geographic Information Systems and Internet-based mapping. Heafner cites extensive research that has shown overall positive outcomes as a result of this integration. She concludes by looking toward the future with the application of geo-technologies in K–12 schools, and asserts the importance of student-centered instruction that is scaffolded by the classroom teacher.

In another review of the literature, Daniel Stuckart and Michael Berson present a compelling argument that research on artificial intelligence has progressed to the point where social studies educators are beginning to see tangible opportunities to individualize and personalize instruction. Focusing on the new gaming technologies, Stuckart and Berson see particularly interesting opportunities for social studies educators. They argue that gaming has emerged from the "weak" school of artificial intelligence that views any intelligence represented in artificial systems as partial representations of human intelligence. This argument is advanced by the authors through an historical review of research and general theory in artificial intelligence. This historical approach is valuable not just as a framework for their argument, but also as a model for scholars to analyze similar areas of technology integration in social studies.

In the last chapter, also focused on a review of research, Fred Koehl and John Lee address the manner in which technological changes in the academic discipline of history have affected the teaching and learning of history. In focusing on the conceptual idea of digital history, Koehl and Lee suggest three primary effects related to traditional academic research, the presentation of historical materials, and transformation in the teaching and learning of history. As a review of research, this work provides others interested in research on specific applications of digital history in the teaching and learning of social studies opportunities to situate their work within larger ideas and frames.

Collectively, these twelve chapters represent our effort to bring together in a single volume reports on how technology is influencing social studies teaching and learning. Given this concentrated effort we feel compelled to present some account of where the field of social studies and technology should go next. We might even begin by asking how future research should be conceptually oriented. One possibility would be to situate research on social studies and technology in the emerging theory of Technological Pedagogical Content Knowledge (TPACK), which suggests that meaningful technology integration emerges from deep consideration of content and pedagogy (Mishra & Koehler, 2006). These considerations are transactional and demand close attention to what is gained and lost regarding content and pedagogy when technology is utilized in instruction. We have also argued elsewhere that the TPACK-oriented use of technology in social studies might be conceptualized of as supporting the special aims of social studies related to facilitating democratic life (Lee, 2008).

Considering technology given the unique and special aims and purposes of social studies is important, but within these aims and purposes there exists practice, and it is this practice that represents the ultimate context for research. In an earlier review of research (Hicks, Friedman, & Lee, 2008), we examined research in social studies focused on uses of technology and student learning. In this work we reviewed research studies that focused on social studies, technology, and student learning. Specifically, we focused on two lines of research pursued by Ann Britt and her colleagues as well as John Saye and Tom Brush, whose work also appears in this volume. We need additional research on social studies and technology that is likewise focused on student learning and similarly structured to build on existing findings.

From a research perspective we also need more clarity, as Britt and her colleagues and Saye and Brush have provided, with regard to specific questions that might frame research in social studies and technology. Furthermore, we need more clarity with regard to the sorts of research methods that might facilitate inquiry into these questions. Given these needs and the work presented in this volume, we would suggest the following broadly conceived questions.

1. How does technology support the use of specific subject matter in the teaching and learning of social studies?
2. How do social studies teachers develop meaningful pedagogical knowledge about how to use technology?
3. What are the limits or ranges of technology use in social studies teaching and learning environments?

Within these three broadly conceived areas, there exist numerous specific questions that focus on discrete technologies or approaches to using various types of technologies in social studies. For example, the first question suggests that there exist technologies that might support specific teaching and learning in social studies. Blogs might be an example of a technology that can support specific teaching and learning activities in social studies, namely political discourse. Researchers could specifically investigate how blogging technology (or some related technological iteration of blogging) supports the exchange of ideas in a social studies class. Such research could be developed in the context of existing work on democratic discussion in the classroom by researchers in social studies, such as the research by Diana Hess (see, e.g., Hess & Posselt, 2002) and Walter Parker (see Parker, 2006) as well as by research in general education (see Billings, L, & Fitzgerald, 2002). We already have some investigations of technology-enabled democratic dialogue and discourse in university-level social studies education courses (see Larson & Keiper, 2002; Merryfield, 2003). The point here is to situate and embed new research in existing research on problems and issues that have deep relevance in curricular content and pedagogical ways of thinking. At the risk of belaboring the point, we would like to offer another example of how research on social studies and technology might emerge from such pedagogical and content related contexts.

Research in historical thinking among children might be one of the richest areas of productive and impactful research that has been conducted in social studies over the last three decades (see Ashby, Lee, & Dickinson, 1997; Barton, 1997; Levstik & Barton, 2002; VanSledright, 2002; Wineburg, 1991). What we know about children's abilities to think historically has dramatically altered the landscape of teaching and learning in social studies. Just take standards in California as an example. In 1998 new standards for History-Social Science were adopted in California. These standards reflected research on historical thinking that elucidated how children in elementary grades could engage with authentic historical materials and develop interpretations through the use of adapted disciplinary thinking in history. For example, the California History-Social Science Content Standards (1998) on Analysis Skills require that students "differentiate between primary and secondary sources," that they "pose relevant questions about events they encounter in historical documents," and that they "identify and interpret the multiple causes and effects of historical events." Curriculum standards such as these in the largest state in the United States suggest that historical thinking and students' work with authentic historical resources is deeply valued by the general public and educational community. Simultaneous to this, an explosion of historical source material has become available through the Internet. In their recent book *Digital History*, Cohen and Rosenzweig (2006) described in detail the wide range of digital historical resources available for students and teachers, going so far as to suggest that "the number of authors of history web pages is likely greater than the number of authors of history books" (p. 6). This confluence research on historical thinking and the availability of authentic historical resources on the Web has created conditions that are ripe for investigation on teaching and learning using digital history resources in social studies.

As research in social studies and technology continues to advance it must remain focused on relevant and meaningful questions that help the education community meet the needs of children in social studies classrooms. Such research needs to draw on existing understandings about how children learn and how teachers teach. We hope that this collection of research reports and analyses will aid in the development of richer and more nuanced research activities in social studies and technology.

REFERENCES

Ashby, R., Lee, P., & Dickinson, A. (1997). How children explain the "why" of history: The Chata research project on teaching history. *Social Education, 61*(1), 17–21.

Barton, K. (1997). I just kinda know: Elementary students' ideas about historical evidence. *Theory and Research in Social Education, 25*, 407–430.

Berliner, D. (2002). Educational research: The hardest science of all. *Educational Researcher, 31*(8), 18–20.

Berson, M. J., & Balyta, P. (2004). Technological thinking and practice in the social studies: Transcending the tumultuous adolescence of reform. *Journal of Computing in Teacher Education 20*(4), 141–150.

Berson, M. J., Mason, C. L., Heinecke, W. F., & Coutts, C. B. (2001). Technology innovation: An examination of beliefs and practices of social studies methods faculty. *The International Social Studies Forum, 1*(2), 89–105.

Billings, L., & Fitzgerald, J (2002). Dialogic discussion and the Paideia seminar. *American Educational Research Journal, 39*(4), 907–941.

Bolick, C. M., Berson, M. J., Coutts, C. B., & Heinecke, W. F. (2003). Technology applications in social studies teacher education: A survey of social studies methods faculty. *Contemporary Issues in Technology and Teacher Education [Online serial], 3*(3). Retrieved April 29, 2008 from: http://www.citejournal.org/vol3/iss3/socialstudies/article1.cfm.

Bolick, C. M., Berson, M. J., Friedman, A. M., & Porfeli, E. J. (2007). Diffusion of technology innovation in the preservice social studies experience: Results of a national survey. *Theory and Research in Social Education, 35*(2), 174–195.

Bolick, C. M., McGlinn, M. M., & Siko, K. L. (2006). Twenty years of technology: A retrospective view of *Social Education*'s technology themed issues. *Social Education, 69*(3), 155–161.

California History-Social Science Content Standards. (1998). Retrieved April 29, 2008 from: http://www.cde.ca.gov/be/st/ss/hstmain.asp.

Cohen, D. J., & Rosenzweig, R. (2006). *Digital history: A guide to gathering, preserving, and presenting the past on the web.* Philadelphia: University of Pennsylvania Press.

Cuban, L. (2001). *Oversold and underused: Computers in the classroom.* Cambridge, MA: Harvard University Press.

Friedman, A. M. (2008). Social studies teachers' use of the Internet to foster democratic citizenship. In P. J. VanFossen & M. J. Berson (Eds.), *The electronic republic? The impact of technology on education for citizenship* (pp. 173–195). West Lafayette, IN: Purdue University Press.

Friedman, A. M., & Hicks, D. (2006). The state of the field: Technology, social studies, and teacher education. *Contemporary Issues in Technology and Teacher Education [Online serial], 6*(2). Retrieved April 29, 2008 from: http://www.citejournal.org/vol6/iss2/socialstudies/article1.cfm

Harris, J. (2005). Our agenda for technology integration: It's time to choose. *Contemporary Issues in Technology and Teacher Education* [Online serial], *5*(2). Retrieved April 29, 2008 from: http://www.citejournal.org/vol5/iss2/editorial/article1.cfm

Hess, D., & Posselt, J. (2002). How high school students experience and learn from the discussion of controversial public issues. *Journal of Curriculum and Supervision, 17*(4), 283–314.

Hicks, D., Doolittle, P., & Lee, J. K. (2004). History and social studies teachers' use of classroom and Web-based historical primary sources. *Theory and Research in Social Education, 32*(2), 213–247.

Hicks, D., Friedman, A. M., & Lee, J. K. (2008). Framing research on technology and student learning in the social studies. In L. Bell, L. Schrum, A. Thompson, & G. Bull (Eds.), *Framing research on technology and student learning in the content areas: Implications for teacher educators* (pp. 51–66). Charlotte, NC: Information Age Publishing.

Hostetler, K. (2005). What is "good" education research? *Educational Researcher 34*(6), 16–21.

Institute of Education Sciences. (n.d.). Who we are. Retrieved April 16, 2008, from: http://ies.ed.gov/ncee/wwc/overview/.

Larson, B. E., & Keiper, T. A. (2002). Classroom discussion and threaded electronic discussion: Learning in two arenas. *Contemporary Issues in Technology and Teacher Education [Online serial], 2*(1). Retrieved July 17, 2008, from: http://www.citejournal.org/vol2/iss1/socialstudies/article1.cfm

Lee, J. K. (2008). Toward democracy: Social studies and technological pedagogical content knowledge. In J. Colbert (Ed.), *The handbook of technological pedagogical content knowledge for teaching and teacher educators* (pp. 151–179). Mahwah, NJ: Lawrence Erlbaum.

Lee, J. K., Doolittle, P., & Hicks, D. (2006). Social studies and history teachers' uses of non-digital and digital historical resources. *Social Studies Research and Practice, 1*(2).

Levine, A. (2008). *2008 Horizons Report.* Retrieved April 28, 2008 from: http://www.nmc.org/publications/2008-horizon-report.

Levstik, L., & Barton, K. (2001). *Doing history: Investigating with children in elementary and middle schools.* Mahwah, NJ: Erlbaum.

Lipscomb, G. (2002). Eighth graders' impressions of the Civil War: Using technology in the history classroom. *Education, Communication & Information, 2*(1), 51. Retrieved April 22, 2008, from: http://www.citejournal.org/vol5/iss2/socialstudies/article1.cfm

Merryfield, M. (2003). Like a veil: Cross-cultural experiential learning online. *Contemporary Issues in Technology and Teacher Education [Online serial], 3*(2). Retrieved July 17, 2006, from: http://www.citejournal.org/vol3/iss2/socialstudies/article1.cfm

Milson, A. J. (2002). The Internet and inquiry learning: Integrating medium and method in a sixth grade social studies classroom. *Theory and Research in Social Education, 30*(3), 330–353.

Mishra, P., & Koehler, M. J. (2006). Technological pedagogical content knowledge: A new framework for teacher knowledge. *Teachers College Record, 108*(6), 1017–1054.

Oppenheimer, T. (1997). The computer delusion. Retrieved on April 23, 2008 from: http://www.theatlantic.com/issues/97jul/computer.htm.

Parker, W. C. (2006). Public discourses in schools: Purposes, problems, possibilities. *Educational Researcher, 35*(8), 11–18.

Project Tomorrow-Net day. (2006). *Learning in the 21st century: A national report of online learning.* Retrieved April 08, 2008, from: http://www.tomorrow.org/speakup/learning21Report.html.

Roblyer, M. D. (2005). Educational technology research that makes a difference: Series introduction. *Contemporary Issues in Technology and Teacher Education [Online serial], 5*(2). Retrieved April 29, 2008 from: http://www.citejournal.org/vol5/iss2/seminal/article1.cfm

Slavin, R. (2002). Evidence-based education policies: Transforming educational practice and research. *Educational Researcher, 31*(7), 15–21.

Strickland, J., & Nazzal, A. (2005). Using webquests to teach content: Comparing instructional strategies. *Contemporary Issues in Technology and Teacher Education [Online serial], 5*(2). Retrieved April 22, 2008, from: http://www.citejournal.org/vol5/iss2/socialstudies/article1.cfm

United States Department of Education. (2003). *Identifying and implementing educational practices supported by rigorous evidence: A user friendly guide.* Retrieved on April 16, 2008, from: http://ies.ed.gov/ncee/pdf/evidence_based.pdf.

VanFossen, P. F., & Shiveley, J. (2003). A content analysis of internet sessions presented at the National Council for the Social Studies. *Theory and Research in Social Education, 31*(4), 502–521.

VanFossen, P. (1999-2000). An analysis of the use of the Internet and World Wide Web by secondary social studies teachers in Indiana. *The International Journal of Social Education, 14*(2), 87–109.

VanSledright, B. (2002). *In search of America's past: Learning to read history in elementary school.* New York: Teachers College Press.

Wineburg, S. (1991). Historical problem solving: A study of the cognitive processes used in the evaluation of documentary and pictorial evidence. *Journal of Educational Psychology, 83,* 73–87.

CHAPTER 2

USING THE AFFORDANCES OF TECHNOLOGY TO DEVELOP TEACHER EXPERTISE IN HISTORICAL INQUIRY

John W. Saye and Thomas Brush

ABSTRACT

This chapter presents a model for developing a professional community of practice for problem-based historical inquiry and focuses on how we might use the affordances of technology to construct an open-ended learning environment that develops teacher expertise in leading problem-based historical inquiry. We apply nine years of research and development in the design, testing, and refinement of a set of theory-based wise practices for technology-enhanced problem-based historical inquiry to a discussion of how technological affordances might be embedded in more robust, holistic on-line learning environments to provide teachers with more vivid visions of alternative practices, overcome practicality concerns that dissuade innovation, and facilitate the collaboration necessary for constructing a shared professional knowledge base for problem-based historical inquiry teaching.

Research on Technology in Social Studies Education, pages 19–37

19

INTRODUCTION

History and social studies instruction as it is commonly practiced in U.S. schools is uninspiring and ineffective. Surveys and national test results consistently report that graduates lack the knowledge, skills, and dispositions necessary for effective self-government (Niemi & Sanders, 2004; Tests, 2002). Competent citizens must be able to apply substantive knowledge and skills to solve complex real-world problems that have no easy answers. To develop such civic competency, many social educators have argued that teachers should engage students in deep, rigorous inquiry into the enduring issues and ethical questions that have confronted societies throughout history (Engle & Ochoa, 1988; Oliver & Shaver, 1966; Saye & Brush, 2004a). However, advocacy for problem-based inquiry learning has had little effect. Opportunities to master substantive content knowledge, learn critical reasoning skills, and develop thoughtful positions on societal issues remain glaringly absent from our nation's schools. Instead, the vast majority of social studies classrooms are dull places that emphasize lower-level factual recall based on teacher-directed lecture, recitation, and individual seatwork (Goodlad, 1984; Kagan, 1993; Shaver, Davis, & Helburn, 1979).

The obstacles to inquiry have been well documented and include institutional constraints such as rigid organizational structures and accountability pressures as well as the motivation, epistemological assumptions, and cognitive development levels of learners. These factors interact with teachers' dispositions, expertise, and beliefs about knowledge, teaching, and learning to help explain teacher resistance to issues-centered inquiry (Brush & Saye, 2000; Onosko, 1991; Rossi, 1995; Saye, 1998b; Schlechty, 1993; Windschitl, 2002).

For the past nine years, the Persistent Issues in History (PIH) project has sought to promote inquiry by helping teachers and learners overcome the obstacles to inquiry (Saye & Brush, 2004a). We refer to our model for historical inquiry as problem-based historical inquiry. Like other versions of historical inquiry, we ask students to interpret historical artifacts and construct historical narratives. However, the central purpose for our inquiry is to use those understandings to make decisions about fundamental societal questions as they arise in particular historical events (Massaro, 1993; Oliver & Shaver, 1996; Saye & Brush, 2004a). For instance, we might ask: "Who was most responsible for the rise and escalation of the Cold War?" Students investigate the early Cold War period in order to form a defensible conclusion on the question. This question represents a larger, enduring social issue: "When are nations justified in intervening in the affairs of other countries?" In such investigations we are careful to respect the unique historical context in which a particular event occurred. However, considering the persistent issue as it is instantiated in the early Cold War can help students reason about later historical instances of the issue such as the Vietnam War and contemporary instances such as U.S. involvement in Iraq.

A large part of our effort has focused on investigating how the affordances of technology might facilitate inquiry. Originally, we concentrated much of our attention on the development of technology-supported learning environments for students that would provide more engaging experiences with social reality and help learners to manage the heavy cognitive load of rigorous inquiry (Brush & Saye, 2001; Saye & Brush, 1999, 2002). However, as we witnessed teachers struggle to envision and implement inquiry, we became convinced that mastery of inquiry-based practices by teachers presented an even greater barrier to disciplined inquiry than the difficulties we had sought to mitigate in student learners. As a result, we have shifted the emphasis of the PIH project to professional teacher development. This chapter presents a model for developing a professional community of practice for problem-based historical inquiry and focuses on how we might use the affordances of technology to construct an open-ended learning environment that develops teacher expertise in leading problem-based historical inquiry.

Our efforts assume that a major reason that inquiry has failed to take hold in the schools rests in the pragmatic, craft knowledge paradigm that typifies school culture. This perspective questions the value of theory-based knowledge produced by university researchers and promoted in colleges of education. Instead, teachers trust the craft knowledge generated by practitioners. Researcher knowledge is public, propositional, and replicable. In contrast, craft knowledge is concrete and tied to problems of practice in specific classrooms (Hiebert, Gallimore, & Stigler, 2002). Those who hold a craft conception of teaching knowledge understand teaching to be a personal, private, pragmatic enterprise learned only from direct experience. Given the practical bent of the teacher culture, a major reason for the lack of inquiry in schools is the lack of inquiry in schools: Teachers lack models in their own schools for envisioning successful inquiry practice. Without demonstrations of effective practice in real classrooms, teachers are unlikely to entertain teaching that deviates so much from the norm (Cuban, 1984; Doyle & Ponder, 1978-79, Elbaz, 1981; Kagan, 1993; Lortie, 1975; McNeil, 1986).

Theorists have argued that reform-based learning strategies might take root if we integrated teachers' practical knowledge with researcher knowledge in ways that produced a professional teacher knowledge base that practitioners would value (Heibert et al., 2002; Saye, 1999). This sort of professional knowledge would retain key characteristics of the craft culture in that it is organized around concrete problems of practice. However, professional knowledge would add to those pragmatic concerns additional elements that have more in common with science. Professional teaching knowledge would be public and stored in ways that make it easily shared and verifiable. The verification process would link concrete examples to generalizable principles that apply beyond a single context. Some advocates have suggested that shared professional knowledge that connects practice to theory might be developed through mentoring, peer teaching, or the formation of collaborative professional communities of teachers and researchers (Clark et al., 1996; Derry et al., 2002; Garet et al., 2001; Martin, 2002; Slavin, 1996).

Our work with teachers has focused on creating a professional knowledge culture for problem-based historical inquiry. Recognizing the pragmatic nature of the craft culture and the difficulty of inciting cultural change (e.g., Sarason, 1982), we have focused on how interactive technologies might augment other professional development strategies to facilitate the change process. Some scholars have theorized that technology might encourage the development of professional teaching knowledge by providing easy access to concrete examples of powerful instruction that allow teachers to envision alternative teaching practices (Hiebert et al., 2002). Others advocates have argued that technology might be used to help overcome practical impediments to inquiry (Dwyer, 1994; Saye, 1998a). We have applied these ideas to collaborations with classroom teachers that design, test, and refine a set of theory-based wise practices for our model of technology-enhanced inquiry. One outcome of that work is a continuously evolving open-ended learning environment (OELE) for professional teacher development: the PIH Network (Saye & Brush, 2004a, 2005).

OELEs harness technology in ways that allow complex concepts to be realistically represented, manipulated, and explored (Land, 2000). Although little research and development have been done with social studies OELEs, substantial work has been done in science and mathematics investigating the potential of OELEs for student learning (e.g., Hickey, Moore, & Pellegrino, 2001; Kolodner et al., 2003; Pedersen & Liu, 2003). We believe that holistic OELEs hold great promise for developing professional teaching knowledge as well. The PIH Network OELE currently features a number of integrated modules including a suite of authoring tools, multimedia cases of wise practice, and communications tools for discussing practice and sharing work in progress. The research we review in this chapter suggests that existing Network resources assist teachers in considering and implementing inquiry practice. However, the PIH OELE remains a work in progress. Our research continues to explore how we might maximize the affordances of technology to create a truly robust OELE for developing professional teaching knowledge for inquiry-based history.

TECHNOLOGICAL AFFORDANCES FOR ENHANCING THE DEVELOPMENT OF PROFESSIONAL KNOWLEDGE

The affordances of technology may enhance the development of professional teaching knowledge in at least three ways: (1) by providing more vivid visions of the possible; (2) by addressing practicality concerns about the feasibility of inquiry; and (3) by facilitating collaborations that overcome teacher isolation and encourage shared knowledge. OELEs allow designers to address each of these needs within a holistic context in which technology tools can be employed flexibly to assist the construction of complex understandings.

Visions of the Possible: Representing Professional Teaching Knowledge in OELEs

Although they hold a great deal of craft teaching knowledge for direct instruction, most teachers approach inquiry-based teaching as novices (Cuban, 1984; Hiebert et al., 2002). When we ask teachers to entertain this alternative model of practice, they must first envision how it might work in the nuanced, multiply confounded world of the classroom. Situated cognition theorists, studying the role that apprenticeship plays in developing expertise in a variety of real-world activities (Brown, Collins, & Duguid, 1989), have urged that the principles of cognitive apprenticeship be applied to more formal learning as well, including teacher education (Korthagen & Kessels, 1999). If knowledge is fundamentally linked to the situation in which it arises and is used, the utility of a cognitive apprenticeship experience is related directly to the scenario's correspondence to how practitioners use the pertinent knowledge in real-world contexts. In the case of teachers seeking to master problem-based historical inquiry, the most relevant situating context is a unit of instruction for students.

An essential first step in guiding novices toward mastery in a given task is to provide a model of exemplary performance. Models of exemplary teacher lessons may be provided through text and images. However, the affordances of interactive technologies allow us to create more realistic representations of this complex social interaction. Some researchers in math, science, and reading have experimented with using technologies to facilitate teacher preparation in this manner (Barab et al., 2001; Derry et al., 2002; Schrader et al., 2003), but few examples exist for history and social studies.

We have experimented for several years with the notion that tangible examples of problem-based inquiry practice captured in classroom video footage might provide authentic models that invite teachers to reconsider their practice. We have evidence that when teachers share video episodes of their teaching among a group of their peers, discussions of practice become qualitatively different. In a study focusing on peer mentoring, we had initial difficulties encouraging teachers to share their experiences and rationales for practice decisions. However, viewing video episodes of their lessons provided a shared context that seemed to encourage teachers to de-privatize their teaching knowledge and engage in rich dialogue that linked particular instances to broader theoretical principles. Most significantly, the public reflections on the video episodes by those teachers whose practice most closely exemplified problem-based historical inquiry professional knowledge seemed to stimulate other teachers to entertain connections between theory and practice that had been missing from their prior conversations (Saye et al., 2009).

The notion of educative curriculum materials for professional teacher development has stimulated us to consider how we might enhance these kinds of experiences to move closer to a powerful professional development OELE for problem-based historical inquiry. Educative curriculum materials promote teacher thinking about practice through work with student learning materials that have been re-purposed with a focus on the teacher as the learner (Davis & Krajcik, 2005). Traditional teacher guides often suggest procedures and activities, but rarely expose the pedagogical rationale and assumptions about knowledge, teaching, and learning that lie behind the design of instructional materials or the recommendations for their use. Educative curriculum materials should deepen teachers' understanding of key disciplinary concepts and frameworks while also encouraging connections between theory and practice that lead to an integrated professional knowledge base for teaching. For instance, the PIH model encourages designing units around central questions that exemplify persistent societal issues. In our model, students first encounter the central question in the introductory unit lesson. Educative materials accompanying the introductory lesson of a PIH unit on the Civil Rights Movement might address the theoretical rationale and supporting research for building units around central questions. Teachers who grasp the rationale for focusing units around a central question have generalizable knowledge that should not only affect the emphasis they give to the central question throughout the Civil Rights unit for example, but their willingness and ability to organize future units around essential ideas.

Although educative curriculum resources may be paper documents that accompany student instructional materials, technological applications could increase the resources' educative power. We are currently building more complex on-line multimedia cases that use hypermedia affordances to link wise practice video to teaching materials, teacher reflections, and student work products in order to test how situating video cases within a more

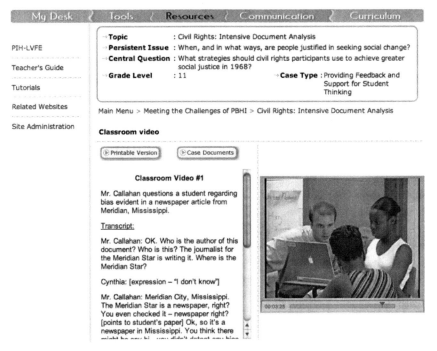

Figure 2.1   Video case of problem-based historical inquiry wise practice.

holistic context might enhance the growth of professional teaching knowledge. For instance, in our investigations of how teachers scaffold inquiry, we identified several teachers who demonstrated considerable scaffolding skills (Saye & Brush, 2006). We filmed one of those teachers engaged in the challenging task of supporting student interrogation of a source document for its subtext. In order to provide a fuller model of exemplary scaffolding of student thinking, we linked that video case to the source document with which the teacher and student are working, a transcript of the discussion, and an audio track of the teacher reflecting on the episode (Figure 2.1). Teachers who have participated in intensive professional development with the PIH project have reported that such models were indispensable in allowing them to overcome procedural, conceptual, and strategic obstacles to adapting their practice for problem-based inquiry (Saye et al., 2009). For instance one of our partners commented:

> History has always been content cans. The challenge was what goes in the can. I knew something was fundamentally wrong with that. The process of clearly articulating that [unit] spine of a Central Question-Culminating Activity will help a lot of teachers jump the hurdle to real planning ... once you formalize it [your planning]; it's repeatable. We become professionals ... And seeing

good models—I couldn't have done it [changed his planning] without seeing [a model].

Although these multimedia cases provide more educative power than video examples alone, we can do more. Through past observations of novices struggling to operate in a given problem domain we can anticipate many of the procedural, conceptual, strategic, and metacognitive difficulties that other novices are likely to encounter. These understandings allow us to embed additional support into authentic teaching scenarios so that it is available when novices are most likely to need it. We are currently developing expanded versions of multimedia cases that are anchored in a unit of instruction and include embedded contextual questions, reflection prompts, models, and explanations that seek to support teachers in linking concrete instances of instruction to broader theoretical principles and foundational subject matter knowledge.

Technology can also provide affordances for professional development OELEs that go beyond modeling and allow virtual apprenticeships to more closely approximate real-time apprenticeship experiences. In real-time apprenticeships, the expert models the task and then observes as novices attempt the same undertaking. In this process, the expert can

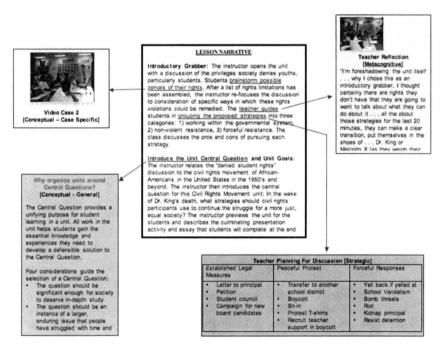

Figure 2.2 Interactive educative curriculum materials.

support novices' development through questioning, coaching, and providing context-specific information. Although it is impossible in on-line environments to replicate fully the quality of this level of support, discussion forums and blogs that are monitored by more experienced teacher, teacher educators, and content experts can provide greater interactivity that more closely approximates a real-time apprenticeship experience. To enhance the interactivity of such interchanges, we are experimenting with the construction of powerful communications interfaces and authoring tools that allow participants to access and link work products and video examples to ongoing on-line discussions. The potential for rich communication presented by such multimedia affordances offers the possibility of new avenues for understanding that in some cases might improve upon the experience available in a real-time apprenticeship. Although this line of investigation is in the developmental phase, our recent work in cultivating inquiry mentors suggests that providing more holistic experiences that link underlying rationales and assumptions to specific instructional examples and creating powerful, transparent tools for facilitating dialogue and representing knowledge hold substantial promise for developing a shared professional knowledge base about inquiry practice (Saye et al., 2009).

Practicality: Scaffolding the Cognitive Load of Student Inquiry

Examinations of teachers attempting inquiry in social studies classes reveal the tremendous cognitive burdens that inquiry practice places upon both students and teachers (Brush & Saye, 2000, 2004; Onosko, 1991; Rossi, 1995; Rossi & Pace, 1998; Saye & Brush, 2002). Teachers must be constantly alert and intellectually agile to monitor and spontaneously support students as they wrestle with complex material and ill-structured social problems. Inquiry teaching also requires substantially more preparation time to develop the deep content knowledge and rich instructional materials necessary to support successful student inquiry. Coupled with issues such as large class sizes and high stakes testing accountability, these cognitive burdens raise genuine questions about the practicality of inquiry-based teaching (Grant et al., 2002; Konopak, Wilson, & Readence, 1994; Saye, 1998b; Schlechty, 1993).

We have experimented with how we might use technological affordances to ease the cognitive burdens that dissuade many teachers from inquiry practice. We have embedded a suite of integrated teacher authoring tools in the PIH Network to facilitate the creation of multimedia digital units, activities, and resources. Hyperlinking and annotation tools allow these digital products to be linked in any way the teacher wishes and facilitate the creation of embedded activity guides, contextual questions and explanations, or other support scaffolds.

As students struggle to construct understandings in an inquiry classroom, demands for teacher assistance are constant, overlapping, and exhausting. Although many difficulties will be idiosyncratic to individual students, common learner difficulties can be anticipated. By embedding scaffolding support into on-line activities, teachers can create a second stream of classroom expertise that provides students with enough support for common problems so that they can move on independently with their investigations while the teacher is engaged with other learners (Saye, 1998b). We call this premeditated support "hard scaffolding" and distinguish it from "soft scaffolding," which is the spontaneous support that teachers provide based upon an immediate diagnosis of learner needs (Saye & Brush, 2002). Hard scaffolds may give students conceptual guidance about what knowledge to consider, metacognitive guidance about monitoring their thinking, or strategic guidance about how to proceed in problem-solving (Hannafin, Land, & Oliver, 1999). For instance, Figure 2.3 illustrates a metacognitive scaffold that prompts students working with Christopher Columbus' journal to corroborate evidence and consider subtext that may explain changing behaviors among historical actors. Hard scaffolds that require written responses from students can further ease the immediate cognitive demands of soft scaffolding by providing the teacher with an opportunity to review student thinking and plan for a response prior to engaging students in a supporting dialogue (Saye & Brush, 2002, 2004b).

Addressing both the vision and the practicality challenges to inquiry, we have also provided teachers with on-line templates of scaffolds for common historical inquiry tasks. The model units and wise practice video cases available in other areas of the PIH Network's open ended learning environment provide further examples of hard scaffolding and other inquiry strategies that may stimulate teacher thinking and streamline the preparation pro-

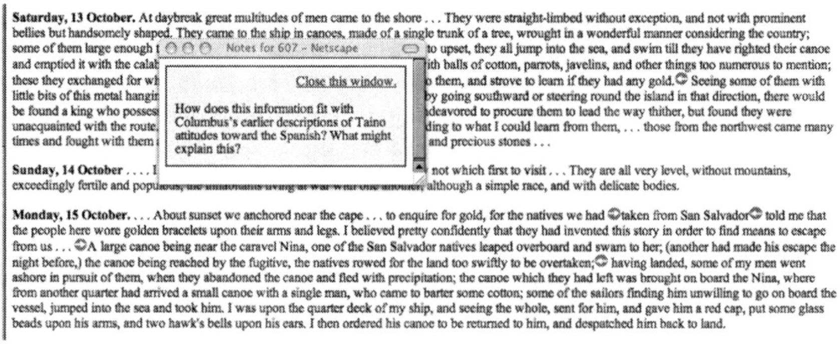

Figure 2.3   Metacognitive hard scaffold.

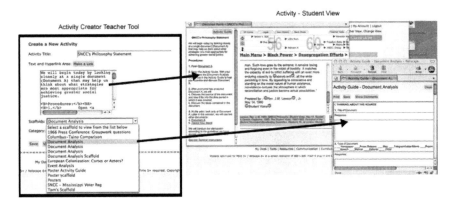

Figure 2.4 Authoring tools: Teacher activity creator.

cess. Teachers have found that these tools and resources do provide some relief from the heavy burdens of preparing, organizing, and implementing inquiry lessons (Saye & Brush, 1999, 2002, 2004b, 2006; Saye et al., 2005).

When joined with authentic models, we hypothesize that mastery of authoring tools such as those featured in the PIH Network will provide teachers with powerful new ways to represent social reality that may encourage them to re-conceptualize the possibilities of lesson content and to experiment with designing richer learning experiences that use technological affordances to engage their students in more authentic encounters with the complexity of the past. Although we have preliminary indications that these tools may be having such a stimulatory effect, we plan more systematic investigations of this question as part of our larger research agenda for developing a professional community of practice (Saye et al., 2009).

Building a Professional Knowledge Community: Collaboration in Constructing Shared Professional Knowledge

Long-term collaborations with a small number of teachers in various schools have established the foundation for a professional problem-based historical inquiry knowledge base and produced the technology-enhanced resources described in the previous sections. Although our collaborators have internalized a holistic view of planning and teaching informed by a unified set of principles for problem-based historical inquiry practice, spreading that vision of practice to the broader corps of social studies teachers has proven difficult.

We have introduced our inquiry framework and supporting on-line resources to in-service and pre-service teachers through publications, course experiences, and intensive summer workshops. These efforts have had some positive effects, but they have not led most teachers to the cultural shift that would result in a truly integrated professional knowledge base for problem-based historical inquiry teaching (Saye et al., 2009). Teachers have adopted specific lessons or strategies without fully grasping the underlying rationale and theoretical principles that link a particular strategy to a conceptually cohesive framework for making practice decisions. When adapted by teachers to fit the assumptions of the traditional craft culture these lessons lose much of their effectiveness.

If teachers are to gain a holistic vision of problem-based historical inquiry teaching practice, they need the same sort of sustained, grounded, and dialogic experience with problem-based historical inquiry practice as our small group of close collaborators. We have begun to experiment with a form of technology-assisted research lesson study as a professional development vehicle that can overcome teacher isolation, share the cognitive burden of conceptualizing inquiry practice, and create a shared knowledge base for problem-based historical inquiry teaching.

The research lesson study concept on which our model is based originated in Japan and has grown in popularity in the United States in the last ten years, but very few projects have an exclusive focus on history. In lesson study, small teams of teachers identify an instructional issue and collaboratively plan a research lesson in which they will test ideas about improving student learning. The research lesson is taught, critiqued, revised, and taught again (Chokshi & Fernandez, 2004; Fernandez, 2002). Refined, field-tested curriculum materials result from the process, but the primary benefit of lesson study should be the dialogue about teaching that causes teachers to develop explanations for instructional outcomes that might be generalized to other lessons: professional teaching knowledge.

Our vision of lesson study differs in several ways from the model most often practiced. It is more tightly focused, more inclusive, and makes greater use of interactive technologies. First, we use lesson study to purposefully examine and refine lessons that elaborate participants' understandings of our framework for professional knowledge for problem-based historical inquiry. Second, we bring the expertise of diverse knowledge communities together in a continuing dialogue about practice. Most commonly lesson study involves a small group of teachers at one school. Although occasionally a teacher educator or a disciplinary expert may join as a full partner in a lesson study group, individuals from those knowledge communities more often serve as outside consultants when the group has a specific need for their expertise. Rather than serving as consultants, historians and teacher educators in our model are full partners with teachers in all stages of the lesson study. Third, we expand collaboration beyond the small local work group to broader national communities. Truly reliable professional knowledge must apply beyond the local communities of practice. This principle does not devalue the knowledge that arises from local contexts. Technology can broaden the applicability of locally generated knowledge by providing mechanisms for representing and sharing the processes and products of local efforts so that they can be continually tested and refined in other contexts (Hiebert et al., 2002; Saye et al., 2009). The Lesson Study Research Group at Teachers' College has begun experimenting with very basic technology applications to support lesson study. They offer a listserv and a gateway to several forums about lesson study as well as a space for posting work for others to review. However, more robust, integrated, interactive applications of technologies in OELEs can provide teachers with more powerful experiences that encourage more authentic national professional knowledge communities.

We are currently forming a local lesson study group to test and refine the problem-based historical inquiry professional knowledge base. A major focus of our lesson study project is experimenting with ways in which interactive technologies embedded in an OELE can facilitate the process of professional knowledge construction locally and provide powerful tools to facilitate participation by teachers in other national contexts. As we envision the technological infrastructure for supporting virtual communities of practice, we are building upon communications and authoring tools that we have already developed for the PIH Network OELE. We plan an interactive lesson study database as a new feature of the PIH Network. The database will feature user-friendly indexing, authoring, and communications tools to assist and document local lesson study collaboration and to disseminate lesson study processes and products to teachers and teacher educators nationally so that we might facilitate the multiple trials in diverse contexts that are necessary to build a true professional teaching knowledge base.

We foresee each research lesson as an indexed case that allows remote users to participate virtually in all aspects of a local group's lesson study. Indexed content and pedagogical knowledge would include video of each stage of the local lesson study; planning, implementation, debriefing, and refinement. Planning documents, final lesson materials, and student work products would be indexed by lesson study stage. Users would have ready access to content expertise on the research lesson topic. Also included in the lesson index would be video of historian-led sessions on the lesson topic as well as suggested historical source documents, readings, and content websites.

Existing PIH Network communications tools and authoring tools will be integrated with the lesson study database to allow users to access, annotate, and link any database item to a forum posting. Community members can also link to a public folder workspace where users can post new work to be reviewed, discussed, and refined in collaboration with other members. We anticipate that these affordances will allow multiple remote users to join a local lesson study group in discussing a featured research lesson at any stage in the lesson study process. Furthermore, remote users can use database resources to replicate the lesson in their own context and post their results. Comparing results to those in the local site will refine and expand the knowledge base for problem-based historical inquiry teaching.

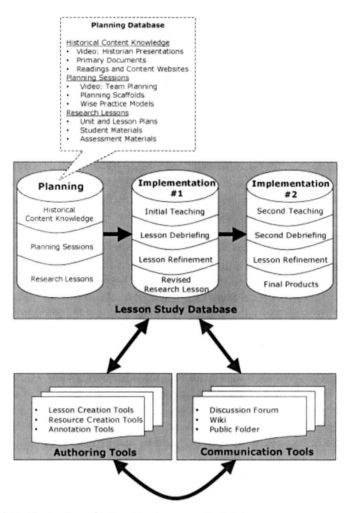

Figure 2.5   Illustration of interactive lesson study database.

CONCLUSION

Although we have worked for a number of years with the challenges of assisting teachers in developing expertise in problem-based historical inquiry, much remains to be done. Our early investigations suggest great potential for joining interactive technologies in integrative ways to promote expertise, but our OELE is at this point rudimentary. Building upon the challenges and potential identified by our work and the work of others, we are pursing complementary projects for developing technology-enhanced educative curriculum materials and interactive research lesson study. As each project matures, it should bolster the other in ways that increase the robustness of the overall PIH Network OELE. The understandings embedded in educative curriculum materials for existing PIH units might serve as exemplars that facilitate the lesson study process as teams of teachers begin to conceptualize new instruction. On the other hand, the professional knowledge generated from lesson study might be used to develop or enrich educative materials for that lesson topic for use by other teachers.

Promoting teacher change represents one of the most daunting challenges for advancing the civic mission of social education. Numerous studies over the last forty years have helped us to understand the complex reasons for the resilience of traditional practices. Resistance to change is rooted in the organizational structures and cultural expectations of the schools and the broader society (Cuban, 1984; Onosko, 1991), teacher and learner beliefs and dispositions (Kagan, 1993; Lortie, 1978; Saye, 1998b), and the cognitive demands that challenging learning places upon teachers and learners (McNeil, 1986; Saye & Brush, 2006). The landscape is littered with failed efforts at reform. We believe that interactive technologies, skillfully employed, offer an opening that might overcome obstacles that have doomed past initiatives aimed at promoting more challenging, authentic social studies instruction. Current technologies allow us to create learning experiences that were unavailable to past curriculum reformers. We invite others in the field to join us in exploring ways we might employ these powerful tools to enable the sort of teaching required for nurturing informed democratic citizenship.

ACKNOWLEDGMENT

Portions of this work were supported by grants from the National Endowment for the Humanities (Grant ED-22175-02), Fund for the Improvement of Postsecondary Education (Grant P116B041038), Apple Computer, Auburn University College of Education, Indiana University, and Auburn City Schools.

REFERENCES

Barab, S., MaKinster, J., Moore, J., & Cunningham, D. (2001). Designing and building an on-line community: The struggle to support sociability in the Internet Learning Forum. *Educational Technology Research and Development, 49*(4), 71–96.

Brush, T. A., & Saye, J. W. (2000). Implementation and evaluation of a student-centered learning unit: A case study. *Educational Technology Research and Development, 48*(3), 79–100.

Brush, T. A., & Saye, J. W. (2001). The use of embedded scaffolds with hypermedia-supported student-centered learning. *Journal of Educational Multimedia and Hypermedia, 10*(4), 333–356.

Brush, T. A., & Saye, J. W. (2004). Supporting learners in technology-enhanced student-centered learning environments. *International Journal of Learning Technology, 1*(2), 191–202.

Brown, J. S., Collins, A., & Duguid, P. (1989). Situated cognition and the culture of learning. *Educational Researcher, 18*(1), 32–42.

Clark, C., Moss, P. A., Goering, S., Herter, R. J., Lamar, B., Leonard, D., Robbins, S., Russell, M., Templin, M., & Wascha, K. (1996). Collaboration as dialogue: Teachers and researchers engaged in conversation and professional development. *American Educational Research Journal, 33*(1), 193–231.

Chokshi S., & Fernandez, C. (2004). Challenges to importing Japanese lesson study: Concerns, misconceptions, and nuances. *Phi Delta Kappan, 85*(7), 520–525.

Cuban, L. (1984). *How teachers taught.* New York: Longmans.

Davis, E. A., & Krajcik, J. S. (2005). Designing educative curriculum materials to promote teacher learning. *Educational Researcher, 34*(3), 3–14.

Dewey, J. (1933). *How we think.* New York: D. C. Heath.

Derry, S. J., Siegel, M., Stampen, J., & the STEP Research Group. (2002). The STEP system for collaborative case-based teacher education: Design, evaluation and future directions. *Proceedings of computer support for collaborative learning (CSCL) 2002* (pp. 209–216). Mahwah, NJ: Erlbaum.

Doyle, W., & Ponder, G. (1977-78). The practicality ethic in teacher decision-making. *Interchange, 8*(3), 1–12.

Dwyer, D. (1994). Apple classrooms of tomorrow: What we've learned. *Educational Leadership, 51*(7), 4–10.

Elbaz, F. (1981). The teacher's practical knowledge: Report of a case study. *Curriculum Inquiry, 11*(1), 43–71.

Engle, S., & Ochoa, A. (1988). *Educating citizens for democracy: Decision-making in social studies.* New York: Teachers College Press.

Fernandez, C. (2002). Learning from Japanese approaches to professional development: The case of lesson study. *Journal of Teacher Education, 53*(5), 393–405.

Garet, M. S., Proter, A. C., Desimone, L., Birman, B. F., & Yoon, K. S. (2001). What makes professional development effective? Results from a national sample of teachers. *American Educational Research Journal, 38*, 915–945.

Grant, S. G., Gradwell, J., Lauricella, A. M., Derme-Insinna, A., Pullano, L., & Tzetzo, K. (2002). When increasing stakes need not mean increasing standards: The case of the New York state global history and geography exam. *Theory and Research in Social Education, 30*(4), 488–515.

Goodlad, J. (1984). *A place called school: Prospects for the future.* New York: McGraw-Hill.

Hannafin, M., Land, S., & Oliver, K. (1999). Open learning environments: Foundations, methods, and models. In C. Reigeluth (Ed.), *Instructional design theories and models* (Vol. 2, pp. 115–140). Mahway, NJ: Lawrence Erlbaum.

Hickey, D. T., Moore, A. L., & Pellegrino, J. W. (2001). The motivational and academic consequences of elementary mathematics environments: Do constructivist innovations and reforms make a difference? *American Educational Research Journal, 38*(3), 611–652.

Hiebert, J., Gallimore, R., & Stigler, J. W. (2002). A knowledge base for the teaching profession: What would it look like and how can we get one? *Educational Researcher, 31*(5), 3–15.

Kagan, D. M. (1993). *Laura and Jim and what they taught me about the gap between educational theory and practice.* Albany: SUNY Press.

Kolodner, J., Camp, P., Crismond, D., Fasse, B., Gray, J., Holbrook, J., Puntambekar, S., & Ryan, M., (2003). Problem-based learning meets case-based reasoning in the middle school science classroom: Putting learning by design into practice. *The Journal of the Learning Sciences, 12*(4), 495–547.

Konopak, B., Wilson, E., & Readence, J. (1994). Examining teachers' beliefs, decisions, and practices about content area reading in secondary social studies. In C. Kinzer & D. Leu (Eds.), *Multidimensional aspects of literacy research, theory, and practice* (pp. 127–136). Chicago: NRC.

Korthagen, F., & Kessels, P. (1999). Linking theory and practice: Changing the pedagogy of teacher education. *Educational Researcher, 28*(4), 4–17.

Kuhn, D. (1999). A developmental model of critical thinking. *Educational Researcher, 28*(2), 16–26, 46.

Land, S. M. (2000). Cognitive requirements for learning with open-ended learning environments. *Educational Technology Research and Development, 48*(3), 61–78.

Lortie, D. (1975). *School-teacher: A sociological study.* Chicago: University of Chicago Press.

Martin, A. (2002). Mentoring and teacher induction: Hearing the voices of change. In F. Kochan (Ed.), *The organizational and human dimensions of successful mentoring programs and relationships* (Ch 13, pp. 185–201). Greenwich, CT: Information Age Publishing.

Massaro, T. M. (1993). *Constitutional literacy: A core curriculum for a multicultural nation.* Duram and London: Duke University Press.

McNeil, L. M. (1986). *Contraditions of control: School structure and school knowledge.* New York: Routledge and Kegan Paul.

Niemi, R. G. & Sanders, M. S. (2004). Assessing student performance in civics: The NAEP 1998 civics assessment. *Theory and Research in Social Education, 32*(3), 326–348.

Oliver, D. W., & Shaver, J. P. (1966). *Teaching public issues in the high school.* Boston: Houghton Mifflin.

Onosko, J. (1991). Barriers to the promotion of higher order thinking in social studies. *Theory and Research in Social Education, 19*(4), 341–366.

Pedersen, S., & Liu, M. (2003). Teachers' beliefs about issues in the implementation of a student-centered learning environment. *Educational Technology Research and Development, 51*(2), 57–76.

Rossi, J. A. (1995). In-depth study in an issues-centered social studies classroom. *Theory and Research in Social Education, 23*(2), 87–120.

Rossi, J. A., & Pace, C.M. (1998). Issues-centered instruction with low achieving high school students: The dilemmas of two teachers. *Theory and Research in Social Education, 26*(3), 380–409.

Sarason, S. (1982). *The culture of the school and the problem of change.* Boston: Allyn & Bacon.

Saye, J. W. (1998a). Creating time to develop student thinking: Team-teaching with technology as an instructional partner. *Social Education, 62*(6), 356–362.

Saye, J. W. (1998b). Technology in the classroom: The role of dispositions in teacher gatekeeping. *Journal of Curriculum & Supervision, 13*(3), 210–234.

Saye, J. W. (1999). School-based collaborations: Building an authentic model for problem-based instruction. *The Journal of Social Studies Research, 23*(2), 11–18.

Saye, J. W., & Brush, T. A.. (1999). Student engagement with social issues in a multimedia-supported learning environment. *Theory and Research in Social Education, 27*(4), 472–504.

Saye, J. W., & Brush, T. A. (2002). Scaffolding critical reasoning about history and social issues in multimedia-supported learning environments. *Educational Technology Research and Development, 50*(3), 77–96.

Saye, J. W., & Brush, T. A. (2004a). Promoting civic competence through problem-based history learning environments. In G. E. Hamot & J. J. Patrick (Eds.), *Civic learning in teacher education* (Vol. 3). Bloomington, IN: ERIC Clearinghouse for Social Studies/Social Science Education.

Saye, J. W., & Brush, T. A.. (2004b). Scaffolding problem-based teaching in a traditional social studies classroom. *Theory and Research in Social Education, 32* (3), 349–378.

Saye, J. W., & Brush, T. A. (2005). The persistent issues in history network: Developing civic competence through technology-supported historical inquiry. *Social Education, 69*(4), 168–171.

Saye, J. W., & Brush, T. A.. (2006). Comparing teachers' strategies for supporting student inquiry in a problem-based multimedia-enhanced history unit. *Theory and Research in Social Education, 34*(2), 183–212.

Saye, J., Kohlmeier, J., Brush, T. Mitchell, L., & Farmer, C. (2009). Using mentoring to develop professional teaching knowledge for problem-based historical inquiry. *Theory and Research in Social Education, 37*(1), 6–41.

Schlechty, P. (1993). On the frontier of school reform with trailblazers, pioneers, and settlers. *Journal of Staff Development, 14*(4), 46–51.

Schrader, P., Leu, Jr., D., Kinzer, C., Ataya, R., Teale, W., Labbo, L., & Cammack, D. (2003). Using Internet delivered videocases to support pre-service teachers' understanding of effective early literacy instruction: An exploratory study. *Instructional Science, 31*, 317–340.

Shaver, J. P., Davis, O. L., & Helburn, S. W. (1979). The status of social studies education: Impressions from three NSF studies. *Social Education, 4*(3), 150–153.

Slavin, R. E. (1996). Research on cooperative learning and achievement: What we know, what we need to know. *Contemporary Educational Psychology, 21*, 43–69.

Tests: most students lack basic history knowledge. (2002). Retrieved August 6, 2008 at: http://archives.cnn.com/2002/fyi/teachers.ednews/05/10/history. scores.ap/index.html

Windschitl, M. (2002). Framing constuctivism in practice as negotiation of dilemmas: An analysis of the conceptual, pedagogical, cultural, and political challenges facing teachers. *Review of Educational Research, 72*(2), 131–175.

CHAPTER 3

STUDENT-CREATED DIGITAL DOCUMENTARIES IN THE HISTORY CLASSROOM

Outcomes, Assessment, and Research Design

Thomas Hammond and Bill Ferster

ABSTRACT

The student creation of digital documentaries, which are brief narratives that draw upon primary source images and incorporate a voice-over narration, offer unique possibilities for enhancing student outcomes from history instruction. Determining the effectiveness of digital documentaries in instructional practice will require a contextualized, multidimensional analysis and a sustained research effort using a variety of designs. This chapter provides a framework for this research, identifying key constructs and highlighting methodological challenges.

Research on Technology in Social Studies Education, pages 39–66
Copyright © 2009 by Information Age Publishing
All rights of reproduction in any form reserved.

39

INTRODUCTION

We live in an increasingly media-infused culture. In response, some social studies educators have adopted a goal of empowering students to become critical consumers of digital media. With the advent of the Internet and accessible media creation tools, young people are able to become media creators as well. According to the Pew Foundation's Internet and American Life Project (Lenhart & Madden, 2005), almost one-third of all teenagers download video from the Internet, and an equal amount create and share their own media on the Internet, whether as artwork, stories, photos, or videos. This interest and activity in student-created digital media have begun to affect the history classroom. Innovative teachers are seeking to leverage their students' skills and interest in media creation by asking them to create digital movies that address topics within the curriculum. The term we are using to describe these movies is *digital documentaries* (Hofer & Owings-Swan, 2005).

A digital documentary is a historical account that draws upon primary source images and incorporates a voice-over narration to explore some facet of history. The point of view used in the narration can be the traditional scholarly, third-person omniscient used in history writing and conventional documentaries, or it can be a first-person exploration of the topic. First-person narratives could take the form of a dramatic re-enactment of a historical episode from the point of view of a historical actor (e.g., Oppenheimer watching the Trinity tests) or from the point of view of the author ("What I find the most interesting about the Manhattan project is…"). Regardless of the topic or point of view, digital documentaries are short, preferably two to three minutes in length.

Digital documentaries can be created by teachers or students. Teachers can create digital documentaries to present a range of topics including local-history topics, such as the implementation of Jim Crow laws in the local community, or customized versions of commercially-produced educational media, such as the Discovery Channel's UnitedStreaming service. Our primary interest, however, lies in student-created digital documentaries. Specifically, we have three questions to explore within this chapter:

1. What outcomes can we expect from students creating digital documentaries in social studies?
2. What forms of measurement or assessment can we use given expected outcomes from digital documentary use in social studies?
3. What are some considerations for the design of large-scale evaluation of digital documentary programs in K–12 schools?

Prior to exploring these issues, however, we consider the value of digital documentaries as an educational tool.

WHY STUDENT-CREATED DIGITAL DOCUMENTARIES?
WHY NOW?

Digital documentaries are a development from work in digital storytelling. Dana Atchley was the pioneer of the form in his 1994 "multimedia auto-biography," titled *NEXT EXIT* (Atchley, 1994). Atchely and Joe Lambert were founders of the Center for Digital Storytelling, which has developed a program of digital storytelling workshops and an articulation of seven critical elements for high-quality digital stories (Lambert, 2003). Language-arts teachers have embraced the concept of digital storytelling in their classrooms as a tool to elicit reflective writing, particularly from students reluctant to express themselves verbally using traditional writing techniques (Kajder, 2006).

Digital storytelling is now undergoing the same diffusion process as previous technical innovations. Free online video-sharing services such as YouTube have emerged as part of mass culture. YouTube receives thousands of uploads daily and serves millions of video clips; the site was singled out by TIME magazine for being the hallmark of a new generation (Grossman, 2006). Advertisers are using online shared videos for viral marketing (Ratliff, 2006). This online content is emerging from growing base of young users, as young people create and upload videos, pictures, podcasts, and other digital media (Lenhart & Madden, 2005). Unsurprisingly, workshops and roundtables on digital storytelling are becoming common features at education conferences. For example, a search for "digital storytelling" in the Education and Information Technology Library sponsored by the Association for the Advancement of Computing in Education returned 32 conference proceedings from 2001 onwards. The same search in the H. W. Wilson education full-text database returned 36 articles spanning multiple content areas (health education, social studies, language arts, and more).

A critical element in the diffusion of digital storytelling is the recently emerged ubiquity of free digital video editing environments. Apple revolutionized the concept of digital home video when it began offering iMovie as a standard feature of its operating system. Microsoft responded by developing and bundling Movie Maker with its XP operating system, following it with Microsoft Photo Story. A second generation of free web-based digital video editors is emerging. For example, JumpCut (http://www.jumpcut.com) provides not only free hosting but also allows users to edit the video and share both the final product and its individual components with others. The authors of this chapter have developed a web-based digital movie-maker designed specifically for use by K–12 teachers and students (Ferster, Hammond, & Bull, 2006).

Given the explosion of activity in digital movie-making, a strategy must be developed for studying the integration of student-created digital video into the K–12 classroom. The history curriculum is a logical place to begin this study for pedagogical, technological, and disciplinary reasons. First, instruction on the discipline of history is ripe for innovation (Martorella, 1997). Student outcomes from history instruction have been a perennial source of dissatisfaction, both in the United States and abroad. Even in the early 1900s (and probably since antiquity), both pundits' and history educators' complaint has been, "Kids don't know history" (Wineburg, 2001, p. viii; see also Paxton, 2003). Given the perceived lack of success from traditional methods of instruction, a new technique for teaching and learning merits a trial, particularly if it has a demonstrated positive effect on student outcomes.

Second, a set of pedagogical factors also suggest the introduction of digital documentary-making in history education. Researchers have noted the value of student writing as a strategy for social studies instruction (Risinger, 1992; Smith & Niemi, 2001). Student creation of digital documentaries provides a rich arena for eliciting student writing. Cognitive scientists have found that students learn better from words and pictures than words alone, and learn better from graphics and narration than from graphics and text (Mayer, 2005). History education researchers' careful observations of students' internalization of historical information reveal a tendency toward misrepresentation. Students may miss the main narrative and instead focus on a sub-narrative, or they may recast an institutional narrative into a personal narrative (Barton, 1997). In other studies, researchers have found that students invent details to create a more cohesive narrative or integrate material from other sources (i.e., the "Disney effect," VanSledright, 2002, p. 63; see also Wineburg, 2001, Ch. 10). The most common format for measuring student outcomes from history instruction—the multiple choice test—does not allow instructors to examine and respond to this phenomenon. In contrast, student-created digital documentaries, being whole products, provide a framework in which students fully articulate their understandings, exposing the ways in which they make sense of classroom instruction. Assessments made using student-created digital documentaries, therefore, obtain a truer picture of students' knowledge and understanding of history.

Finally, two developments in the technological environment of K–12 teachers and students support the integration of digital movie-making into the history classroom. The first development is the emergence of available digital source materials. Online archives such as the Library of Congress' American Memory, the Virginia Center for Digital History, and the National Archives provide access to hundreds of thousands of high-quality, primary source images (McMichael, Rosenzweig, & O'Malley, 1996; VanFossen & Shively, 2000). These "digital" history resources (Lee, 2002) provide educators with countless instructional opportunities, including digital documentary creation. The second technological development is the emergence of tools to support documentary-making. Computer availability and Internet access are becoming more common in American schools and society (Rainie & Horrigan, 2005; Wells & Lewis, 2006). Large-format displays, such as digital projectors and interactive whiteboards, are available in more and more classrooms. Digital video editors such as Windows Movie Maker and iMovie are now part of the standard software package installed on new computers. The impact of these tools is easily visible outside of the classroom—digital media creation and consumption have become a staple feature of young people activities outside of school (Lenhart & Madden, 2005).

Finally, the nature of historical investigation and the habits of mind necessary for the discipline are well suited to the tasks of digital movie creation. The entire enterprise of history rests upon integrating and interpreting evidence—often mere fragments—into existing schema, unmaking and reshaping assumptions as we glean understanding from the sources. Feminist historian Joan Wallach Scott asserts, "History functions through an inextricable connection between reality and interpretation" (quoted in VanSledright, 2002, p. 3). When students create digital documentaries, they are aware that they, too, are engaged in this process of integrating evidence (the images) and interpretation (their narration) to frame a cohesive account. In fact, as historian Ed Ayers (1999) notes, "history may be better suited to digital technology than any other humanistic discipline" (para. 4).

History teachers and students are already engaged in exploring the possibilities of addressing content through digital movies. The National History Day competition includes a documentary category that grows in popularity every year. A cursory search of the Internet will turn up a wide variety of student-produced videos that appear to have been produced as part of a class activity. In our local area of central Virginia, we are working with growing numbers of teachers who have integrated student creation of digital video as part of one or more units of study.

While examining these models, we have been intrigued by the possibilities of articulating a clearly-defined role for student-created digital documentaries in the curriculum. However, before such a proposal can be taken seriously, we must lay out a research agenda to explore the student outcomes from creating these products and connect them both to the local curriculum and to the larger goals of history education in the 21st century.

STUDENT PROCESS, STUDENT OUTCOMES, AND DIGITAL DOCUMENTARY

What outcomes can we expect from students creating digital documentaries in social studies? To answer this question, we must identify the student behaviors involved in the process of creating a digital documentary. Are students searching for source material, and thus applying research skills, or are they working from a preselected list provided by the teacher? When working with the images, are students using a sourcing heuristic (a set of questions to guide them through the analysis and interrogation of the image and its context; examples include SCIM-C [Hicks, Doolittle, & Ewing, 2004] and APPARTS [College Board, 2001]) or are they accepting the images as iconic representations of pre-existing ideas–or is there something else going on? As we identify these behaviors, we have found it necessary to introduce certain constraints on the product and process we are discussing to focus the discussion. Teachers can implement student-created digital documentaries in many ways; we will focus on the variations we have observed in our work with classroom teachers.

The first constraint is that we will only consider student work that is produced as an individual product. In our experience student digital media products are commonly produced as group projects: teachers place students in pairs or small groups, and the students collaborate to draft the script, compose the visuals, and so forth. Teachers view the works in progress, provide feedback, and spur refinement of the students' products. While this interaction is, as Ayers (1999) suggested, entirely appropriate for the study of the humanities, it creates a complex research situation. Any group-created product will reflect the historical knowledge and understandings contributed by each student, but we cannot know with certainty whether the knowledge is held by one student or both students, or what role the teacher played. Furthermore, if the teacher has played a role in editing the images or narrative, then the final product is even more collaborative. In contrast, the tests given by history teachers and the assessments used by education researchers examine individuals' knowledge, understandings, and skills. Therefore, for research purposes, it is preferable that students individually produce the digital documentary.

A second constraint is the source and number of the images to be used by students in constructing their digital documentaries. We are interested in the means by which students are locating images, whether via a search engine, an archive, or a preset list. For example, a Google search for images of Pocahontas will turn up hundreds of thousands of images while a search through the National Archives Research Catalog will generate only a handful. The movies can therefore differ given the source of the images. Furthermore, each environment can influence a user search for historical information. Google provides rapid access to information (depending upon the topic), but the information is often decontextualized. Archival searches provide access to resources and context, but can be difficult to navigate for non-expert users, and can actually provide too much detail. Teacher-selected resources, however, allow for the appropriate mix of information and context (Lee & Molebash, 2004; Lee & Clarke, 2003). An additional possibility is that the image list is generated through a collaborative effort as teachers and students mine the Internet or an archive for images and build up needed contextual information, often as part of an inquiry-driven lesson. Therefore, we will constrain our focus by considering products produced using a teacher-selected or collaboratively-created image list.

A third constraint that we will place on our consideration of student-created digital documentaries emerges from the questions about the differing effects from *creating* a narrative versus the effects of *watching* another student's work. Once students have completed their digital documentaries, the teacher often reserves time for students to present their projects to the rest of the class. A distinction therefore needs to be made between the student outcomes from making an individual project and the outcomes from watching others' projects. If the final products are posted to the Internet, the question becomes especially important, as students may be watching and learning from one another's work outside of class. While this is an admirable pedagogical goal, it poses a dilemma for researchers. Therefore, we will simply address this situation by considering only the learning outcomes from making the digital documentaries, not from watching others.

Finally, a fourth constraint on our work will involve the exclusion of the technology itself from the analysis. True, the digital editing environment used may alter the product: a digital documentary made using a tool with fewer graphical features will probably differ from a product made using one that can do more, at least superficially. However, we are interested in students historical knowledge and understandings as they produce digital documentaries; the editing environment used to produce these documentaries must be observed and described—in particular regarding the teacher's scaffolding process—but the technical expertise displayed in the final products is not the focus of the analysis.

Working within these four simplifying constraints, the student outcome variables can now be identified. At least three constructs could serve as dependent variables in a research study: historical content knowledge, disciplinary skills, and expressive skills. Historical content knowledge includes both discrete facts (Abraham Lincoln was assassinated in 1865 by John Wilkes Booth) and substantive concepts (federalism, slavery, regionalism). Another term for this category of knowledge is first-order conceptual and narrative ideas and knowledge. This information is typically the focus of K–12 history instruction and assessment (VanSledright & Limon, 2006, p. 546). Disciplinary thinking includes discipline-specific operations (questioning and integrating evidence, treating historical accounts as tentative judgments, creating interconnected webs of strong and weak causation, organizing ideas by chronology or geography or change, etc.). Many descriptions of historical thinking exist (Donovan & Bransford, 2005; National Center for

History in the Schools, 1996; National Council for the Social Studies, 1994; VanSledright & Limon, 2006; Wineburg, 2001), so researchers must identify and describe the particular definition they are using. Expression skills include capabilities in writing (grammar, organization of ideas), speaking (enunciation, pacing), and media composition (integration of visuals and narration, purposeful use of editing, sequence and pans and zooms). These skills are more commonly associated with language arts (or film studies) than history education, but in the context of student-created digital documentaries, they are a logical outcome variable.

Each of the three dependent variables will be influenced by the conditions under which the student produced the digital documentary. Are the students creating movies as part of a culminating, end-of-instruction product or are the movies created during instruction? Which constructs—among content knowledge, thinking skills, and expression skills—are privileged in the classroom curriculum? We think of these constructs as environmental factors, which might further be thought of as independent variables. We have identified five of these environment factors that can be monitored or controlled in a research study.

- *Prior experiences:* What formal (classroom context) or informal (family, community, or personal context) opportunities has the student had to develop his or her historical content knowledge, disciplinary thinking, or expression skills?
- *Curriculum & assessment regimen:* Is the student accustomed to learning and producing discrete, a-contextual items or whole accounts? In other words, is the student expected to learn isolated facts and then answer multiple-choice test items on these facts, or is he or she expected to study historical accounts and produce a whole product (such as an essay or skit or poster) that responds to these accounts?
- *Instructor:* What training, skills, or attitudes does the instructor have that may impact the student? For example, does the instructor feel that the student is capable of historiography? Does the instructor feel that the students are capable and responsible of forming an integrated narrative, with a meaningful beginning, middle, and end?
- *Instruction:* In the student current classroom context, what explicit instruction has he or she received regarding historical content knowledge, disciplinary thinking, and expression skills? For example, what sources of information were available? Did the instruction involve analysis of primary sources? Interpretation of visual images? Organization and expression of ideas?
- *Production process:* What expectations were placed upon the student for the project—how long was the product to be? How broad was

the topic? How much time did the student have to produce the digital documentary? What steps were involved in the process? In what order were the steps arranged? What formative feedback was offered? Was the project completed using only class time or did the student also work outside of school?

THE MEASUREMENT AND ASSESSMENT OF STUDENT-CREATED DIGITAL DOCUMENTARIES

What forms of measurement or assessment can we use to observe outcomes from digital documentary use in social studies? Every analysis of student outcomes is fraught with challenges. What forms of evidence are credible— can we rely upon self-report? Do multiple-choice tests assess content knowledge or test-taking skills? Multiple-choice tests should be taken as only one

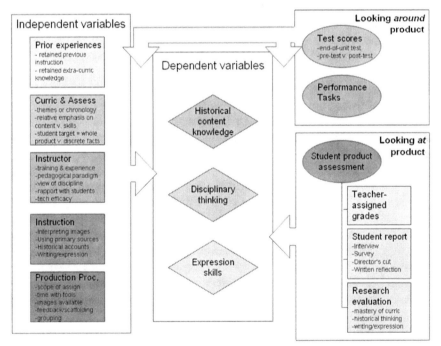

The independent variables describe the conditions under which digital documentaries are made; the dependent variables are the internal bases of knowledge and skill that students use in constructing digital documentaries; changes in the dependent variables can be observed using the measures in the right-hand boxes.

Figure 3.1 Operationalization of constructs and measures involved in student creation of digital documentaries.

indicator of knowledge, and not as a conclusive measure (Amrein & Berliner, 2002; Nuthall & Alton-Lee, 1995). More exhaustive tests, such as performance tasks, can be used (Barton & Levstik, 1996; Brophy & Alleman, 2000; Lee & Ashby, 2000; Wineburg, 1990). However, how much disruption of the class room environment is ethical? What amount of imposition upon students' or teachers' time will be accepted? Regardless of the weighing of these factors, two avenues are available for assessing the student outcomes from producing a digital documentary. One is to look *around* the product, and one is to look *at* the product (see Figure 3.1).

Looking Around the Product

What student behaviors are evident before and after producing the digital documentary? In most classrooms, the student will experience an end-of-unit test; what evidence of historical content knowledge or skills is on display in the student responses to the test item? Of course, this assessment does not control for previous instruction (information the student learned before beginning the unit) or for content (some units may be more difficult to understand than others). Accordingly, a researcher should pretest students if possible.

Many pretest/posttest instruments can be employed. The most expedient format is multiple-choice items, such as those used on all large-scale standardized tests (e.g., Advanced Placement exams, the National Assessment of Education Progress, and state-level end-of-year tests). Constructed-response items such as short-answer questions or essays provide an opportunity to obtain a rich, open-ended sample of students' understanding. A performance task provides an even more thorough exploration of understanding and thinking. In these tasks, students respond to a prompt or a series of prompts and explain their reasoning. Prompts can include texts, as in the case of Wineburg (2001, Ch. 3) primary source analysis or Lee and Ashby (2000) secondary-source responses, or visuals, as in Barton and Levstik (1996) picture-sorting task or Brophy and Alleman (2000) image prompt. Students are directed to "think aloud," verbalizing their thoughts as they read a text, place an image chronologically, or answer questions framed by photographs or drawings of cultural universals.

In general, test items are useful for assessing students' historical content knowledge, while performance tasks provide greater access to students disciplinary thinking. Expression skills, or at least the written component, can be assessed through instruments such as the National Writing Project's adaptation of the 6+1 Traits Writing Model (National Writing Project, 2006). For a more social studies-specific writing evaluation, teachers and researchers can adapt the rubrics employed by the College Board on their Advanced Placement (AP) history exams (e.g., College Board, 2006). Note that these rubrics are tied to the expository context—for example, they require a thesis statement—and the specific characteristics of the question asked, such as comparing and contrasting. Accordingly, teachers and researchers working outside of the AP context must adapt these rubrics to suit the circumstances.

A final element to consider, when looking around the product, is the time scale. Posttests should ideally consider not just what a student knows, understands, and can do immediately after completing the digital documentary or at the end of the current unit of study, but what the student retains in the longer run. Ideally, posttests should be repeated after several months to observe the true effects. Lee and Molebash (2004) most interesting findings emerged from a posttest several months after the initial task.

Looking at the Product

What historical content knowledge, disciplinary thinking, and expression skills are evident in the student digital documentary? Obviously, the teacher-assigned grade will be vital here as a source of triangulating data. Different teachers will look for different elements. For example, one teacher may emphasize factual accuracy, while another may emphasize expression skills. And even if the project was intended to address disciplinary thinking, the teachers' summative assessment may tilt toward emphasizing the more easily discerned right/wrong aspects of a product, such as factual accuracy or correct grammar. After all, teachers grading decisions "must be not only made but justified" (Anderson & Krathwohl, 2001, p. 247).

Student self-report presents a fruitful opportunity to shed further light on their learning. Traditional forms of self-report include surveys or reflective essays. An exciting opportunity provided by the medium of digital video is a "Director Cut" that asks the student to revisit a completed digital documentary and explain his or her thinking process: why were these images chosen? What informed the sequencing of images? Why were these particular pans and zooms applied upon the images? What else was the student thinking or feeling that didn't make it into the movie? Of course, more traditional forms of self-report such as surveys and interviews would serve just as well. Qualitative analysis can then be conducted to provide additional information regarding the student content knowledge, disciplinary thinking, and expression skills.

The most critical lens on the product is the researcher's independent assessment. The goal is to obtain a third-party view on the knowledge and understandings on display in a given digital documentary. In some ways, the research assessment mirrors a historian's use of evidence, asking questions that the original creators of an artifact never intended. Like a historical study, then, the researcher must approach an assessment carefully, viewing the product on several levels and always in the context of other information. Ideally, the research assessment will take place through a web of instruments, each built upon a foundation of rich contextual information. One possible design for our evaluation process includes assessment in three areas; content knowledge, disciplinary knowledge, and writing skills.

Assessment of the Content Knowledge Displayed

This assessment could take the form of a simple listing of facts and concepts mentioned in the digital documentary. Assuming that such a listing can take place, however, the next questions are far more difficult to answer. Once we've identified what is present, how do we weigh it? Is a three-minute movie that addresses 15 facts and concepts better than, worse than, or the same as a one-minute movie that addresses five facts and concepts? What degree of quality of content knowledge is displayed? What if the student made a factual error ("Pearl Harbor was attacked on December 6, 1941") but appeared to grasp the overall concept ("While this attack was the culmination of rising tensions between Japan and the United States, it came as a shock to the American public")? Does the quantity and quality of content knowledge displayed meet the goals of instruction?

The most authentic frame for making this assessment is the student local curriculum. While this decision limits the basis of comparison to other products generated under the same curriculum (i.e., digital documentaries produced by 7th-graders in Virginia public schools can be compared only to those produced by other 7th-graders in Virginia public schools), it makes the assessment far more valid. Only the local curriculum can meaningfully specify both the scope and the quality of the content knowledge that the student is expected to display. Other content frames can be used, whether E.D. Hirsch's Core Knowledge series or the National Assessment of Educational Progress (NAEP) U.S. History Framework. However, any assessment conducted with such a frame will need to provide a rationale for its use and will not be able to reflect upon the goals of the local curriculum. For an example of what a content knowledge rubric based upon the local curriculum might look like, see Appendix A. Assuming that a suitable instrument for assessing the historical content knowledge displayed in a digital documentary can be developed, many questions might be addressed. Are students mastering, failing to master, or exceeding the goals of their local history curriculum? What patterns exist in students' knowledge? What patterns exist in students' interest or attention?

Assessment of Disciplinary Thinking Displayed

Ideally, this level of evaluation would draw upon the literature describing the nature of historical thinking (Donovan & Bransford, 2005; Wineburg, 2001) and encompass the desired outcomes of professional associations such as the National Council for the Social Studies (1994).

Assuming that such an instrument can be developed, it would allow comparison across curricula. After all, historical thinking is a more universal concept—if one could measure its pattern of presence or absence in a digital documentary, comparisons could be made between, say, 7th-graders products in Virginia and 11th-graders products in New York. For an example of what a historical thinking skills rubric might look like, see Appendix B.

Any interpretation of these measurements should take place within the context of the goals of instruction. If the instructor emphasized facts and chronology and made no effort to develop students' awareness of evidence or the nature of historical accounts, the evaluation should not bemoan students' lack of deep historical thinking skills. In contrast, if the teacher did explicitly address, for example, the importance of perspective-taking in interpreting testimony, then students' products should be expected to reflect this instruction. Given an instrument to measure the disciplinary thinking displayed in a digital documentary produced within a described context of instruction, many interesting questions can be addressed. For example, if the classroom instruction addressed aspects of historical thinking, is the impact of this instruction evident in the work produced by students? What patterns exist in students' acquisition and application of the habits of mind specific to history? If instruction in disciplinary thinking can produce measurably different results in students' work, how enduring are these changes? Do students maintain this frame of reference over time and across different topics or does it decay or vanish? If classroom instruction focuses on content knowledge and does not address disciplinary thinking, are students capable of displaying increasingly sophisticated understandings of history?

Assessment of the Writing Skills Displayed

Fortunately, many well-established assessments exist to measure the writing skills displayed in a digital documentary. Researchers can take a student final script or a transcript of the narration and use an instrument such as the modified 6+1 traits rubric used by the National Writing Project (2006) or the rubrics for narrative, informational, or persuasive writing (depending upon the task assigned to the students) used by the NAEP Writing assessment (National Assessment Governing Board, 1998). After selecting a valid and reliable instrument for measuring students writing skills (or other expression skills), researchers can ask questions such as whether students who create digital documentaries display increasing levels of writing proficiency in their scripts. Assuming that a relationship between creating digital documentaries and demonstrated writing skills exists, does this pattern spill over to other content areas? In other words, do students who create digital documentaries display stronger writing skills in their language assignments than students who do not create digital documentaries? Finally, can creating digital documentaries act as a gateway to stronger writing skills for students who are resistant to writing or have received little benefit from traditional writing instruction?

Assessment of Other Outcomes

This description of various assessment schemes is not meant to be exhaustive. Obviously, researchers may want to make additional product assessments depending upon their interests. For example, researchers may be interested in generic thinking skills, rather than the discipline-specific historical thinking skills, and therefore use a rubric based on Bloom's taxonomy of educational objectives in the cognitive domain (or some variation thereof). Other researchers may be interested in exploring aspects of expression beyond writing, and develop product assessments that address students' oral fluency or their skillful use of images and motion. Other outcomes of interest can be student attitudes, engagement, completion rate, or even attendance.

Development and Use of Instruments

Any assessment rubric, whether addressing content knowledge, disciplinary thinking, or expression skills, should be tested and refined before being employed. Multiple raters should examine each student product, and inter-rater agreement should reach a level of reliability appropriate for research, suggested by a Kappa value (Cohen, 1960) greater than .65 (Bakeman & Gottman, 1997, p. 66). While two scorers may not return identical scoring sheets, their assessment evaluation should nevertheless tell the same story: this student product did or did not display strong historical content knowledge, a certain pattern of historical thinking, strong or weak writing skills.

Regardless of the construct studied or the instrument used, any assessment should take place within the context of the actual classroom instruction. While blind assessments of products may be desirable in some instances, the interpretation of their results should be made in reference to the

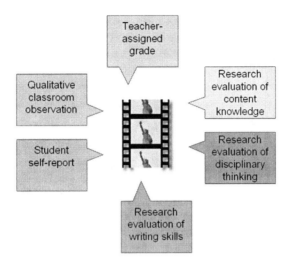

Figure 3.2 Contextual, multi-dimensional evaluation of student-created digital documentary. (Image of the Statue of Liberty supplied by Latvian.)

curriculum, instruction, and assessment the students experienced. Accordingly, any research that generates student-created digital documentaries for assessment must include qualitative descriptions of the classroom. Interpretations should be based upon a constellation of data (Figure 3.2), not on information from a single measure, such as historical content knowledge.

DESIGNS FOR LARGE-SCALE EVALUATIONS

After exploring student-created digital documentaries' potential student outcomes and measures, we next turn to research design. What are some considerations for the design of large-scale evaluation of digital documentary programs in K–12 schools? Given our interest in identifying student outcomes from creating digital documentaries, we will focus on quasi-experimental designs. While purely descriptive studies will be important and useful in identifying what students and teachers think about history, the nature of digital documentaries and the connection between the two as well as making causal inferences about student outcomes requires comparison between groups. These comparisons should look across groups' performance in producing digital documentaries (i.e., looking at the product) and/or at pre- and posttests (looking around the product) to explore relative differences in content knowledge, disciplinary thinking, and/or expression skills. Again, the groups' performance must be presented in context, such as curricular expectations, patterns in instruction and assessment, and so forth.

Because we are interested in classroom instruction, quasi-experimental designs will be far more common than experimental designs. Experimental designs looking for outcomes at the student level typically create equivalent groups by randomly assigning students to the experimental and control conditions. This practice is very rarely feasible within the context of K–12 curricular instruction. Accordingly, the following quasi-experimental designs should provide useful results.

Evaluation Design: Controlled-Comparison

In a controlled comparison study the experimental class or section receives the treatment condition (creation of digital documentaries) while the other receives a more traditional style of instruction, preferably by the same teacher covering the same content in the same amount of time (see Table 3.1). Note that this design works best when looking around the product, as the strongest causal inferences can be drawn if pretest data is available. Of course, student products can also be compared to further explore content knowledge, disciplinary thinking, and/or expression skills.

Multiple Baseline Design

Multiple baseline design involves the examination of a particular treatment at different times under circumstances. Applying this procedure to digital documentaries, an initial digital documentary performance baseline can be established and then the use of student-created digital documentaries can be introduced at different times in an instructional sequence (see Table 3.2). The difference in performance between the baseline and experimental conditions can then be compared to suggest each condition's efficacy. This design allows each class grouping to serve as its own control. Again, pre- and posttest data (looking around the product) is preferable,

TABLE 3.1 Controlled-Comparison Quasi-Experimental Design

	Pre-tests (content knowledge tests, performance tasks)	Instruction involving student-created DDs	Post-tests (content knowledge tests, performance tasks)
Experimental classroom	O	X	O
Control classroom	O		O

TABLE 3.2   Multiple-Baseline Quasi-Experimental Design

	obs	inst	obs	inst	obs	inst	obs	inst	obs
Classroom A	O	X	O	X	O	X	O	X	O
Classroom B	O		O	X	O	X	O	X	O
Classroom C	O		O		O	X	O	X	O
Classroom D	O		O		O		O	X	O

Legend: ▨ = baseline condition; ■ = experimental condition.

but sometimes only post-test-only data is available. Examination of such data in the form of student products can provide important insight. Assuming repeated production of digital documentaries, as in Table 3.2, comparisons can be made across iterations of the activity, allowing researchers to observe growth (or decay) in students' content knowledge, disciplinary thinking, and/or expression skills. This design mitigates the effects of different instructors, instruction and participants. Ideally, this design would take place within the context of a single instructor or at least a single curriculum. Otherwise, possible interactions between the treatment (student creation of digital documentaries) and the content area will be unexplored, since the content being learned will vary at each stage of instruction.

Comparison Between Differing Instructional Techniques

In this strategy, different variations in digital documentary projects are implemented to determine which implementations are more effective. Possible variations include:

- *Point of view.*   Use of formal, third-person point of view vs. first-person point of view (student or historical actor)
- *Image list.*   Use of tightly constrained image lists vs. more open-ended lists.
- *Production process.*   Digital documentaries created more or less scope of student decision-making, for example, documentaries with tightly-focused topics and/or time frames vs. those created in longer-term time frames and/or open-ended topics.

These comparisons will be especially useful for teasing out the impacts of different aspects of the independent variables, such as production process, and determining which implementations of digital documentaries may be more appropriate for different grade levels or different curricula. Hypothesizing about the isolated effects of the independent variables, however, can only take place after many quasi-experiments with detailed descriptions of the class room context. After all, one instructor's results with constrained vs. open-ended image lists may be affected by other independent variables, such as student prior knowledge; in other contexts and with a different configuration of variables, the outcomes may be different. Only many comparisons, within many different contexts, can provide the necessary depth for making assertions.

Blocking by Achievement-level Grouping

Many school systems track or group students by variables such as reading ability. Research in these situations—whether following a controlled-comparison, multiple-baseline, or differential instructional technique design—should be alert to interaction effects and consider how student outcomes from a given implementation can differ by grouping. For example, students in lower achievement-level groups, such as those with weaker reading skills, may benefit from the visually-oriented nature of digital documentaries, while students in higher achievement-level groups may not, who may do well in all treatment conditions. Insofar as these different tracking or grouping practices result in different instruction and expectations, the analysis of students performance should be analyzed within track level, both to avoid false positives (or negatives) and to be alert to aptitude-treatment interaction.

As mentioned previously, further variations will take place due to the degree of collaboration among students (as they work as individuals, pairs, or small groups), the sources and number of images used, time given to watching others' work, and the technology used (desktop-based tools such as Movie Maker or iMovie vs. web-based tools such as PrimaryAccess). Each design described above will require its own careful consideration of the questions addressed and the methods required to gather and to analyze data. Furthermore, any analysis must be made in the context of the described context of curriculum, instruction, and assessment.

Additional Comments on Design

Both designs will be vulnerable to similar threats, such as the novelty effect (from working with digital video in class), Hawthorne effect, selection bias, resentful demoralization, mortality (as students change schools or classes), or even the simple effects of history during the school year. For example, as springtime arrives, and high-stakes tests loom on the horizon, the classroom atmosphere can change dramatically. Researchers should be sensitive to these threats and address them in their analyses.

Regardless of the design of any one study, we encourage collaboration, distribution, and replication. First, researchers should work in collaboration with one another. The variables involved are complex, the constructs under study are subtle, and the measurements being used are imprecise at best. No single study or single researcher or single publication can authoritatively address even one strategy for student-created digital documentaries. Second, digital video can be extremely portable. Student work (and contextual data) generated in one location can be made available to researchers in other locations for evaluation and discussion. In this way, the research effort can be distributed over many researchers and many sites, allowing for both a richer discussion of the ways digital documentaries are being used in classrooms and vastly improved measurements of students' content knowledge, thinking skills, and expression skills. Finally, studies should be replicated. Given the fact that we are working with intact groups (i.e., students assigned to a teacher as part of a school's normal scheduling process), any identified positive difference in student outcomes needs to be tested using different students, a different instructor, a different school, or even a different curriculum before it can begin to be accepted as relevant to the K–12 community as a whole. Replication will also be essential to allaying the threats to validity mentioned above.

CONCLUSIONS

Digital video provides an exciting canvas for students and teachers. Classroom innovators are already integrating digital video into history instruction throughout the country. To determine whether this activity is not only interesting but *useful*, a sustained, focused research effort must be made. This chapter explored three questions. The first and most important question is, *What outcomes can we expect from students creating digital documentaries in social studies?* Exploring this complex question will require different implementations, different research designs, and different methodologies. The second question, therefore, is *What forms of measurement or assessment can we use given expected outcomes from digital documentary use in social studies?* When moving beyond single classroom studies, *What are some considerations for the design of large-scale evaluation of digital documentary programs in K–12 schools?*

A coordinated body of research on student-created digital documentaries requires an agenda or unifying strategy. This chapter seeks to be an initial step in formulating such an agenda by highlighting key constructs, identifying challenges to research, and offering suggestions on methodology. It is not conclusive but an open invitation to interested parties to enrich and elevate the present document through the addition of new perspectives and considerations, such as Mishra and Koehler's conceptualization of teachers' Technological Pedagogical Content Knowledge (2006). While many research questions and designs are possible and indeed necessary, best practices will be vital. For example, all research should strive to meet agreed-upon standards of quality, such as a comprehensive reporting criterion: providing complete information about the setting, participants, intervention, measures, and methods of analysis (Roblyer, 2005). Sustained, complementary, and high-quality research efforts will be required to best determine the full pedagogical potential of this exciting new medium of student-created digital documentaries.

In addition to the measurement and design work described in this chapter, the authors have developed and field-tested a web-based application for creating digital documentaries (Ferster, Hammond, & Bull, 2006). They have conducted two rounds of classroom-based quasi-experiments and are developing a larger-scale study (Hammond, 2007). Potential collaborators and interested parties are invited to use the application, review the existing research, and discuss future research.

APPENDIX A

Sample Rubric for Scoring Historical Content Knowledge in a Student-Generated Digital Documentary Using the Local Curriculum as the Frame

The following rubric is based upon the Virginia Department of Education's *History and Social Science Standards of Learning Enhanced Scope and Sequence: United States History: 1877 to Present* (2004; available from http://www.pen.k12.va.us/VDOE/EnhancedSandS/history-ss.shtml).

Instructions:

I. First, read the curriculum guide. Next, review the student product. Make any general notes about
   – How well the product addresses the curriculum

- Where the product falls short of the curriculum (e.g., addresses topic but does so poorly or with inaccuracies)
- Where the product exceeds the curriculum

II. Place a check by each item that is present in the product, then add up the TOTAL checks and TOTAL POSSIBLE checks.

		Student performance expressed as a percentage: total addressed divided by total possible:
Total number of curriculum criteria addressed		
Total possible number of curriculum criteria addressed		
Total running time of product (in minutes or fractions of a minute)		
Curriculum addressed per minute: Percentage score of curriculum guide divided by running time		

III. Finally, address the quality/accuracy with which the product addresses each point. Scoring:

+1	Convinces the reader that the student understands both particulars (discrete facts) and substantive concepts (abstractions) identified by the curriculum
0	Suggests to the reader that the student has errors in either the particulars (discrete facts) and substantive concepts (abstractions) identified by the curriculum
−1	Suggests to the reader that the student has errors in both the particulars (discrete facts) and substantive concepts (abstractions) identified by the curriculum

Digital documentary		Curriculum Guide (applicable sections)	prs	abs	Rating (+1, 0, −1)
	Skills	Make connections between past and present.			
		Sequence events in United States history from 1877 to the present.			
(Narration associated with image 1)	Content	Identify some effects of segregation on American society. Include the following: • Separate educational facilities and resources for white and African American students • Separate public facilities (e.g., restrooms, drinking fountains, restaurants) • Social isolation of races.			
(Narration associated with image 2)		Describe how the African American struggle for equality became a mass movement. Include the following: • Opposition to *Plessy v. Ferguson* — "Separate but equal" • *Brown v. Board of Education*, desegregation of schools • Martin Luther King, Jr. — Passive resistance against segregated facilities; "I have a dream…" speech • Rosa Parks — Montgomery bus boycott • Organized protests, Freedom Riders, sit-ins, marches • Expansion of the National Association for the Advancement of Colored People (NAACP)			
(Narration associated with image 3)					

Image	Narration	Description
(film strip)	(Narration associated with image 4)	Describe the following legislation resulting from the Civil Right Movement that ensured constitutional rights to all citizens regardless of race: • Civil Rights Act of 1964 • Voting Rights Act of 1965
(film strip)	(Narration associated with image 5)	Identify how women were disadvantaged in the work place. Include the following: • Discrimination in hiring practices against women • Lower wages for women than for men doing the same job.
(film strip)	(Narration associated with image 6)	Explain how women activists were inspired by the achievements of the Civil Rights Movement and took action to gain equality for themselves, particularly in the workplace. Include the following improvements in women's conditions that resulted from this action: • National Organization for Women (NOW) • Federal legislation to force colleges to give women equal athletic opportunities • The Equal Rights Amendment, despite its failure, and a focus on equal opportunity employment created a wider range of options and advancement for women in business and public service.
(film strip)	(Narration associated with image 7)	

APPENDIX B

Sample Rubric for Scoring Historical Thinking Skills in a Student-Generated Digital Documentary

Instructions:

I. First, read or observe the product and offer a holistic response regarding the student's level of demonstrated historical thinking.

II. Next, for each stem, identify the behaviors present using the key below.

Behavior	Description	Example
Perspective-taking	Every product gets ONE, for taking its initial perspective—usually, but not always, the third-person objective, historical point of view Do note where the text departs from this, shifting to EXPLICITLY consider the point of view of a historical actor, or moving from one "take" to another	
New Topic		
Elaborating detail		
Chronological reference	evidence of use of time as an organizing concept	
Geographical reference	evidence of awareness of space, or use of space as an organizer	
Causal assertion	at the *topic* level; topic A causes topic B or influences topic B—not at the elaborating detail level	
Reference to evidence		
Reference to nature of historical accounts	Evidence of awareness that • history is a human construction • many judgments are tentative and arguable • accounts may be colored by the motivations of the authors • events generally have multiple causes • historical outcomes were not inevitable, and the future is not predetermined	
Assertion of significance (thesis?)	author is loading a concept with emotional weight	

#	Stem	Scoring	Notes
1		New topic?: _____ Elaborating detail? Chronological reference? Geographical reference? Causal assertion? Perspective-taking (change in POV)? Reference to sources? Reference to nature of hist accts? Thesis/Assertion of significance?	
2		New topic?: _____ Elaborating detail? Chronological reference? Geographical reference? Causal assertion? Perspective-taking (change in POV)? Reference to sources? Reference to nature of hist accts? Thesis/Assertion of significance?	
3		New topic?: _____ Elaborating detail? Chronological reference? Geographical reference? Causal assertion? Perspective-taking (change in POV)? Reference to sources? Reference to nature of hist accts? Thesis/Assertion of significance?	
4		New topic?: _____ Elaborating detail? Chronological reference? Geographical reference? Causal assertion? Perspective-taking (change in POV)? Reference to sources? Reference to nature of hist accts? Thesis/Assertion of significance?	
5		New topic?: _____ Elaborating detail? Chronological reference? Geographical reference? Causal assertion? Perspective-taking (change in POV)? Reference to sources? Reference to nature of hist accts? Thesis/Assertion of significance?	

REFERENCES

Amrein, A., & Berliner, D. (2002). High-stakes testing, uncertainty, and student learning. *Educational Policy Analysis Archives, 10*(18). Retrieved March 1, 2007 from: http://epaa.asu.edu/epaa/v10n18

Anderson, L., & Krathwohl, D. (2001) *A taxonomy for learning, teaching, and assessing.* New York: Addison Wesley Longman, Inc.

Atchley, D. (1994). Some thoughts on technology. *Morph Outpost.* Retrieved March 1, 2007 from: http://www.nextexit.com/nextexit/morph.html

Ayers, E. (1999). *The pasts and futures of digital history.* Retrieved July 12, 2005 from: http://www.vcdh.virginia.edu/PastsFutures.html

Bakeman, R., & Gottman, J. (1997). *Observing interaction: An introduction to sequential analysis* (2nd ed.). New York: Cambridge University Press.

Barton, K. (1997). Bossed around by the Queen: Elementary students' understanding of individuals and institutions in history. *Journal of Curriculum and Supervision, 12,* 290–314.

Barton, K., & Levstik, L. (1996). Back when God was around and everything: The development of elementary children's understanding of historical time. *American Educational Research Journal, 33,* 419–454.

Brophy, J., & Alleman, J. (2000). Primary-grade students knowledge and thinking about Native American and pioneer homes. *Theory and Research in Social Education, 28*(1), 96–120.

Cohen, J. (1960). A coefficient of agreement for nominal scales. *Educational and Psychological Measurement, 20,* 37–46.

College Board. (2001). Improving student comprehension: Primary sources. In *The AP vertical team guide for social studies* (pp. 15–17). New York: Author.

College Board. (2006). *AP world history 2006 scoring guidelines.* Retrieved August 30, 2008 from: http://www.collegeboard.com/prod_downloads/ap/students/worldhistory/ap06_sg_world_history.pdf

Donovan, M.S. & Bransford, J.D. (2005). *How students learn: History, mathematics, and science in the classroom.* Washington, DC: National Academies Press.

Ferster, B., Hammond, T., & Bull, G. (2006). PrimaryAccess: Creating digital documentaries in the social studies classroom. *Social Education, 70*(3), 147–150.

Grossman, L. (2006, December 13). TIME person of the year: You. *TIME, 168*(26).

Hammond, T. (2007). *Media, scaffolds, canvases: A quantitative and qualitative investigation of student content knowledge outcomes in technology-mediated seventh-grade history instruction.* Unpublished doctoral dissertation, University of Virginia.

Hicks, D., Doolittle, P. E., & Ewing, T. (2004). The SCIM-C strategy: Expert historians, historical inquiry, and multimedia. *Social Education, 68*(3), 221–225.

Hofer, M., & Owings-Swan, K. (2005). Digital moviemaking he harmonization of technology, pedagogy and content. *International Journal of Technology in Teaching and Learning, 1*(2), 102–110.

Kajder, S. (2006) *Bringing the outside in: Visual ways to engage student readers.* Portland, ME: Stenhouse.

Lambert, J. (2003). *Digital storytelling cookbook and travelling companion.* Berkeley, CA: Digital Diner Press.

Lee, J. (2002). Digital history in the History/Social Studies classroom. *The History Teacher, 35*(4), 503–518.

Lee, J., & Clarke, W. (2003). High school social studies students uses of online historical documents related to the Cuban Missile Crisis. *The Journal of Interactive Online Learning, 2*(1). Retrieved October 24, 2005 from: http://www.ncolr.org/jiol/issues/PDF/2.1.3.pdf

Lee, J., & Molebash, P. (2004). Outcomes of various scaffolding strategies on student teachers' digital historical inquiries. *Journal of Social Studies Research, 26*(1), 25–35.

Lee, P., & Ashby, R. (2000). Progression in historical understanding among students ages 7–14. In P. Stearns, P. Seixas, & S. Wineburg (Eds.), *Knowing, teaching, and learning history: National and international perspectives* (pp. 199–222). New York: New York University Press.

Lenhart, A., & Madden, M. (2005, November 2). *Teen content creators and consumers.* Retrieved January 2, 2006 from: http://www.pewinternet.org/pdfs/PIP_Teens_Content_Creation.pdf

Martorella, P. (1997). Technology and the social studies r: Which way to the sleeping giant? *Theory and Research in Social Education, 25*(4), 511–514.

Mayer, R. (2005). Introduction to multimedia mearning. In R. Mayer (Ed.), *Cambridge handbook of multimedia learning* (pp. 1–16). Cambridge: Cambridge University Press.

McMichael, A., Rosenzweig, R., & O'Malley, M. (1996). Historians and the web: A beginner's guide. *Perspectives* (American Historical Association Newsletter), 34(January 1996). Retrieved July 13, 2006, from: http://www.historians.org/perspectives/issues/1996/9601/9601COM3.CFM

Mishra, P., & Koehler, M. (2006). Technological pedagogical content knowledge: A framework for teacher knowledge. *Teachers College Record, 108*(6), 1017–1054.

National Assessment Governing Board. (1998). *Writing framework and specifications for the 1998 National Assessment of Educational Progress.* Retrieved May 17, 2006 from http://www.nagb.org/pubs/writing.pdf

National Center for History in the Schools. (1996). *National standards for history* (Basic edition). Los Angeles: National Center for History in the Schools.

National Council for the Social Studies. (1994). *Expectations of excellence: Curriculum standards for social studies.* Washington, DC: National Council for the Social Studies.

National Writing Project. (2006). *Local site research initiative report: Cohort II, 2004–2005.* Berkeley, CA: National Writing Project. Retrieved May 6, 2006, from: http://www.writingproject.org/cs/nwpp/download/nwp_file/5683/LSRI-CohortllSummaryReport.pdf?x-r=pcfile_d

Nuthall, G. & Alton-Lee, A. (1995). Assessing classroom learning: How students use their knowledge and experience to answer classroom achievement test questions in science and social studies. *American Education Research Journal, 32*(1), 185–223.

Paxton, R. (2003). Don't know much about history—never did. *Phi Delta Kappan, 85*(4), 264–273.

Ratliff, B. (2006, February 3). Critic's notebook: A new trove of music video in the web's wild world. *The New York Times.*

Rainie, L., & Horrigan, J. (2005). *A decade of adoption: How the internet has woven itself into American life*. Retrieved July 13, 2006, from: http://www.pewinternet.org/pdfs/Internet_Status_2005.pdf

Risinger, C. F. (1992). *Trends in K–12 social studies*. Bloomington, IN: Clearinghouse for social studies/social science education. ED 351278.

Roblyer, M. D. (2005). Educational technology research that makes a difference: Series introduction. *Contemporary Issues in Technology and Teacher Education, 5*(2), 192–201.

Smith, J., & Niemi, R. (2001). Learning history in school: The impact of course work and instructional practices on achievement. *Theory and Research in Social Education, 29*(1), 18–42.

VanFossen, P., & Shiveley, J.M. (2000). Using the Internet to create primary source teaching packets. *The Social Studies, 91*, 244–252.

VanSledright, B. (2002). *In search of America's past: Learning to read history in elementary school*. New York: Teachers College Press.

VanSledright, B., & Limon, M. (2006). Learning and teaching social studies: A review of the cognitive research in history and geography. In P. Alexander & P. Winne (Eds.), *Handbook of educational psychology* (pp. 545–570). Mahwah, NJ: Lawrence Earlbaum Associates.

Wells, J., & Lewis, L. (2006). *Internet access in U.S. public schools and classrooms: 1994–2005* (NCES 2007-020). U.S. Department of Education. Washington, DC: National Center for Education Statistics.

Wineburg, S. (1990). *Historical problem solving: A study of the cognitive processes used in the evaluation of documentary evidence*. Unpublished doctoral dissertation, Stanford University.

Wineburg, S. (2001). *Historical thinking and other unnatural acts: Charting the future of teaching the past*. Philadelphia, PA: Temple University Press.

CHAPTER 4

CONCEPTUAL CHANGE AND THE PROCESS OF BECOMING A DIGITAL HISTORY TEACHER

Philip E. Molebash, Rosemary Capps, and Kelly Glassett

ABSTRACT

The process of training pre-service social studies and history teachers to effectively infuse technology into their practice is complex. In most cases, we are not only asking teachers to increase their knowledge and proficiency in using classroom technologies, we are also asking them to make conceptual changes in their overall perceptions of teaching. Schools and colleges of education sometime have only months to produce desired changes in perceptions and practice; therefore, we must carefully consider what types of experiences we should give pre-service teachers to accelerate the change process. We open this chapter by closely examining the literature concerned with the conceptual change and diffusion of innovation processes that social studies teachers are likely to take part in on their path toward becoming a "digital" history teacher. We then introduce and explain the use of Web Inquiry Projects as a strategy we used in pre-service teaching methods courses as a way to give future teachers the experiences they need to understand and see the viability of historical inquiry as a preferred method for teaching and learning, and to effectively leverage technology for this purpose. We close the chapter by introducing a conceptual change model centered on the concerns teachers

Research on Technology in Social Studies Education, pages 67–97

have as they become effective digital history teachers. The four reflexive and recursive stages to this model are orientation, understanding, feasibility, and progression.

INTRODUCTION

Jeremy Hersch is a real second-year high school history teacher, and the following is a true account of two hours of a typical day in his U.S. History class:

> Jeremy wanted his U.S. History students to not just understand the potential devastating effects of nuclear weapons; he also wanted them to experience the subtle fear of worldwide annihilation many people felt during the Cold War era. As a result he stayed up late last night putting a multimedia-filled presentation together. The results of his efforts could not have been any more effective. For 45 minutes the class was hooked. It was exactly the type of use of PowerPoint that his social studies methods instructor would have been proud of, for it wasn't PowerPoint that had the students hooked; rather, it was the topic and the variety of ways Jeremy presented it that mattered. In his presentation, Jeremy included several video clips such as a short segment from Terminator 2, the 1960s classic 'Duck and Cover,' footage of Hiroshima and Nagasaki soon after the bombs were dropped, and President Kennedy's address to the nation during the Cuban Missile Crisis. Of course, integrated into each slide were Jeremy's comments to provide historical context; yet even more important to him were the questions—an onslaught of student-generated questions. Getting students to feel comfortable asking any question other than, "What's going to be on the test?" took Jeremy months to accomplish, and getting them to ask good questions took even longer. But his efforts were finally paying off, for the questions were evidence that his students were taking interest in, and more important, ownership of the topic.

> With the presentation behind them, and the hook swallowed, Jeremy was satisfied that his students were properly motivated and prepared to do research for their upcoming mock trial entitled "Truman on Trial." In this assignment, students were to either prosecute Harry Truman for the murder of thousands of Japanese civilians as a result of dropping nuclear bombs on Hiroshima and Nagasaki, or they were to defend Truman's actions as the far lesser of two evils. Jeremy reminded his students of the assignment's specifics before they moved next door to the computer lab to do research for next week's trial. Although Jeremy's wish to have more than one computer in his classroom was likely years away, he was somehow able to monopolize the scheduling of the school's only multimedia lab.

> In the lab, students worked both individually and in groups, applying the historical research skills Jeremy had practiced with them all year long. A few students were unsure of how to defend Truman, so Jeremy spent some time

guiding them to a web site that discussed the alternative plan for a land invasion of Japan and the devastating projections of casualties attached to such an invasion. Before long, these students were off and running with a new idea.

Jeremy had a hard time believing how popular his class was. Only in his second year of teaching, he had nearly 300 students apply for one of only 70 slots available in the two sections he offered. At the end of the year, students' transcripts were still going to simply say "U.S. History," but they knew they were going to get the opportunity to do much more than if they were enrolled in the 'regular' sections of U.S. History. They were going to 'do history' as opposed to simply learn about history, and, best of all, they were going to create a digital video documentary for their year-end project. It took less than one year for word to spread around campus that Mr. Hersch's class was one that you wanted to take, not because it was easy but because it was relevant and fun. The net result was a class full of engaged students, and the key to it all, for Jeremy, was technology.

For social studies teacher educators who dream of generating effective technology-using teachers, Jeremy exemplifies what many of us seek. He has made technology a transparent means to the end of enhancing the learning of history among his high school students. We can be encouraged by the fact that Jeremy's philosophy of teaching and his vision for his classroom practice shifted significantly during his pre-service training. But what precisely changed within Jeremy that has transformed him into the teacher he is today, and what experiences caused these changes? Why don't more teachers make such fundamental shifts in their philosophy and practice? More important, what can social studies teacher educators do to ensure that a greater percentage of teachers make the changes we desire? These questions are difficult to answer, but resting at the core of this investigation is a topic that, although highly relevant, is somewhat foreign to social studies education. This topic, as this chapter's title signifies, is conceptual change as it related to the uses of technology and pedagogy.

Given that multimedia and information technologies are central to the conceptual changes that must take place in teachers if they are to effectively teach digital history, the theories pertaining to how individuals adopt technological innovations naturally complemented our research efforts to provide a new educational conceptual change model. We will therefore spend ample time in this chapter discussing general Diffusion of Innovation theory (Rogers, 2003), and the Concerns-based Adoption Model (Hall, George, & Rutherford, 1977; Hall & Hord, 2001; Hord et al., 1987), specifically as each theory can be applied to Conceptual Change theory (Posner et al., 1982).

On a more practical level, we will discuss how we have used Web Inquiry Projects (WIPs) (Molebash et al., 2002) as a strategy for facilitating conceptual change in pre-service teachers. Finally, based upon our research, we will propose a new conceptual change model relevant to the preparation of digital history teachers. Our hope is that this model will assist social studies teacher educators as they prepare new teachers to be capable and willing to make digital historical inquiry an everyday part of their students' learning.

THEORETICAL FRAME OF CONCEPTUAL CHANGE

Constructivist theorists, researchers, and practitioners see learning as an active creative process in which learners' prior knowledge affects how and what will be subsequently learned (DeVesta, 1987; Eggen & Kauchak, 2004). In keeping with the constructivist interest in what happens within the individual mind, educational theorists often pay attention to the contents and processes of change in the mind. This is clearly a radical constructivist assumption, and we would like to avoid the inner versus outer debate of constructivism by providing a compromise. We propose that constructions of knowledge are indeed ultimately a personal choice, but that the social environment heavily influences these choices. On a practical level, this "holistic constructivist" (Molebash, 2002) view leaves the door open for educators to create classroom (i.e., social) environments that can affect conceptual (i.e., individual) change in learners.

Posner et al. (1982) wrote the seminal work in the area of conceptual change, suggesting that concepts, the central assumptions and paradigms that frame our understanding of the world, are built into mental structures, and that they are deeply resistant to change. Posner et al. suggested four conditions that should exist to facilitate conceptual change: Dissatisfaction, Intelligibility, Plausibility, and Fruitfulness, defined thus:

- Dissatisfaction: Learners must have accumulated questions unsolved by their existing concepts.
- Intelligibility: Learners must be able to make sense of a new concept before they can explore its possibilities.
- Plausibility: A new concept must be able to solve the problems or questions that existing concepts could not.
- Fruitfulness: A new concept must have the potential to lead to new questions, products or areas of inquiry.

Many have interpreted the Posner et al. model as linear; however, we find it more productive to see these stages as reflexive and recursive. We will explore this later in this chapter. Posner et al. (1982) defined conceptual change as a rational process of exposure to, consideration of, and conscious assimilation or accommodation of new ideas. More recent conceptual change models have both contested and complemented this "cold" definition. Pintrich, Marx, and Boyle (1993) suggested that conceptual change is a "hot" process influenced by learning contexts, individual goals and motivational beliefs (p. 170). Dole and Sinatra (1998) added that the process of conceptual change involves weighing cognitive and motivational issues, including depth of learner cognitive engagement and strength of learner commitment to old ideas. Gregoire (2003) proposed that conceptual change is influenced by affective factors such as learner appraisal of the degree to which new ideas challenge the self and the degree to which learners can meet this challenge. From these various conceptual change propositions, we can begin to see a line of reasoning that suggests that the process of effecting conceptual change is deeply rooted in the experiences educators provide learners. This requires us to move beyond mere theoretical models and into practical applications of conceptual change.

Drawing on Posner et al.'s (1982) conditional framework to apply the ideas of conceptual change to teachers, Feldman (2000) explained that teachers base their classroom decisions on their own practical theories about what works and what does not, and he suggested that these practical theories are as durable as any other conceptions. In order to change their practical theories, he said, teachers must find that new ideas, techniques and conceptions of teaching are sensible, beneficial, and illuminating or explanatory. It seems logical, then, that talking about techniques and conceptions of teaching—as we are not shy of doing in teacher education—is not enough by itself. What pre-service teachers need are practical inquiry learning experiences to buttress the constructivist and inquiry conversations we frequently have in teacher education classes.

Before we continue to explore what these practical inquiry-learning experiences should include, we provide the reader with a working definition of conceptual change. For the purposes of this chapter, we turn to Dhindsa and Anderson's (2004) definition: "Conceptual change is interpreted as a context-appropriate change in the breadth and composition of conceptual knowledge occasioned by challenging experiences that require learners to rethink their understandings based on evidence from experience" (p. 64). For conceptual change in pre-service teachers, we turn to Yip's (2004) description of the desired goal:

> This "conceptual-change" view of learning emphasizes the impact of the learner's preconceptions in the process of learning as well as the need for an instructional strategy promoting active construction of new knowledge rather than just the passive transmission of information. (p. 77)

In other words, the general aim of teaching for conceptual change in pre-service teachers is to apply proven instructional strategies for the purpose of shifting their ideas of teaching and learning from didactic methods to more inquiry-oriented approaches. With regards to teaching for conceptual change in pre-service history teachers, the aim might more specifically be to shift their ideas regarding the nature of historical inquiry, thereby opening up the door to methods of teaching and learning history that lead students to ask relevant historical questions and interpret primary source artifacts to answer these questions. Technology becomes a logical extension of such an aim, for it has made available millions of digitized primary historical sources to students as well as provided ample pedagogical support for how to analyze and interpret them.

We use these definitions and goals as a starting point from which to explore the published research on the factors involved in facilitating conceptual change in pre-service teachers. An analysis of these factors will thereby justify our use of Web Inquiry Projects (WIPs) (Molebash et al., 2002) as a practical instructional strategy to be used in teacher education for this purpose, as called for by Yip (2004).

Factors to be Considered

In our attempts to facilitate the conceptual change that we desire in history teachers, we see a host of factors at play. Some are external and part of the social environment that, as teacher educators, we can control. Others are more internal, and based upon epistemological beliefs that have been ingrained in teachers long before they come to our teacher education courses. Often it is the external factors we directly control that have influence upon the internal factors that we hope to indirectly affect. External factors can include types of assignments given in class, practice and feedback, time allowed, use of technology, and teacher educator beliefs and presentation. As we aim to overcome the prior learning and teaching experiences pre-service teachers bring with them, we ultimately hope to positively change their overall epistemological beliefs, as well as hasten their adoption of technology into their teaching.

Types of assignments. Research indicates that assignments such as observations, reflections, and lesson plans, if well designed, can promote conceptual change in pre-service teachers because such assignments can encourage deep engagement, weighing of opposing arguments, and justification of opinions—all conducive to conceptual change (Dole & Sinatra, 1998). Observations can serve as useful venues for encountering different ideas of appropriate teaching methods, selection of curriculum, and evaluation of students. As Van Sickle and Kubinec (2003) noted, "it is most important to see the practices to gain a mental picture of what teaching and learning look, feel, sound, and act like with students. Thinking about it and planning without having seen the practices create[s] a very different picture in [the] mind" (p. 260). Observing model teachers who are more experienced at incorporating inquiry-oriented teaching strategies can provide pre-service teachers with models from which to take ideas. The more often pre-service teachers can observe others, the more chances they will have to consider whether they are satisfied with their old ideas, and the more experience they will have to enhance the intelligibility of the new teaching ideas that they encounter.

However, observations alone may not be enough to prompt deep conceptual change. Pre-service teachers who discuss, reflect, and write about what they have observed in others' classrooms can be led to explicitly confront both their own beliefs and other explanations for the same phenomena, an important step in conceptual change. Furthermore, we add that active observation is needed. By this we mean pre-service teachers should experience learning in inquiry-oriented ways, and from this lens they can reflect upon their experience from both the learner and teacher's perspective. Entwistle and Walker (2000) warn that teacher educators should be clear about the purpose of reflection—they should not just tell pre-service teachers to self-reflect for teaching solutions because lack of experience may leave pre-service teachers with few new ideas for reflection. By making observation an active experience, pre-service teachers are far more capable of looking within because their reflection will be based upon personal, as opposed to secondhand experience. Therefore, as they provide pre-service teachers with authentic inquiry learning experiences, teacher educators could assign reflections in which student teachers compare and contrast their own conceptions of the inquiry they just experienced to their previous and typically more traditional learning experiences. Once pre-service teachers have had opportunities to experience, observe, discuss, reflect on and write about teaching, they are better prepared to create their own lesson plans, for which they must make pedagogical decisions as to content and presentation. If teachers are required not only to plan but also to justify their choices, these assignments can promote conceptual change.

Practice and feedback. In keeping with the supposition that experience matters, pre-service teachers should have opportunities to put into action lesson activities that mirror their inquiry learning experiences— there is no better way to test the Posner et al. (1982) stages of *Plausibility* and *Fruitfulness* of a new idea than to try it out in the classroom. To this end, many pre-service teachers are assigned to work in K–12 classrooms under the supervision of a practicing teacher. These field placements are meant to provide for practice and feedback, valuable components in conceptual change. Unfortunately, we have to be realistic about the realities of these field placements. Rarely will pre-service teachers be given opportunities to enact inquiry in their student teaching, often because of curriculum constraints placed upon them by cooperating teachers. Furthermore, feedback from cooperating teachers on implemented inquiry activities may yield little meaningful direction, because cooperating teachers sometimes lack inquiry experiences themselves and therefore adhere to predominantly didactic teaching practices. In effect, depending upon student teaching could perhaps do more harm than good in our conceptual change efforts. This is all the more reason to provide as many authentic inquiry learning experiences, including reflection, in our teaching methods courses. We will point out, however, that when inquiry-oriented feedback is provided in student teaching on what works, what does not, and why, experimenting with implementing inquiry techniques is invaluable (Smith, Baker, & Oudeans, 2001).

Time. Other research also indicates that time may be the crucial factor in whether or not all of the other efforts described so far actually make a difference. As Artiles and McClafferty (1998) pointed out, just getting teachers used to new ideas is not enough—we want to see a corresponding change in practice. Correa, Hudson, and Hayes (2004) suggest that one semester is a good start, but one semester or even one year is not generally enough time to allow for more than the beginning stages of conceptual change. Tal, Dori, and Keiny (2001) also challenge the longevity of conceptual change after short programs. Deeper and more lasting change that will affect teaching practices may take several years to mature (Englert, Raphael, & Mariage, 1998; Entwistle & Walker, 2000; Fonder-Solano & Burnett, 2004; Van Sickle & Kubinec, 2003). Artiles and McClafferty (1998) further explain the implications of these studies for pre-service teachers: at the end of one or two semesters, pre-service teachers may still be in the midst of reconfiguring their conceptions to accommodate the new ideas that their experience has introduced. In order to solidify the ideas and the practices that follow, pre-service teachers need considerable additional time for observation, discussion, practice and reflection (Borko, Davinroy & Bliem, 2000; Smith et al., 2001). In our research with the application of Web Inquiry Projects (WIPs) in teaching methods courses, we find time to be a critical factor as well. We will expand on this issue later.

Use of technology. Technology can provide expanded opportunities for observation, reflection, and exposure to new ideas described above as important for the process of conceptual change in pre-service teachers. Developing teachers who incorporate digital historical inquiry methods into their teaching requires that they not just shift their teaching philosophies from objectivism to constructivism, they must also embrace a myriad of relatively new multimedia and information technologies. Fortunately, these two goals do not have to be exclusive. Research shows us that constructivist teachers are more likely to embrace technology, and conversely, technology has the potential to facilitate the desired shift in teaching philosophies toward constructivism (Molebash, 2004; Wenglinsky, 2005).

Teacher educator beliefs and presentation. Beyond curricular adjustments, such as types of assignments and use of technology, is the factor of teacher educator beliefs and presentation, which can exert considerable influence on pre-service teachers' conceptions of teaching and learning. Many pre-service teachers have experienced years of didactic teaching as learners, and as noted above, such repeated observations over prolonged periods of time lead to conceptions that didactic teaching is the acceptable and realistic norm instead of one possible way to approach teaching (Trigwell, Prosser, & Waterhouse, 1999). No matter the content and concepts presented in teacher preparation classes, if pre-service teachers do not have a model of teaching for conceptual change in their teacher educators, they will have a much more difficult time changing their ideas and future teaching practice (Prosser, Martin, & Trigwell, 2005).

Prior learning experiences. Before understanding changes in mental concepts, we need to understand what conceptions pre-service teachers hold of teaching and learning. Pre-service teachers frequently assume that the way they experienced a subject is the way it must be experienced, and their resistance to new ideas makes it very difficult to overcome years of practice and observation in didactic classrooms (Agee, 1998; Campanario, 2002; Volkmann & Zgagacz, 2004). Molebash (2004) found that pre-service elementary teachers' perceptions of social studies, social studies teaching, and technology integration were conditioned by their previous K–12 experiences, whether positive or negative. Too often teachers covet these experiences and subsequently develop their own nonreflective teaching knowledge framework to match (Clark & Peterson, 1986; Feiman-Nemser, McDiarmid, Melnick, & Parker, 1989; Jackson, 1986; Lortie, 1975; Wilson, Miller, & Yerkes, 1993). For conceptual change to occur in pre-service teachers, we must provide "second-order changes" (Ertmer, 2005, p. 26) because they require confronting "fundamental beliefs, [require] new ways of both seeing and doing things" (p. 26), and cause these teachers to reflect upon their prior ways of doing and thinking. They are thereby more likely to see those prior practices as inadequate and seek to change.

Epistemological beliefs. Intimately tied to pre-service teachers' prior learning experiences are their epistemological beliefs. These beliefs have a direct effect on how easily or quickly pre-service teachers undergo conceptual change (Sinatra & Kardash, 2004). Abd-El-Khalick and Akerson (2004) studied pre-service teachers in a conceptual change-oriented science teaching methods class, and they found that students who saw teaching as *clearing up misconceptions* and who held deep processing orientations—those who actively sought to reconcile inconsistent ideas—developed more accurate and elaborate views of the nature of science over the course of the class. We propose that similar approaches ought to be taken with pre-service teachers and the nature of historical inquiry. Entwistle and Walker (2000) described the process of conceptual change as a nested hierarchy of developmental stages, saying that those who had only begun to think about possible changes from transmission teaching will have a more difficult time making major changes because they will not yet be ready for major changes. Those who have already explored alternative conceptions will have an easier transition into constructivist methods. Epistemological beliefs not only affect the process of change, they also affect teaching decisions, and they can interfere with the implementation of new approaches if the two underlying ideologies are not consistent, "result[ing] in only incremental, or first-order, changes in teaching style [that] remain far removed from the best practices advocated in the literature" (Ertmer, 2005, p. 26).

ADOPTION THEORIES

Current literature has explored many aspects of conceptual change but has done little to connect it to the theories related to the adoption of innovations. Digital history involves inquiry learning, which is an innovative approach to most pre-service teachers. Digital history also involves innovative uses of technology; therefore, we offer an overview of the two adoption theories most relevant to our research.

Diffusion of Innovations

Rogers (2003) distinctly separates the diffusion process from the adoption process (as opposed to diffusion alone). While the diffusion process permeates through society and groups, the adoption process is most relevant to the individual. Rogers defines the adoption *process* as "the mental process through which an individual passes from first hearing about an innovation to final adoption" (p. 35). The five steps in this process are: Knowledge (awareness), Persuasion (interest), Decision (evaluation), Implementation (trial), and Confirmation (adoption). Throughout the adoption process the individual seeks knowledge and skills and will proceed through the various steps and eventually adopt—or reject—an innovation.

Rogers also developed five variables that affect the adoption *rate* of any particular innovation. These include: Perceived attributes of innovations, Type of innovation or decision, Communication channels, Nature of the social system, and Extent of change agents' promotion efforts. Numerous scholars have effectively utilized Rogers's framework to demonstrate the adoption and use of educational technology (e.g., Anderson, Varnhagen, & Campbell, 1998; Chuang, Thompson, & Schmidt, 2003). Also, Rogers's template has helped explain how the characteristics of educational products and programs interact with other factors to affect the diffusion process of educational technology (e.g., Degennaro & Mak, 2002/2003; Meehan, 1976; Odabasi, 2000).

Some researchers argue that diffusion of innovation theory is, at best, a descriptive tool that is less than strong in its explanatory power, less than useful in predicting outcomes, and less than able to provide guidance for accelerating the rate of adoption (Davison et al., 2001; Joseph & Reigeluth, 2005). Nonetheless, it provides a valuable "hook" on which to hang research and practice. While Rogers provides a generic model of the process of the adoption of an innovation, some case studies show that alternative models may be more applicable to school systems (e.g., Dooley, 1999; James et al., 2000; Joseph & Reigeluth, 2005). These models vary from the one proposed by Rogers (2003) by specifically addressing educational technology and attempting to identify more specific factors that will lead to the adoption of innovation in school settings. Rogers's model, as well as some of its offshoots, assisted us in considering the factors that affect history teachers' adoption or rejection of digital historical teaching methods. However, teacher professional development is a complex human system, and therefore the simplicity of Rogers's model, which would otherwise be its strength, limits it to some degree. We therefore extend our discussion of the adoption of innovations to include the Concerns-based Adoption Model (Hall, George, & Rutherford, 1977; Hall & Hord, 2001; Hord et al., 1987).

Concerns-Based Adoption Model

The Concerns-based Adoption Model (CBAM) (Hall et al., 977; Hall & Hord, 2001; Hord et al., 1987) acknowledges that learning brings change and that supporting people in change is critical for learning to take hold. This model holds that people considering and experiencing change evolve regarding the questions they ask and the way they use the particular change. With regards to preparing pre-service teachers to teach in innovative ways that often include the use of multimedia and information technologies, CBAM can be particularly informative in developing effective programs of study and guiding research as it revolves around conceptual change.

CBAM describes adoption of innovation in terms of *levels of use*. It includes eight categories with corresponding behavioral indicators (Hall & Hord, 2001; Hord et al., 1987); these are:

1. Non-use: The user has no interest.
2. Orientation: The user shows initiative to learn more about an innovation.
3. Preparation: The user has definite plans to use the innovation.

4. Mechanical: The user changes to better organize an innovation.
5. Routine: The user has established a pattern of use.
6. Refinement: The user makes changes to increase outcomes.
7. Integration: The user makes deliberate efforts to coordinate with others.
8. Renewal: The user seeks more effective alternatives to the established use of the innovation.

The concept of "concerns" has been described as follows: "Depending on their personal make-up, knowledge, and experience, each person perceives and mentally contends with a given issue differently; thus there are different kinds of concerns" (Hall & Hord, 2001, p. 59). There are seven stages of *concern* that the authors contend correspond to adoption of innovations (Hall & Hord, 2001; Hord et al., 1987); these are:

1. Awareness: The potential user is not concerned.
2. Informational: The potential user would like to know more about it.
3. Personal: The potential user asks, "How will using it affect me?"
4. Management: The user asks, "Am I spending all my time getting materials ready?"
5. Consequence: The user asks, "Is use affecting learners?"
6. Collaboration: The user asks, "How can I relate what I am doing to what others are doing?"
7. Refocusing: The user thinks, "I have some ideas that would make things even better."

These stages have major implications for adoption of innovative pedagogy and uses of technology in education. First, they point out the importance of assisting people at whatever stage they are and answering the questions they ask when they ask them. Second, this model suggests the importance of paying attention to implementation over several years, because it takes at least three years for early concerns to be resolved and later ones to emerge (Hall & Hord, 2001). Furthermore, concerns of management can last at least a year, especially when teachers are implementing a school year's worth of new curricula or when new approaches to teaching require practice, each approach bringing new surprises (Hall & Hord, 2001). Third, with all the demands placed on teachers, it is often the case that once their methods become routine they never have the time and convenience to focus on whether—and in what ways—students are learning.

Change entails an unfolding of experience and a gradual development of skill and sophistication when using an innovation. An individual's concerns can progress from those typical of nonusers to those associated with fairly sophisticated use. When we introduce innovative inquiry-oriented teaching strategies that include the use of multimedia and information technologies, such as we do when we prepare teachers to teach using digital historical methods, we must account for concerns related to content knowledge, pedagogical knowledge, pedagogical content knowledge (Shulman, 1987), and technological pedagogical content knowledge (Mishra & Koehler, 2006).

The theory and research behind CBAM shows that there is a general pattern to the intensity of the different stages of concern and that changes in this pattern can be linked to the change process as it unfolds (Hall & Hord, 2001). As teachers begin to use the new program or innovation, concerns become more intense in the area of *Management* (task concerns), and as they become more experienced and skilled with an innovation, the tendency is for concerns at the lower stages to decrease in intensity while those in higher stages, such as *Consequence, Collaboration,* and *Refocusing,* become more intense (impact concerns) (Hall et al., 1977; Hall & Hord, 2001).

This theory indicates that learning experiences evolve over time, take place in different settings, rely on varying degrees of external expertise, and change with participant needs (Hall & Hord, 2001). It depicts change as a process that takes "3-to-5 years" (p. 6) to complete. CBAM seems to be best utilized when one wants to monitor change efforts, which is precisely what our present research requires and why it plays such an important part in our developing conceptual change model.

WEB INQUIRY PROJECTS

Based upon a meta-analysis of the aforementioned research on conceptual change, Diffusion of Innovations, and CBAM, we concluded that providing future teachers with multiple, varied inquiry learning experiences in their training would be vital to the process of stimulating conceptual change in the way they perceive the viewing of history, and consequently how they will teach history. Therefore, four years ago, we made Web Inquiry Projects the central theme of our social studies methods courses.

Web Inquiry Projects (WIPs) are simply defined as "open inquiry learning activities that leverage the use of uninterpreted online data and information" (Molebash et al., 2002). In the history classroom, they shift the locus of students' studies from learning about history to doing history. WIPs require students to play an active role in asking historically relevant questions, determining procedures necessary for answering these questions, and locating the online primary resources needed to answer the questions. The focus in a WIP is on the process of performing historical inquiry and the historical narrative that follows.

WIPs are not precisely lesson plans, in that they do not give step-by-step directions for teachers or students to follow as they complete a historical inquiry. To give students all of the pieces to the process of a historical inquiry would be to remove the inquiry from the activity. WIPs, instead, provide teachers with a detailed example of how a historical inquiry would be completed, from the beginning of asking historical questions, all the way through primary source analysis and the presentation of findings. The goal of a WIP is to have learners play significant roles at each stage of the inquiry, so a WIP exists to enable a teacher to insert the necessary scaffolding at each stage in the process to ensure that students are successful. Only one portion of a WIP is usually given directly to students, the Hook, as a way to provoke historical questioning. The goal is to elicit questions from students similar to those presented in the WIP, and then to guide students through an inquiry similar to the one presented. Including the Hook, there are seven stages to WIPs:

1. Hook: sparks students' interest in the topic with the goal of eliciting inquiry-oriented questions from them.
2. Questions: possible historical inquiry questions.
3. Procedures: procedures for how to successfully complete the investigation.
4. Data Investigation: a list of web sites with relevant primary source data.
5. Analysis: a sample of a completed historical inquiry analysis.
6. Findings: a sample of answers to the historical questions and/or ideas for how students could present an historical narrative that displays an understanding of the content.
7. New Questions: new questions arising as a result of the inquiry.

We propose that in order for teachers to be prepared to carry out digital history instructional activities in a WIP-like manner with their students, they must first experience WIPs in their social studies methods courses. That is, they must perform a historical inquiry of their own, where they ask the historical questions, go through the steps necessary to answer these questions, and produce a high-quality historical narrative.

For three years we have made WIPs the central theme of pre-service teachers' social studies methods courses. In addition to participating in several WIP-like experiences over the course of the semester, teachers must also complete a series of eight assignments that ultimately yield a completed WIP—that is, they perform a thorough digital historical inquiry. The eight assignments are as follows:

1. Topic/Big Idea: Rather than simply choose an historical time period or event for the topic of their WIP, pre-service teachers must develop a Big Idea addressed by the topic or event (see Engle &

Ochoa, 1988). As an example, for topics related to the Cuban Missile Crisis a Big Idea might be, "Leaders make difficult decisions that affect many people."

2. Inquiry Questions: Pre-service teachers must produce at least two inquiry questions that address the topic and Big Idea. For the above example, an inquiry question specifically related to the topic might be, "How was the Cuban Missile Crisis resolved?" A question that addresses the Big Idea might be, "How do we make difficult decisions?"

3. Children's Thinking: In order to better understand children's historical thinking, pre-service teachers take their inquiry questions and ask representative students these questions (see Barton, 2005). Pre-service teachers must then reflect upon these responses either in a research paper or in an edited digital video.

4. Procedures   Before pre-service teachers are allowed to begin their quest for answers, they must first define a set of procedures for how they are going to do so. They must decide what information they need to find and how they will perform their analysis once they find this information.

5. Data Investigation Concept Map: Pre-service teachers search the Internet for digitized primary source artifacts that will help answer their inquiry questions. Potential resources are put into an electronic graphic organizer.

6. Historical Analysis: Pre-service teachers use the primary sources and put into practice the historical research strategies their methods instructor has taught them. Often a series of concept maps are created during the analysis. Ultimately, pre-service teachers provide answers to their inquiry questions, sometimes written as short historical narratives (see Hicks, Doolittle, & Ewing, 2004; Wineburg, 2001).

7. Hook: Pre-service teachers consider and plan for how they would spark their future students' interests in the Topic/Big Idea to elicit the desired historical inquiry questions.

8. Development of Web Site: The products of all of the above steps are put into a web site.

The conceptual categories of (a) content knowledge, (b) pedagogical knowledge, (c) pedagogical content knowledge (Shulman, 1987), and (d) technological pedagogical content knowledge (Mishra & Koehler, 2006) form a useful framework for justifying the use of WIPs in teaching methods courses. Content knowledge is the depth and breadth of knowledge in a content area such as English, history, etc. Ideally, teachers know facts and concepts of the discipline, frameworks for explaining such disciplinary facts and concepts, and the path new content must take to become part of the discipline (Shulman, 1987). If teachers do not have this knowledge they cannot teach their discipline effectively or integrate technology effectively (Chua & Wu, 2005). General pedagogical knowledge—such as learning theories, individual cognitive development, and classroom management—serves teachers across all subject areas when making general pedagogical choices. Pedagogical content knowledge is specific for each content area: Teachers within a discipline make pedagogical decisions about instruction and learning based on (a) what they believe are the purposes for teaching the content, (b) what knowledge they believe students should be developing (noting what has been taught in previous and subsequent grade levels), (c) what discipline-based teaching materials are available, and (d) what representations or activities they have successfully used in the past (Eggen & Kauchak, 2004). Technological pedagogical content knowledge emphasizes the need to situate technology knowledge within content and pedagogical knowledge (Mishra & Koehler, 2006).

According to Borko and Putnam (1995, 1996) and Bransford and Schwartz (1999), a teacher's prior knowledge affects future learning. In learning situations, teachers interpret, question, and evaluate new knowledge through previously acquired knowledge and experiences (Bransford & Schwartz, 1999). Additionally, an important part of teachers' lifelong learning is the "expansion and elaboration of their professional knowledge base" (Borko & Putnam, 1995, p. 36). Overall, knowledge is essential because teachers use it to determine actions in the classroom. Wenglinsky (2005) argues that teachers need to understand the "curriculum and how instructional practices other than educational technology fit in" (p. 28) before they can begin to integrate technology effectively. We advance that the use of WIPs just described affect all four categories of content knowledge, pedagogical knowledge, pedagogical content knowledge, and technological pedagogical content knowledge.

RESEARCH METHODS

The research reported in this chapter is focused on conceptual change among pre-service teachers enrolled in an undergraduate teacher education program. Our study included 124 pre-service teachers enrolled in one semester social studies methods courses. Of these participants, 88 were enrolled in elementary methods and 36 were enrolled in secondary methods. These methods courses included a range of activities focused on technology. All students completed Web Inquiry Projects as a major component of the classes. The WIP project served as a context for developing knowledge about teaching with technology.

Participants took a pre-survey during the first class meeting and a post-survey approximately one week after the completion of the course. Surveys asked a variety of questions related to teachers' prior learning experiences, their attitudes toward inquiry learning, their current teaching philosophy, and their current vision of an ideal learning environment. Participants were given a writing prompt for a weekly reflective journal that they turned in as an assignment. Prompts queried them on their experiences participating in inquiry learning activities in the methods course. All assignments, particularly the completed WIPs, were used in analysis. In order to gain more insight on survey responses and reflection journals, and the effects or lack of effects of developing a WIP, one-third of the participants were also interviewed after both surveys were collected and analyzed. Our research continued with six elementary and six secondary participants who were followed through their first two years of in-service teaching. We purposively chose these 12 participants after the methods courses were completed based upon our perception of how far through the adoption process they had progressed. Four were resistant to inquiry learning and technology integration, four were considering adopting inquiry and technology integration, and four were early adopters who were eager to make inquiry and technology an active part of a digital history classroom. These twelve teachers' classrooms were observed five hours apiece on days that they described as typical of their approach to teaching history. In addition, each was interviewed two times, and each allowed the researchers to analyze developed lessons and student products.

In our efforts to develop a conceptual change model that describes the complex process new teachers go through as they either adopt or reject the innovative pedagogical strategies and uses of technology that they experienced in their pre-service training, we have previously applied Erickson's (1986) method of analytic induction to analyze our data (see Molebash, 2004). In analytic induction the researcher must establish an evidentiary warrant for assertions by repeatedly reviewing the data corpus to test for validity of assertions by seeking confirming and disconfirming evidence. Over the span of the past three years we have iterated toward a conceptual change model. In this work, we have applied our previous findings (Molebash, 2004) toward the development of a specific Concerns-Based Conceptual Change Model.

CONCERNS-BASED CONCEPTUAL CHANGE MODEL

Not everybody changes, and when change does occur it can take as much as three to five years (Englert et al., 1998; Entwistle & Walker, 2000; Fonder-Solano & Burnett, 2004; Hall & Hord, 2001; Van Sickle & Kubinec, 2003). How much an individual changes and how fast is predicated on their strength of commitment to their prior pedagogical conceptions and the intensity of their concerns for pedagogy and learners. The years of learning how to be a teacher before pre-service teachers enter their teacher training called the "apprenticeship of observation" by Lortie (1975), is for most teachers the biggest obstacle between them and an inquiry-oriented pedagogy (p. 61). For a few, however, past experiences can be the catalyst for embracing inquiry. Regardless of whether or not they adopt or reject digital historical inquiry methods, the teachers we studied all navigated or are still navigating their way through a process of conceptual change that is heavily influenced by the intensity of their concerns for pedagogy and learners. There are four major stages to the model we propose:

- Orientation
- Understanding
- Feasibility
- Progression

While there is both an intuitive and empirically based order to these stages, we stress the reflexive and recursive nature of the overall model. *Orientation* is a stage that informs all three of the other stages, and therefore, in our model, though it is most prominent initially, it persists throughout. *Understanding* and *Feasibility* are closely tied to each other and prove to be the lifeblood behind any conceptual change that occurs. Most conceptual change models use the term *Fruitful* as a descriptor for a final stage, which gives the appearance of an established endpoint to the process. Our conceptual change model, however, includes *fruitful* only as the first indicator of a more forward-looking stage we entitle *Progression*. We found it necessary to label our final stage with a term that suggests change to be an ongoing part of teachers' careers. This is how we justify the reflexive nature of our model. Figure 4.1 presents a simple visual representation of our model as it transpires over time. We deliberately have not included specific time frames

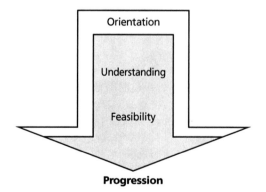

Figure 4.1 Concerns-based conceptual change model.

for each stage because of the reflexive and recursive nature of the model and because of the unpredictability of how fast—or slow—individuals accept or reject change.

Within each stage are several connected variables with which participants expressed concern. Because the participants in this study were navigating through the stages in so many different ways and at different paces, and because they expressed similar concerns but at varied levels, we discuss our model in light of the behavioral indicators that describe how participants contended with the concerns they had.

Orientation

Launching the process of change involves being exposed to new ideas, explanations, concepts, tools, and strategies. A variety of indicators presented themselves as teachers became oriented to digital historical inquiry approaches to learning. These orientation indicators often permeated across the other conceptual change stages.

Unconcern. Because most participants entered social studies methods with their own perceptions of what the course was supposed to be about, initially they were unconcerned and were therefore somewhat ambivalent toward the historical inquiry strategies presented to them. This was particularly true of pre-service secondary teachers, who believed their content expertise and passion for history was sufficient. Eventually, and often quickly, lack of concern gave way to a holistic concern of how digital history might impact them as a teacher.

Disorientation. As they experienced inquiry, a side to learning that was new to them, many became disoriented and uncertain about what it meant to be an effective history teacher. For some, this unsettling feeling persisted throughout the entire methods course and into student teaching.

Dissatisfaction. Many, but not all, participants became dissatisfied with their prior, more traditional philosophies of teaching and learning. Although dissatisfaction is often considered a requisite condition for conceptual change to occur, we found that even though it often evidenced itself in the process, a number of teachers did move to other stages without first experiencing dissatisfaction with their prior conceptions. Instead, they replaced what they considered to be a legitimate philosophy with a better philosophy.

Curiosity. Becoming aware of innovative inquiry approaches to teaching history sparked a curiosity to want to know more in nearly every participant. Curiosity evidenced itself across the continuum, from day one of the methods course for some, but for others up to three years later.

Excitement. Embraced by a small majority of participants was excitement for the possibilities of digital history. Like the variable of curiosity, excitement evidenced itself at unpredictable times. For those entering their teacher training already thinking "outside the box," there was immediate excitement in finally being able to put theories and proven strategies behind their thinking. On the other end of the continuum were teachers who first needed a year or more of real classroom experiences to support what they had been exposed to in their training before excitement presented itself.

Fear. Sometimes teachers responded to the inquiry experiences in their teacher training with a fear that they would not be capable of creating inquiry learning environments for their future students. This fear was usually a result of the lack of personal experience they had with learning in inquiry-oriented ways.

Understanding

All proposed conceptual change models contain a stage synonymous to Posner et al.'s (1982) stage of *Intelligibility*. In our research, we discovered that in order for participants to accommodate the changes we desired, they need adequate knowledge of content, pedagogical content (Shulman, 1987), and technological pedagogical content (Mishra & Koehler, 2006). As participants were oriented to digital historical methods using the WIP model, many become curious and excited almost immediately, perhaps even believing these methods would be *Feasible* in their own teaching (see next stage); however, they were far from fully understanding how to put these methods into practice. Participants' experiences in their teacher training, particularly the WIP-inspired theme of their social studies methods course, often combined with later teaching experiences in the K–12 classroom, were necessary in order for these teachers to acquire a solid understanding in the three areas. Some teachers, particularly elementary pre-service teachers, lacked content knowledge, or at least a context understanding of important historical events. Others' pedagogical knowledge and pedagogical content knowledge was underdeveloped. And for nearly every participant, technological skills and knowledge and the complex notion of technological pedagogical content knowledge were lacking. Vital to processing the requisite knowledge in these areas and putting this knowledge into practice was a metacognitive awareness that they did indeed need this knowledge. We found that teachers who developed expertise across these areas, or at least who monitored whether or not they were growing in understanding, were most likely to employ digital history in their teaching. In so doing, they were actively monitoring the *Feasibility* of making digital history a part of their teaching repertoire.

Content and context expertise. The pedagogy of historical inquiry instruction allows requires that teachers possess rich and multifaceted content knowledge. Most teachers in our study felt that their content knowledge was inadequate to teach historical inquiry and even more traditional and less demanding instructional approaches such as lecture. This belief was most pronounced among pre-service elementary teachers. Context knowledge, the ability to place historical events in time and space even if the event under analysis is not thoroughly known, was also a concern. After teachers mastered a particular historical topic as a result of completing their WIP, they felt much more confident in their ability to lead students through a historical inquiry activity on the topic.

Pedagogical and pedagogical content expertise. Participants entered social studies methods familiar with a host of constructivist/inquiry teaching strategies, for they were discussed often in their prior pre-service coursework. Rare, however, were opportunities to witness teaching models for inquiry, and even rarer were experiences in prior classes to participate in inquiry learning activities. Despite their theoretical understanding of effective inquiry pedagogy, they felt uncertain about their ability to make inquiry a part of their teaching. They described, even two years later, the experience of participating in a variety of inquiry learning activities in their social studies methods course, culminating with the creation of a WIP, as crucial to their understanding of how to connect inquiry pedagogy to the teaching of historical content. As one teacher said,

> The WIP was more than I expected, because I was forced to learn and to think about the whole process of how I was learning. I'd probably lecture to my kids all the time, just like my history teachers did to me. Now even on the days when I do lecture, I stop, listen to them [students], and constantly try to think of a way to make them want to own the history.

Technological and technological pedagogical content expertise. Because technology plays a vital role in digital history, teachers believed that they first needed to understand and feel comfortable using a variety of multimedia and web-based technologies. For all but a handful of participants, gaining expertise with technology was considered to be the first major obstacle in accommodating change that required the use of technology. As a result of learning to use technology in the context of digital history, they quickly recognized, however, the distinct difference between knowing how to use technology and knowing how to use technology to teach history. The majority felt liberated by this recognition, for they believed it freed them from feeling like they had to know how to use technology in every possible way. Instead, they saw more value in gravitating toward a subset of technology tools that fit within the context of digital history.

Feasibility

Working in tandem with the prior described stage of *Understanding* is the stage of *Feasibility*. Here participants often expressed that as they grew in their understanding of digital history, they could not help but to continually assess its potential worth in their future or current teaching. *Understanding*, by itself, was not sufficient for participants to make accommodations in their teaching, for many made clear statements about the value of taking an inquiry approach to history, some even seeing it as the superior approach, but they still sometimes leaned toward concluding that "it just isn't for me." Therefore, they also needed to answer the personal question, "Does this approach to teaching history make sense for me?" Although this same question presents itself on the surface in the early stages of *Orientation* (see above), we discovered deeper levels of concern with this question at this stage, both at the micro and macro level. At the micro level were concerns focused mostly on the question, "How will embracing digital history affect me?" At the macro level were concerns focused on the question, "How will making digital history a part of my teaching affect my students?"

Management. Nearly every participant discussed at least some concern over a variety of task concerns related to their ability to manage making digital history a part of their regimen. Time was the chief concern, which included more specific concerns of lesson planning, setup, and cleanup. Even early adopter participants brought up time as a concern, particularly as it involved coordinating their schedules with other teachers in order to make digital history cross curricular. Evidencing itself with nearly half of those interviewed was a concern over how doing digital history might take away from time needed to prepare students for mandated tests. This concern was less focused on how students would perform on these tests, and rather, more focused on how it might detract from the teachers' assessment by superiors, such as school principals.

Teaching beliefs. During the ever-present *Orientation* stage, participants are compelled to compare and contrast their prior learning experiences with the ones they experienced during their teacher training, and later as they taught in their own classroom. As such, they discussed having to continuously assess whether or not their epistemological beliefs agreed with digital history pedagogy. Ultimately, in order for digital history to be feasible to them, they often needed to ask whether or not digital history fit, as most teachers called it, their "teaching style." Most acknowledged that their initial vision for the type of teacher they thought they were going to be needed to change in order for them to be effective digital history teachers. For those who have made this transformation, comments were made that they felt that they had no choice but to change their "style" because as they came to understand digital historical inquiry and how it could be superior to traditional methods (see *Understanding* stage), their teaching beliefs changed, and their "style" naturally changed to follow suit.

Learning outcomes. As we have stated, participants typically agreed on a theoretical level that inquiry-oriented approaches to learning history were superior to more didactic methods, yet they still questioned how digital history would impact learners in a practical sense. There was a deep concern among those who have yet to embrace digital history over how students would perform on mandated tests. For those practicing digital history, experience had informed them that student' performance on mandated tests would either improve or be unaffected as a result of their adoption of digital history. In lieu of worrying over test results, these teachers instead felt concern for preparing students for 21st century careers. This concern caused teachers to develop a deeper commitment to digital historical inquiry, for they believed that through this approach they were doing a better job preparing their students to think independently, ask questions, do research, and defend answers—skills and strategies they considered critical to being a contributing member to today's workforce. Along this line, they were also concerned about converting students' tacit knowledge into action—that is, they wanted their students to become effective and contributing democratic citizens.

Collaboration. Because authentic inquiry learning is rare in today's schools, we found a significant minority of the participants worried that, if they taught using an inquiry approach, their fellow teachers and administrators might misinterpret their inquiry approach as "lazy teaching." Consequently they wondered how they could adequately justify what they were doing or wanted to do. As one participant said, "It doesn't matter whether or not inquiry is the right thing to do. If my principal kills it then I can't do it." Participants also suggested that because of inadequate technology resources at their schools, they needed to collaborate with technology coordinators in order to secure necessary computer resources to make digital history possible.

Progression

Just as with the original Posner et al. (1982) conceptual change model, we found *fruitful* to be an accurate descriptor to illustrate the successful occurrence of conceptual change. For those teachers who tested the *Feasibility* of digital history in a particular learning activity and experienced success, nearly every single one concluded that digital history was going to continue to work in other contexts as well. However, we discovered the term *fruitful*, by itself, inadequately described the progression of thinking we heard from those participants who have made digital history a part of their teaching.

From these teachers we learned that their efforts to become effective history teachers were just beginning, and that their teaching would continue to evolve for the duration of their careers. Their behaviors and concerns at this stage were now focused on how to improve inquiry learning among their students.

Fruitful. As mentioned, those teachers who tested the *Feasibility* of digital history methods and experienced success continued to apply these methods in other contexts. However, rather than accept a personal status quo with regards to their newfound successes, their focus oriented itself toward continually making adaptations to their teaching.

Adaptation. Even after completing a successful digital history activity with students, teachers' chief concern was assessing what worked and what did not, and based upon this self-evaluation, they hoped to discover new ideas to make the next activity even better. At this step their concern was centered on refocusing their efforts, being innovative, and becoming more willing to take risks.

Collaboration. For those in the *Progression* stage, we saw a deepening of the concern for collaboration than they had during the *Feasibility* stage. Instead of being concerned with justifying what they were doing to colleagues and superiors, they moved forward with a desire to relate and build upon what they were doing with what other teachers were doing. Moreover, they expressed a desire to collaborate with other teachers in their school, their district, or nationally to develop themselves further. Secondary teachers also expressed a desire to collaborate with English teachers in order to create integrated humanities units.

Orientation. In order to show the recursive nature of our model, it is necessary to close our model where we began—at *Orientation.* With change a permanent fixture in teachers' lives, they will constantly be required to reorient themselves to different approaches to teaching and learning.

IMPLICATIONS

For 25 years, conceptual change has been used as a theoretical construct in a variety of educational fields, from which curricula and programs have been built for the purpose of invigorating desired change. Though developed from research performed with college physics students, the original Posner et al. (1982) model has proven to be quite durable and valid in its application to other disciplines. The model we propose is based on empirical research performed in another discipline, and is informed by previous conceptual change models as well as the frameworks of Diffusion of Innovations (Rogers, 2003) and the Concerns-based Adoption Model (Hall et al., 1977; Hall & Hord, 2001; Hord et al., 1987). We anticipate that the

Concerns Based Conceptual Change Model we have presented will be durable and have external validity much like the Posner et al. (1982) model. In fact, our preliminary research with pre-service teachers in other content areas is leading us toward a more general model that closely resembles the one presented in this chapter.

We feel it necessary to reemphasize the reflexive and recursive nature of conceptual change, particularly in our model. Because of the temporal suggestion made by the term *stage*, we struggled with labeling *Orientation* a stage, for it occurs throughout our entire model. When we moved to our next stages of *Understanding* and *Feasibility*, we found that although they are distinct from each other, they also work in concert with each other. Our final stage, *Progression*, includes *fruitful* as an indicator that conceptual change has indeed occurred, but it also includes the indicators of *adaptation* and *collaboration* to indicate that change has become a permanent fixture in many of our participants' lives. We finished the *Progression* stage model back at the beginning—*orientation*—for at this point teachers have accepted the cliché that "the only thing constant in life is change" and thus they must reorient themselves to change all the time. Finally, we made a valuable discovery in our research that *dissatisfaction*, a requisite stage in most other conceptual change models, might not ever happen. Teachers sometimes see the change process as simply replacing one good idea with a better idea. We therefore made *dissatisfaction* merely a possible behavioral indicator of the omnipresent *Orientation* stage.

We started this chapter with several questions. The most important was "What can social studies and history teacher educators do to ensure that a greater percentage of teachers make the changes we desire?" Although we are several years from confidently concluding whether or not our use of WIPs in pre-service teachers' methods courses has increased this percentage, we are currently seeing evidence that some teachers have indeed changed, and many others are considering it. Based upon this research, we estimate that one in five teachers whose methods course included WIPs have already made digital history a *fruitful* part of their teaching practice and therefore are in the stage of *Progression*. Approximately three in five navigate at least as far as the stage of *Understanding* within one year of the start of their social studies methods course; they require student and in-service teaching experiences (approximately three years from the beginning of their social studies methods course) to test *Feasibility*. Of this group, it appears that approximately half have traveled a step farther through the stage of *Feasibility* and will soon be testing the waters of *Progression*. From this, we estimate that overall between 40% and 50% of our participants will navigate to *Progression* within five years. The remaining 50% or 60% will reject the innovation of digital history.

Teacher educators should remember the implications of conceptual change theory's roots in cognitive constructivism, which sees cognitive constructions as individually oriented. Thus, the process of conceptual change will always be a process that is somewhat unique to each learner or teacher (Tal et al., 2001). However, the durability and external validity of most conceptual change models shows that we can create environments in which individuals experience change in similar ways. Differences to consider might include that some learners will change their beliefs first but not practice, and others will change practice but cling to their underlying beliefs, producing "change without difference" (Woodbury & Gess-Newsome, 2002, p. 763). In addition, the rates of and reactions to change will differ: some learners will not change much, some will change more than others, some will be distressed by the change and resist it, and some will relish it (Ho, Watkins & Kelly, 2001). We used WIPs to stimulate conceptual change, yet we hope to see other approaches build upon this and other proven strategies in the effort to produce a larger number of effective digital history teachers.

We see the teaching methods course as the most likely environment for teacher educators to confront teachers' misconceptions about teaching and the use of technology, but it takes more than exposure to and conversations about inquiry-oriented strategies. Rather, in order to produce the conceptual change we strive for, teacher educators must be models for inquiry learning and pre-service teachers must be given opportunities to effectively relearn how to learn. In our research, we are discovering that providing pre-service teachers with multiple learning experiences using inquiry methods and using technology to enhance these experiences is proving to be successful in facilitating the conceptual change we desire. These inquiry experiences must be content-specific so that teachers' expertise can grow in all the necessary areas of content/context knowledge, pedagogical and pedagogical content knowledge (Shulman, 1987), and technological and technological pedagogical content knowledge (Mishra & Koehler, 2006).

We close with a short discussion on perhaps the least studied, yet likely very important piece to the conceptual change story—the complex and often conflicting nature of the K–12 educational system. The educational system is not a single social system. It is a decentralized organization with embedded systems consisting of teachers within classrooms, within schools, and within districts. As we track teachers through these systems to examine how they continue to adopt or reject innovative historical teaching methods, we must recognize that every organization has various subsystems whose function is to deliver the products or services that are essential to the organization's basic mission or primary task. These subsystems develop their own individual cultures and those cultures are often the primary targets of organizational transformation efforts (Schein, 1999). These organizations also contain countless communities that may include students, parents, pre-service teachers, teacher aides, in-service teachers, technology mentors, curriculum coordinators, content experts, and administrators, all of whom fall somewhere along a spectrum ranging from novice learners to expert learners (Fullan, 2001). Therefore, any conceptual change model is subject to the priorities held anywhere in the educational system. For example, the various forms of mandated testing associated with the current educational assessment trend in our country evidenced themselves as obstacles between teachers' desire to adopt digital history into their teaching and their practice of doing so. Therefore, we must not only continue to develop and assess programs of study in our teacher education programs, such as we have done with Web Inquiry Projects; we must also look to the systemic factors which either encourage or inhibit conceptual change from occurring.

REFERENCES

Abd-El-Khalick, F., & Akerson, V. L. (2004). Learning as conceptual change: Factors mediating the development of preservice elementary teachers' views of nature of science. *Science Education, 88*(5), 785–810.

Agee, J. M. (1998). Negotiating different conceptions about reading and teaching literature in a preservice literature class. *Research in the Teaching of English, 33*(1), 85–120.

Anderson, T., Varnhagen, S., & Campbell, K. (1998). Faculty adoption of teaching and learning technologies: Contrasting earlier adopters and mainstream faculty. *The Canadian Journal of Higher Education, 28*(23), 71–78.

Artiles, A. J., & McClafferty, K. (1998). Learning to teach culturally diverse learners: charting change in preservice teachers' thinking about effective teaching. *The Elementary School Journal, 98,* 189–220.

Barton, K. (2005). Teaching history: Primary sources in history: Breaking through the myths. *Phi Delta Kappan, 86*(10), 745–751.

Borko, H., Davinroy, K. H., & Bliem, C. L. (2000). Exploring and supporting teacher change: Two third-grade teachers' experiences in a mathematics and literacy staff development project. *The Elementary School Journal, 100*(4), 273–306.

Borko, H., & Putnam, R. T. (1995). Expanding a teacher's knowledge base. In T. R. Guskey & M. Huberman (Eds.), *Professional development in education* (pp. 35–65). New York: Teachers College Press.

Borko, H., & Putnam, R. T. (1996). Learning to teach. In D.C. Berliner & R.C. Calfee (Eds.), *Handbook of educational psychology* (pp. 673–708). New York: Macmillan.

Bransford, J. D., & Schwartz, D. L. (1999). Rethinking transfer: A simple proposal with multiple implications. In A. Iran-Nejad & P.D. Pearson (Eds.), *Review of research in education* (pp. 61–100). Washington, DC: American Educational Research Association.

Campanario, J. M. (2002). The parallelism between scientists' and students' resistance to new scientific ideas. *International Journal of Science Education, 24*(10), 1095–1100.

Chua, B. L., & Wu, Y. (2005). Designing technology-based mathematics lessons: A pedagogical framework. *Journal of Computers in Mathematics and Science Teaching, 24*(4), 387–402.

Chuang, H., Thompson, A., & Schmidt, D. (2003). Issues and barriers to advanced faculty use of technology. *Technology and Teacher Education Annual* (pp. 3449–3452). Charlottesville, VA: Association for the Advancement of Computing in Education.

Clark, C., & Peterson, P. (1986). Teachers' thought processes. In M.C. Wittrock (Ed.), *Handbook of research on teaching* (pp. 255–296). New York: Macmillan.

Correa, V.I., Hudson, R.F. & Hayes, M.T. (2004). Preparing early childhood special educators to serve culturally and linguistically diverse children and families: Can a multicultural education course make a difference? *Teacher Education and Special Education, 27*(4), 323–341.

Davison, R., Kock, N., Loch, K. D., & Clarke, R. (2001). Research ethics in information systems: Would a code of practice help? *Communications of the Association for Information Systems, 7*(4), 1–39.

Degennaro, A., & Mak, B. L. (2002/2003). A *diffusion* model for computer art in education. *Journal of Educational Technology Systems, 31*(1), 5–18.

DeVesta, F. (1987). The cognitive movement and education. In J. Glover & R. Ronning (Eds.), *Historical foundations of educational psychology* (pp. 203–233). New York: Plenum Press.

Dhindsa, H.S., & Anderson, O.R. (2004). Using a conceptual-change approach to help preservice science teachers reorganize their knowledge structures for constructivist teaching. *Journal of Science Teacher Education, 15*(1), 63–85.

diSessa, A. A., & Sherin, B. L. (1998). What changes in conceptual change? *International Journal of Science Education, 20*(10), 1155–1191.

Dole, J. A., & Sinatra, G. M. (1998). Reconceptualizing change in the cognitive construction of knowledge. *Educational Psychologist, 33*(2–3), 109–128.

Dooley, K. E. (1999). Towards a holistic model for the diffusion of educational technologies: An integrative review of educational innovation studies. *Educational Technology and Society, 2*(4), 34–46.

Eggen, P. D., & Kauchak, D. P. (2004). *Strategies for teachers: Teaching content and thinking skills* (4th ed.). Needham Heights, MA: Allyn & Bacon.

Engle, S., & Ochoa, A. (1988). *Educating citizens for democracy: Decision-making in social studies.* New York: Teachers College Press.

Englert, C. S., Raphael, T. E., & Mariage, T. V. (1998). A multi-year literacy intervention: Transformation and personal change in the community of the early literacy project. *Teacher Education and Special Education, 21*(4), 255–277.

Entwistle, N. J., & Walker, P. (2000). Strategic alertness and expanded awareness within sophisticated conceptions of teaching. *Instructional Science, 28*(5/6), 335–361.

Erickson, F. (1986). Qualitative methods in research on teaching. In M. C. Wittrock (Ed.), *Handbook of research on teaching* (3rd ed., pp. 119–161). New York: Macmillan.

Ertmer, P. A. (2005). Teacher pedagogical beliefs: The final frontier in our quest for technology integration? *Educational Technology Research and Development, 53*(4), 25–39.

Feiman-Nemser, S., McDiarmid G. W., Melnick, S. L., & Parker, M. (1989). *Changing beginning teachers' conceptions: A description of an introductory teacher education course.* (Research Report No. 89-1). East Lansing; Michigan State University, The National Center for Research on Teacher Education.

Feldman, A. (2000). Decision making in the practical domain: a model of practical conceptual change. *Science Education, 84*(5), 606–623.

Fonder-Solano, L. & Burnett, J. (2004). Teaching literature/reading: A dialogue on professional growth. *Foreign Language Annals, 37*(3), 459–469.

Fullan, M. (2001). *The new meaning of educational change* (3rd ed.). NEW YORK: Teachers College Press.

Gregoire, M. (2003). Is it a challenge or a threat? A dual-process model of teachers' cognition and appraisal processes during conceptual change. *Educational Psychology Review, 15*(2), 147–179.

Hall, G. E., George, A. A., & Rutherford, W. C. (1977). *Measuring stages of concern about the innovation: A manual for use of the SoC Questionnaire.* University of Texas: Austin Research and Development Center for Teacher Education. (ERIC Document Reproduction Service No. ED147342)

Hall, G. E., & Hord, S. M. (2001). *Change in schools: Facilitating the process.* Albany: State University of New York Press.

Hicks, D., Doolittle, P. E., & Ewing, T. (2004). The SCIM-C strategy: Fostering historical inquiry in a multimedia environment. *Social Education, 68*(3), 221–225.

Ho, A. S. P., Watkins, D., & Kelly, M. (2001). The conceptual change approach to improving teaching and learning: an evaluation of a Hong Kong staff development programme. *Higher Education, 42*(2), 143–169.

Hord, S. M., Rutherford, W. L., Huling-Austin, L. & Hall, G. E. (1987). *Taking charge of change.* Alexandria, VA: ASCD.

Jackson, P. (1986). *The practices of teaching.* New York: Teachers College Press.

James, R. K., Lamb, C. E., Bailey, M. A., & Householder, D. L. (2000). Integrating science, mathematics, and technology in middle school technology-rich environments: A study of implementation and change. *School Science and Mathematics, 100*(1), 27–35.

Joseph, R., & Reigeluth, C. M. (2005). Formative research on an early stage of the systemic change process in a small school district. *British Journal of Educational Technology, 36*(6), 937–956.

Lortie, D. (1975). *Schoolteacher: A sociological study.* Chicago: University of Chicago Press.

Meehan, M. L. (1976). An innovative competency-based vocational education model diffuses itself. *Journal of Industrial Teacher Education, 13*(2), 34–46.

Mishra, P., & Koehler, M. J. (2006). Technological pedagogical content knowledge: A framework for integrating technology in teachers' knowledge. *Teachers College Record, 108*(6), 1017–1054.

Molebash, P. E. (2002). Constructivism meets technology integration: The CUFA technology guidelines in an elementary social studies methods course. *Theory and Research in Social Education, 30*(3), 429–455.

Molebash, P. E., Dodge, B., Mason, C., & Bell, R. (2002). Promoting student inquiry: Webquests to web inquiry projects (WIPs). *Society for Information Technology in Teacher Education, 2002* [CD ROM]. Charlottesville, VA: Association for the Advancement of Computing in Education.

Molebash, P. E. (2004). Preservice teacher perceptions of a technology-enriched methods course. *Contemporary Issues in Technology and Social Studies Teacher Education, 3*(4), 412–432.

Odabasi, H. F. (2000). Faculty use of technological resources in Turkey. *Innovations in Education and Training International, 37*(2), 103–107.

Pintrich, P. R., Marx, R. W., & Boyle, R. A. (1993). Beyond cold conceptual change: The role of motivational beliefs and classroom contextual factors in the process of conceptual change. *Review of Educational Research, 63,* 167–199.

Posner, G. J., Strike, K. A., Hewson. P. W., & Gertzog, W. A. (1982). Accommodation of a scientific conception: Towards a theory of conceptual change. *Science Education, 66*(2), 211–227.

Prosser, M., Martin, E., & Trigwell, K. (2005). Academics' experiences of understanding of their subject matter and the relationship of this to their experiences of teaching and learning. *Instructional Science, 33*(2), 137–157.

Rogers, E. M. (2003). *Diffusion of innovations* (5th ed.). New York: The Free Press.

Schein, E. (1999). *Process consultation revisited: Building the helping relationship.* New York: Addison-Wesley Longman.

Shulman, L. S. (1987). Knowledge and teaching: Foundations of the new reform. *Harvard Educational Review, 57*(1), 1–22.

Sinatra, G., & Kardash, C. M. (2004). Teacher candidates' epistemological beliefs, dispositions, and views on teaching as persuasion. *Contemporary Educational Psychology, 29*(4), 483–498.

Smith, S. B., Baker, S., & Oudeans, M. K. (2001). Making a difference in the classroom with early literacy instruction. *Teaching Exceptional Children, 33*(6), 8–14.

Tal, R. T., Dori, Y. J., & Keiny, S. (2001). Assessing conceptual change of teachers involved in STES education and curriculum development—the STEMS project approach. *International Journal of Science Education, 23*(3), 247–262.

Trigwell, K., Prosser, M.T., & Waterhouse, F. (1999). Relations between teachers' approaches to teaching and students' approaches to learning. *Higher Education, 37*(1), 57–70.

Van Sickle, M. L., & Kubinec, W. (2003). Transformation teaching. *Journal of College Science Teaching, 32*(4), 258–263.

Volkmann, M .J., & Zgagacz, M. (2004). Learning to teach physics through inquiry: The lived experience of a graduate teaching assistant. *Journal of Research in Science Teaching, 41*(6), 584–602.

Wenglinsky, H. (2005). *Using technology wisely: The keys to success in schools.* New York: Teachers College Press.

Wilson, S. M., Miller, C., & Yerkes, C. (1993). Deeply rooted change: A tale of learning to teach adventurously. In D. K. Cohen, M. W. Mclaughlin, & J. E. Talbert (Eds.), *Teaching for understanding: Challenges for policy and practice.* San Francisco: Jossey-Bass.

Wineburg, S. (2001) *Historical thinking and other unnatural acts.* Philadelphia, PA: Temple University.

Woodbury, S., & Gess-Newsome, J. (2002). Overcoming the paradox of change without difference: A model of change in the arena of fundamental school reform. *Educational Policy, 16*(5), 763–782.

Yip, D. Y. (2004). Questioning skills for conceptual change in science instruction. *Journal of Biological Education, 38*(2), 76–83.

SECTION 2

RESEARCH ON STUDENTS' LEARNING IN SOCIAL STUDIES WITH TECHNOLOGY

CHAPTER 5

STUDENT AND TEACHER PERCEPTIONS OF THE WEBQUEST MODEL IN SOCIAL STUDIES

A Preliminary Study

Phillip J. VanFossen

ABSTRACT

WebQuests have become ubiquitous and are the default Internet-based curriculum model. Touted by advocates as increasing student learning and motivation, little empirical study of this model has been done. This preliminary study was an attempt to add to the sparse research literature on WebQuests. Following an intensive summer institute on Internet technology in citizenship education, 32 teachers (grades 3–11) developed and implemented WebQuests with their students ($n = 796$). After participants implemented these WebQuests, data were collected from students and teachers on various aspects of the WebQuest model including student enjoyment, perceived student learning, and student involvement relative to a 'regular' lesson. Results were mixed. A majority of students enjoyed the WebQuest model, felt they

Research on Technology in Social Studies Education, pages 101–126
Copyright © 2009 by Information Age Publishing

learned more, and felt they had more control over their own learning using the model compared to a traditional lesson. The participating teachers also had generally positive reactions to student use of the model. However, a number of students (and a few of the participating teachers) had less positive reactions. Data suggested that the model may not be uniformly accepted by all students. In addition, data called into question some widely held beliefs concerning the innate motivational benefit of the WebQuest model. Moreover, these results suggested more detailed investigation of the manifestation of the model; namely, that not all WebQuests are created equal. Further study of the impact of the WebQuest model on student learning and motivation in other contexts is strongly recommended.

INTRODUCTION

While it remains true that a significant 'digital divide' continues to exist in terms of access to the Internet in the United States, the Internet (and the World Wide Web) has become increasingly pervasive part of Americans' daily lives. Whether using the WWW for e-commerce, to access a wide array of online multimedia, or to simply communicate with friends and family, many Americans consume Internet services on a daily basis. Indeed, estimates place the number of those the United States with Internet access at 112 million and the number of Americans who regularly use the Internet at 185 million (Information Please, 2005).

Moreover, data suggest that Internet access may be even more ubiquitous in American schools. In 2003, for example, 100% of all public schools in the United States reported having Internet access.[1] In addition, 93% of all K–12 public school classrooms in the United States reported having some type of Internet access in 2003, and 95% of these classrooms reported having broadband connectivity. Most important, however, the ratio of public school students to instructional computers with access to the Internet fell from 12.2 students in 1998 to 4.4 students in 2003 (National Center for Educational Statistics, 2003; Parsad & Jones, 2003).

In part because of its interactive and multimedia nature, the Internet has been increasingly touted as an important component of both elementary and secondary education. Becker (1999), in a nationwide study of Internet use by American teachers, concluded that "along with word processing, the Internet may be the most valuable of the many computer technologies available to teachers and students" (p. 32). These arguments are certainly not new, and a number of educational benefits have been ascribed to Internet use in K–12 classrooms. Wilson (1995) argued that the Internet has the ability to break down the classroom's physical limitations and to allow students access to experiences well beyond the limited resources available in classrooms and media centers. Braun, Fernlund and White (1998) believed that the use of Internet resources can develop students' inquiry and analytical skills. Moreover, many have argued that because of the very nature of the Internet—its relatively unrestricted access to information and media—the social studies, with its goal of citizenship education, is the school discipline most likely to make use of the medium (Shiveley & VanFossen, 2001).

In spite of the promising rhetoric, however, studies have indicated that K–12 teachers do not integrate Internet use in their classrooms with much regularity. Becker (2001) found that nearly 75% of teachers in grades four through twelve either never used the Internet in their classes or used it only occasionally. In a 2003 study of K–5 teachers in Indiana, VanFossen (2005) found that while 95% of K–5 respondents reported Internet access in their classroom (65.5% with a 'fast, reliable connection') and more than half reported participating in multiple training sessions on using the Internet, 80% had never used the Internet in their classes, or had used it only rarely. Other studies have reached similar findings (Diem, 2000; Hack & Smey, 1997; Hicks, Doolittle, & Lee, 2004; Wiesenmayer & Meadows, 1997; Zenanko, King, & Nelson, 1996).

Among the most common barriers to Internet integration cited by K–12 teachers are a lack of training, concern over student access to inappropriate Internet sites, and concern over the amount of time needed to developed effective Internet-based instruction. For example, VanFossen (2000) reported that many secondary social studies teachers felt that the benefits associated with using the Internet did not offset the significant time required to find useful web sites.

THE WEBQUEST MODEL

In 1995, in response to some of these issues—especially the frustration felt by teachers over failed Internet searching—Bernie Dodge and Tom March developed a curriculum model that was designed to harness the power of the Internet and to encourage inquiry-based, critical thinking activities. The curriculum model they developed—the WebQuest—has become nearly as ubiquitous in schools as access to the Internet itself.

Dodge (1998) has described WebQuests as inquiry-oriented activities in which some or all of the information that learners interact with comes from resources on the Internet. Because Dodge questioned the benefit of requiring students (or teachers) to do exhaustive 'surfing' for resources on the Internet, WebQuests were designed to be entirely self-contained instructional modules. The assignments and the resources needed to complete them would all be located at the WWW sites students would access. In this way, WebQuests provide an all-important organizing framework for harnessing the vast resources of the Internet. Moreover, the WebQuest model allows teachers to control and preview questionable Internet content (another 'barrier' to Internet use often mentioned by K–12 teachers). K–12 teachers can access hundreds of thousands of examples of the WebQuest model that already exist on the Internet. Indeed, a Google® search for 'WebQuests' (conducted September 20, 2005) resulted in more than 1,010,000 hits (554,000 of which were social studies related) including teacher-created WebQuests and commercially produced WebQuests, as well as everything in between.

Dodge (1998) outlined six key elements (called 'building blocks') that must be in any WebQuest:

1. An introduction that sets the stage and provides some background information for the learner.
2. A task that is doable and interesting.
3. A set of information sources needed to complete the task. Many (though not necessarily all) of the resources are embedded in the WebQuest document itself as anchors pointing to information on the World Wide Web. Information sources might include web documents, experts available via e-mail or real-time conferencing, or searchable databases on the Internet, as well as books and other documents physically available in the learner's setting. Because links to these resources are included in the WebQuest, the learner is not left to wander aimlessly through the Internet.
4. A description of the process the learners should go through in accomplishing the task. The process should be broken out into clearly described steps.
5. Some guidance on how to organize the information acquired. This can take the form of guiding questions, or directions to complete organizational frameworks such as timelines, concept maps, or cause-and-effect diagrams. This is the scaffolding that allows learners to extend themselves in producing new products or projects.
6. A conclusion that brings closure to the WebQuest, reminds the learners about what they've learned, and perhaps encourages them to extend the experience into other domains.

Dodge also described several additional elements that, while not critical to WebQuest success, might contribute to the experience for students: (a) WebQuests are most likely to be group activities, and (b) WebQuests might be enhanced by using motivational elements such as giving the learners a role to play (e.g., scientist, detective, reporter), and a scenario to work within (e.g., "you've been asked to propose a new state mineral for Indiana"). A more complete description of the model can be found at the WebQuest Page (http://webquest.org/index.php).

Research Literature Related to WebQuests

On its face, the WebQuest model has been presented as a powerful tool for developing critical thinking (Vidoni & Maddux, 2002); a useful example of problem-based learning strategies (Brucklacher & Gimbert, 1999; Mathison & Pohan, 1999); and as interesting and motivating approach for both teachers and students (Yoder, 1999). However, a review of the literature on WebQuest use in K–12 classrooms reveals that these, and most other reports of the model's use, while generally positive, tend to be based on cursory or anecdotal data. These reports almost always present intuitive, rather than data-based, arguments for the WebQuest model.

In point of fact, very few studies have actually examined the impact of this Internet-based curricular model on student learning, attitudes, or motivation. Indeed, very few empirical studies have been conducted on the actual effectiveness of the WebQuest model with students. McGlinn and McGlinn (2004), in their review of the literature on WebQuests and the social studies, concluded that "although educators increasingly recognize WebQuests as resources for teachers, little research has been conducted on their effectiveness" (p. 4836). Milson (2002) also provided a summary of these concerns when he noted, "the WebQuest approach appears to be in widespread use, yet the literature largely reports anecdotal accounts of success rather (than) independent research on this instructional technique" (p. 335). Milson concluded that "a need exists for classroom-based research to investigate the effectiveness of this technique" (p. 335). Brucklacher and Gimbert (1999) echoed this call for empirical investigation into the effectiveness of the WebQuest when they asked: "Are educators who use … the Internet better educators? Are students who use … the Internet better learners? They can be" (p. 42). Vidoni and Maddux (2002) concluded that further research on the WebQuest model was needed in order to confirm claims that its use helped foster critical thinking among students or led to increased student learning or motivation. Vidoni and Maddux (2002) implied that without such research-based confirmation, the use of WebQuests might simply represent the latest educational fad. The trouble is, very little evidence exists—one way or the other—on the effectiveness of the Web-Quest model or to support its use in K–12 classrooms.

Indeed, few studies have examined the impact of Internet-based projects (such as the WebQuest) on student learning; one of these was conducted by the Center for Applied Special Technology (CAST). In a controlled study of student access to the Internet while participating in a project unit on civil rights, CAST found that students exposed to the Internet resources scored significantly higher on post-unit measures (Follensbee et al., 1997). In one of the few empirical studies of the impact of the actual WebQuest model on social studies students, Milson (2002) studied a sixth grade classroom as students worked through a WebQuest on ancient Egypt over the course of eight days. Subsequent interviews with students following the WebQuest indicated that (a) students had different perceptions of the value of the use of the Internet; (b) students generally chose lower order, or "path-of-least-resistance" strategies when using the WebQuest; and (c) students approached and perceived the value of WebQuest investigations differently. Given these findings, Milson's (2002) conclusions were mixed and were not the "zealous support" found in many reports of WebQuest use (p. 348). Rather, Milson stressed his "cautious optimism" for the WebQuest's value as an instructional approach (p. 348).

In another study, Strickland (2005) compared learning between students exposed to a WebQuest about the Texas Revolution and those who learned about it by creating a poster. Strickland found that students who had participated in the WebQuest actually scored significantly *lower* on the end-of-unit assessment than those who had participated in the traditional task. Strickland concluded that these results suggested that the WebQuest model may not be effective for introducing students to large amounts of information. Strickland also called into question the motivational impact of the WebQuest model, noting that the WebQuest was "designed to make the topic more interesting... however, the experimental group never seemed very interested in the assignment" (p. 142). Strickland further cautioned against an uncritical view of WebQuests as motivational devices, especially for students who already have access to the Internet at home.

Other studies have produced more positive findings. As part of an action research project, Santavenere (2003) studied three 11th-grade history classes as the students used a WebQuest on World War II. These classes contained students who were "non-college bound or (were) below academic level standing" (p. 22). Santavenere (2003) interviewed a random sample of students from all three classes at two points during the study. Among the questions students were asked was whether they felt they had learned more using the WebQuest approach relative to a traditional lesson. More than 80% of the students interviewed felt they had learned more using the Web-Quest. More than three-quarters of the students interviewed suggested that the WebQuest was more challenging than a traditional lesson. Santavenere (2003) concluded that the use of the WebQuest model had contributed to developing the critical thinking skills of the students involved. Lipscomb (2003) developed and implemented a WebQuest about the U.S. Civil War with his middle school students. Although the study presented no formal data collection, Lipscomb concluded that "they learned a great deal about the Civil War by doing that WebQuest," and that students thought it was "pretty fun" (p. 155). It should be noted that Lipscomb did not compare students who used the WebQuest with those who did not, making such specific claims difficult to support.

RESEARCH QUESTIONS

While the results of these few studies offer some initial conflicting data on the impact of the WebQuest model, much more classroom-based research is needed in order to determine its effectiveness. The purpose of the current, preliminary study is therefore to explore student and teacher perceptions of the WebQuest model on students, and to use these initial data to comment on the efficacy of the model for use in K–12 classrooms. Therefore, the broad research question explored in this study was whether WebQuests promoted greater student engagement than traditional methods of social studies instruction. In order to answer this broad question, the current study sought to answer the following research questions:

1. Do students enjoy learning more using the WebQuest model compared with regular or traditional lessons?
2. Do students feel they learn more using the WebQuest model compared with regular or traditional lessons?
3. Do students who use the WebQuest model feel more involved in their own learning compared with regular or traditional lessons?
4. What aspect of the WebQuest model do students enjoy most? Least?
5. Do teachers feel their students learn more using the WebQuest model compared with regular or traditional lessons?
6. Do teachers feel their students are more involved in their own learning using the WebQuest model compared with regular or traditional lessons?
7. What aspect of the WebQuest model do teachers enjoy most? Least?

METHODS

To answer these questions, the current study collected data from teachers who had developed and implemented WebQuests designed specifically for use with their own students. Teachers in the current study created their WebQuests as part of the 2003 and 2004 summer institutes conducted by the James F. Ackerman Center for Democratic Citizenship at Purdue University. As part of the summer institute, teachers were required to implement the WebQuests they created during the subsequent school year. Following implementation, data from students and teachers were collected using several online questionnaires. These data (including data from several open-ended responses) were analyzed using descriptive statistics, non-parametric analysis, and simple comparative pattern analysis.

The Ackerman Center Summer Institute and Project EnTICE

The James F. Ackerman Center for Democratic Citizenship is an endowed center housed in the College of Education at Purdue University.[2] Its mission is to promote the teaching of citizenship, constitutional principles, and the core beliefs of democracy in grades K–12. The Center accomplishes this mission through outreach and in-service programming for K–12 teachers. The largest of these programs is the Center's annual summer institute. In 2003 and 2004, the Ackerman Center brought 32 teachers from across the state of Indiana to meet for a week of intensive training on integrating Internet technology into citizenship education. This gathering, part of Project EnTICE: Encouraging Technology Integration in Citizenship Education, involved participants developing skills in Internet-based curriculum development, web-publishing, and integrating digital media into their instruction. The primary vehicle for this technology integration was the WebQuest model and participants were required to develop WebQuests that were appropriate for their particular grade level and that were related to citizenship education.[3] Once developed, these WebQuests were peer-reviewed using online rating forms.[4] This review process ensured that the WebQuests adhered—to a certain degree—to the WebQuest model. During the year following their summer institute, participants were given server space at Purdue University and access to the server in order to update the WebQuests they developed.

One example of the type of WebQuest participants developed was "Covering Common Ground: A WebQuest for 4th Grade Hoosiers."[5] Students who participated in this WebQuest were required to work in groups to determine what the Indiana state mineral should be (at the date of the institute Indiana had a state gem, but no state mineral). Each group consisted of a geologist, a researcher, political consultant, and a historian. Within each group, the students determined how they could bring about the necessary change in the Indiana Code needed in order to adopt this mineral and then to compose a letter to send via e-mail to their state representative persuading him or her to write the necessary legislation to take before the Indiana General Assembly.

Participants

The majority (24) of the 32 teachers who participated in Project EnTICE taught either 4th or 5th grade. Of the remaining participants, two taught 3rd grade, three taught 8th grade, two taught 4/5 multiage, and one participant was a high school teacher. All of the participants had at least three years teaching experience, and the vast majority had more than ten. All but six of the participants were female. In a pre-institute survey, most participants rated themselves as 'somewhat comfortable' using both computer technologies generally and using Internet technology specifically. However, no participants had ever created a WebQuest before nor had any done any web publishing.

Data Collection

The current study employed an online instrument created to collect data on student and teacher reaction to participating in the Project EnTICE WebQuests. The instruments were created using the Purdue University College of Education online survey system.[6] This web-based system simplified data collection by allowing participants to build a hyperlink to the online instruments into their respective project WebQuests. The system also simplified data analysis by recording all responses in a database which made data accessible in both hypertext and spreadsheet formats.

Both the teacher and student instruments consisted of eight forced-choice items and two open-ended questions. The forced-choice items focused on student or teacher perceptions of how easy the particular WebQuest was to complete; perceptions of how much students enjoyed using the WebQuest model; and perceptions about the degree of learning that occurred relative to more traditional, (i.e., textbook-based) lessons. The open-ended questions allowed students and teachers to reflect on the specific aspects of the WebQuest they enjoyed most and those they enjoyed least.

The online instrument was completed by students of 29 of the 32 teachers who participated in Project EnTICE. A total of 827 students from these 29 teachers' classes responded to the online instrument. Of these 827 respondents, however, only 796 completed all of the items on the instrument.

Data Analysis

Through the online survey system, participant responses were exported to a Microsoft Excel® spreadsheet and analyzed using SPSS® software. Frequency counts and cross-tabulations were calculated for each fixed-response item. Non-parametric analysis (e.g., chi square) was used in order to determine whether responses differed across grade level or whether students' previous experience with WebQuests was related to student perception of the WebQuest model.

Responses to the open-ended items were analyzed using a very simple comparative pattern analysis (Patton, 1990). Using this technique, the researcher first began to look for recurring regularities in the data. These regularities represented initial categories of classification. Once categories of classification were established, the researcher "work(s) back and forth between the data and the classification system to verify the accuracy of the system" (Patton, 1990, p. 403). In the current study, student responses to open-ended questions were first read multiple times, then coded, and finally initial categories of analysis were determined. Responses were then reread to determine the suitability of the initial categories.

RESULTS

Student Perception of the WebQuest Model Relative to 'Traditional' Lessons

This section reports results related to the first four research questions in the current study. Data indicated that the vast majority of students in the current study were not new to computer or Internet use. Of the 796 students who responded, nearly 90% reported having a computer in their homes. In addition, 92.8% reported using the Internet to complete schoolwork at least 'sometimes.' Additionally, more than half (52%) reported using a WebQuest previously. Perhaps not surprisingly, 8th grade students were more likely to have used the Internet in school while more than two-thirds of 3rd, 5th, and 8th grade students reported using a WebQuest previously.

Table 5.1 reports student perceptions of the difficulty of the WebQuest model by grade level. Overall, more than 75% of students reported that the WebQuests were 'easy' or 'very easy' to complete. Chi square analysis

TABLE 5.1 Student Perceptions of the Difficulty of the WebQuest to Complete

Grade level	Very difficult	Difficult	Easy	Very Easy
3 (*n* = 103)	2.0	15.7	62.7	18.6
4 (*n* = 122)	6.6	28.1	53.7	11.6
4/5 multiage (*n* = 41)	4.9	20.2	63.0	4.9
5 (*n* = 217)	4.1	18.4	63.6	13.4
6 (*n* = 168)	3.6	18.5	69.0	8.9
8 (*n* = 127)	2.4	12.6	69.3	15.7
11 (*n* = 13)	0.0	23.1	61.5	15.4
Totals (*n* = 796)	**3.8**	**20.2**	**63.0**	**12.8**

Percentage responding column spans Very difficult, Difficult, Easy, Very Easy.

Note: $\chi^2 = 45.106$; $p = .006$

($\chi^2 = 45.106$; p = .006) indicated that students in grades six and eight were more likely to find the WebQuest easier to complete than students in other grades represented.

Table 5.2 reports student enjoyment of the WebQuest model compared to a 'regular' or 'traditional' lesson on the same content. Results indicated that more than half of the students enjoyed the WebQuest 'more' or 'much more' than a traditional lesson. Approximately 12% of students reported enjoying the WebQuest *less* than a traditional lesson and while this is a relatively low proportion of students, Chi square analysis ($\chi^2 = 37.735$; $p = .004$) indicated a significant difference in proportions across grade levels. It should be noted that approximately one-quarter of 11th grade students and more than 16% of 4th grade students felt the WebQuest experience was *less* enjoyable than a traditional lesson.

Responses indicated that most students felt they learned more using the WebQuest model, with 59.8% indicating they learned 'more' or 'much more' than they would have in a traditional lesson (see Table 5.3). Thirty-four percent of students, however, indicated that they felt they had learned 'about the same' as they would have in a traditional lesson over the same content, and a small, but persistent, proportion (6.2%) of students indicated they felt they had learned *less* using the WebQuest model. Again, differences in proportions across grade levels were significant ($\chi^2 = 36.834$; $p = .006$). These results suggested that 3rd and 8th grade students were more likely to feel they 'learned less' or 'about the same.'

Students perceived that they were more involved in their own learning during the WebQuest than they might have been during a more traditional lesson (see Table 5.4). Compared to a regular or traditional lesson, more

---

TABLE 5.2   Student Enjoyment of WebQuests Relative to a "Regular" Lesson

Grade level	Less	About the same	More	Much more
		Percentage responding		
3 ($n = 103$)	7.8	34.0	19.4	38.8
4 ($n = 122$)	16.4	29.5	25.4	28.7
4/5 multiage ($n = 41$)	14.6	41.5	26.8	17.1
5 ($n = 217$)	11.1	25.8	30.9	32.3
6 ($n = 168$)	10.7	32.1	32.7	24.4
8 ($n = 127$)	11.1	38.9	35.7	14.3
11 ($n = 13$)	23.1	30.8	38.5	7.7
Totals ($n = 796$)	**11.8**	**31.8**	**29.6**	**26.8**

Note: $\chi^2 = 37.735$; $p = .004$

TABLE 5.3 Student Perception of Amount Learned Using WebQuests Relative to a "Regular" Lesson

	Percentage responding			
Grade level	Learned less	About the same	Learned more	Learned much more
3 (n = 103)	7.8	36.9	37.9	17.5
4 (n = 122)	4.1	23.8	44.3	27.9
4/5 multiage (n = 41)	6.2	24.4	46.3	22.0
5 (n = 217)	6.0	35.5	36.9	21.7
6 (n = 168)	6.0	31.5	47.0	15.5
8 (n = 127)	7.1	47.2	37.0	8.7
11 (n = 13)	7.7	15.4	69.2	7.7
Totals (n = 796)	**6.2**	**34.0**	**41.3**	**18.5**

Note: $\chi^2 = 36.834$; $p = .006$

TABLE 5.4 Student Perception of Degree of Involvement in Own Learned Using WebQuests Relative to a "Regular" Lesson

	Percentage responding			
Grade level	Not very	Somewhat	Quite a bit	Very much
3 (n = 103)	6.8	21.4	51.5	20.4
4 (n = 122)	5.7	12.3	50.8	31.1
4/5 multiage (n = 41)	4.9	34.1	41.5	19.5
5 (n = 217)	6.0	19.8	48.8	25.3
6 (n = 168)	4.8	17.3	57.1	20.8
8 (n = 127)	3.1	28.3	59.1	9.4
11 (n = 13)	0.0	30.8	61.5	7.7
Totals (n = 796)	**5.2**	**20.6**	**52.7**	**21.5**

Note: $\chi^2 = 35.882$; $p = .007$

than 74% of students felt 'quite a bit' or 'very much' involved in their own learning while completing the WebQuest. More than 20% of students felt at least 'somewhat' involved in their own learning. Only slightly more than 5% felt they were 'not very' involved. Interestingly, Chi square analysis ($\chi^2 = 35.882$; $p = .007$) suggested that 4th and 5th grade students (including students in the 4/5 multiage classroom) reported feeling more involved than students in grades 3, 8 or 11.

Aspects of the WebQuest Model Students Enjoyed Most

One of the open-ended questions on the on-line instrument asked students to report what they liked best about participating in a lesson that employed the WebQuest model. Following a simple comparative pattern analysis of these responses, eleven categories emerged (see Table 5.5).

The most common category of student response dealt with the WebQuest tasks themselves. Nearly 19% of students indicated they enjoyed the creativity afforded by working on certain WebQuest tasks. For example, one 5th grade student noted he enjoyed "the freedom to create a card without much time." A second 5th grader responded that "I like doing the 2nd Continental Congress Debate even though the Patriots should have won!" Other students mentioned they enjoyed the opportunity to "be creative" while developing products such as poems, skits and PowerPoint® presentations. One student noted that she liked "seeing the finished products—they were so neat and creative." Another stated, "the best thing about the Web-Quest is that I could get more into the project than in class."

Nearly 14% of students identified learning specific content associated with their WebQuest as the best feature. Students who participated in a WebQuest about Indiana, for example, noted that they liked "learning about the state bird" or "that I learned more about Indiana." Another 5th grade student responded "what I liked about this WebQuest is that I got to learn

TABLE 5.5   Students' Favorite Aspects of the WebQuest Model (*n* = 758)

Aspect	Percentage Students Identifying as Favorite Aspect of WebQuest
Creativity of certain WebQuest tasks	18.9
Learning specific content associated with WebQuest	13.6
Provided easy access to important information/content	10.8
Searching for information	10.1
Flexibility the WebQuest model allowed	8.5
Use of computers to complete the WebQuests	8.1
Learning using the WebQuest was 'fun'	7.8
Enjoyed all elements of the WebQuest	5.7
Exploring interactive media (e.g., digital images, animation, audio) found on WWW	4.4
Efficient use of Internet resources	3.0
Other (e.g., disliked entire WebQuest, 'was kinda boring…', etc.)	10.9

more about the two people who are running for president" and a 5th grade student enjoyed "the pure amount of new information I am learning."

Students also enjoyed how easy the WebQuest model made accessing important information or specific content over the Internet. Nearly 11% of all students indicated that this was the aspect of the WebQuest they liked best. Student responses that fell into this category often described the same benefits to Internet use (e.g., access to unprecedented information and resources) as those cited by Internet advocates such as Wilson (1995) and Braun et al. (1997). For example, one 8th grader noted, "there was information right in front of you and all u (sic) had to do was read the information instead of looking up sites on google (sic) or something." A second student—a 6th grader who participated in a WebQuest about the Holocaust—concluded that the best part was "researching on Jews and Germans and how badly Jews were treated so I can try to prevent it from happening again." A 4/5 multiage student appreciated the way the WebQuest "made information easy to akses (sic) and find, it also made it easy for the teacher to describe where to go."

About 10% of students found the process of using web-based resources (including searching for information using the Internet) to be their favorite aspect of the WebQuest. One student noted "I really liked searching the Internet!" A second student enjoyed "searching the Web" and "finding out cool stuff," while another liked "how it (the WebQuest) told me where I can research things!" Finally, one 5th grade student summed up the category when they wrote:

> My favorite thing to do was looking through and learning all the different things about the presidents and doing the research. I enjoyed it a lot and it is very usful (sic). If I could use a websearch for all my school work it woulbe (sic) a lot better.

Almost 9% of student respondents indicated that they appreciated the flexibility the WebQuest model allowed. In particular some respondents saw this flexibility as encouraging learning because it corresponded to their preferred learning style, whether that was cooperative, inquiry-based activities with student choice or individualized projects that could be done at their own pace:

> I liked that you could go back to anything you wanted and answer the questions on your own time. I liked that you could read this at home and not worry about leaving papers and notebooks at home. I like how the work was and how it was set up. (a 7th grade student)

One student noted a common belief that they liked "working with the group." Another echoed this sentiment saying, "What I liked best was that we got to work together." However, a number of students also indicated they enjoyed working individually, and that the WebQuest model fit this learning style as well. This feeling was evidenced in the response of one 7th grader: "It was an independent kind of project, fitting my style perfectly." An 8th grade student echoed this by noting that she "got to work alone finding out . . . about a Patriot (from the Revolutionary War) that we would not have learned out of a book." Students also appreciated the opportunity the WebQuest gave them to guide some of their own learning by making choices. Other examples of these types of responses included: "the reason I liked the WebQuest was because it felt like you were in control of the project and it was easier to learn things from it," and "the part where you get to choose what you want to learn and what is important." A 5th grader enjoyed the "control over how fast you did the WebQuest. You could take your time if you wanted to assimilate all the information."

Proponents of classroom computer use and the WebQuest model (Vidoni & Maddux, 2002; Santavenere, 2003) often cite the motivational and pedagogical benefits associated with students using computers or with working on the Internet compared to traditional classroom activities. Interestingly, only about 8% of respondents indicated that the aspect of the WebQuest they liked best was that they used computers to complete the WebQuests. One 5th grade student noted that she "liked doing all the stuff with computers." A second 5th grader wrote that "I love working on the computer, so I liked most of it, really." Those who did indicate this aspect stressed that being on the computer was preferable to other activities, for two students noted that "I like using a computer instead of writing" and "I liked it because we didn't have to sit there and listen to the teacher talk and we got to do stuff on our own and use the computer." Another common type of response was from a student who noted that the best thing about the WebQuest was "getting to use the computer" or "that it's on the Internet."

Approximately 8% of respondents indicated that the aspect they liked most about the WebQuest was that, as one 4th grade student put it, "it was fun to learn" using the model. These respondents liked that the WebQuest was, in several students' words, "fun and exciting" and that it offered a "fun and easy" alternative to their regular classroom routine. A 7th grade student noted that "doing the WebQuest was really fun to do. I like it and it let you see much more and learn much more."

Approximately 6% of student respondents could not narrow their choice to a single aspect of the WebQuest model. These students indicated that they "pretty much liked the whole entire thing" or "liked doing everything" and "it was all great." These students generally had a very high opinion of the WebQuest model and, as one 5th grade student put it, "basically, all of it was neat to me. I really enjoyed it."

While the potential interactivity of much of the media found on WWW has often been cited as a factor that can motivate student learning (Becker, 1999; Braun et al., 1998), only about 4% of respondents explicitly noted that this was the aspect of the WebQuest they enjoyed most. Those students who did claim working with interactive WWW resources was enjoyable, were strong advocates of WebQuests. More typically students contrasted the WebQuest with textbook-based lessons. One 7th grade student summed this comparison up by saying "the best aspect of the WebQuest was that learning was interactive, unlike a book, and made the learning fun and easy." This access to multimedia and interactivity (e.g., "pictures and sounds," "slide shows," and "motion clips") was apparently better received than more traditional lessons. A number of students pointed out that the WebQuest model, with its access to multimedia, was, for example, "more exciting than book-work" and "more enjoyable than regular classwork."

A small proportion of student respondents (approximately 3%) felt the best aspect of the WebQuest model was the efficient use of Internet resources. For example, one student noted "the thing I like best about the WebQuest was that all the information was on the same website. I think this made it easier that looking everything up on the Internet without knowing what site to go to." This 'one-stop-shopping' aspect of the WebQuest was also identified by another respondent who stated that she liked that "all of the requirements were easy to see" and the WebQuest "was easy to use and the information was easily accessible."

Aspects of the WebQuest Model Students Enjoyed Least

A second open-ended question asked students to report what they did not like about participating in a lesson that employed the WebQuest model (Table 5.6). Again, student responses were analyzed using a simple comparative pattern analysis. Interestingly, the most frequent type of student response was 'nothing.' Nearly one-fourth of the students indicated that they enjoyed every aspect of the WebQuest learning experience. These respondents stated they "liked everything about it" or that they "did not dislike anything" and that there "was nothing I didn't like about this WebQuest." One student summed up this relative enthusiasm nicely when she stated she disliked "nothing, it was better than a normal boring project."

Curiously, the most common *dislike* among respondents was the specific tasks associated with particular WebQuests. Nearly 22% of respondents identified this aspect of the WebQuest as their least favorite. This result was interesting in that students identified this aspect as their second *favorite* aspect of the WebQuest. Among the examples given by students who disliked the tasks

TABLE 5.6   Students' Least Favorite Aspects of the WebQuest Model (*n* = 727)

Aspect	Percentage students identifying as least favorite aspect of WebQuest
Nothing (i.e., enjoyed entire WebQuest)	24.1
Specific tasks required of WebQuest	21.6
Difficulty of the WebQuest	6.1
Lack of resources; not enough information to complete task	5.5
Time the WebQuest took	5.0
Searching for information	4.8
Specific design aspects or multimedia components	4.4
Too much information to work effectively with	3.8
Technical difficulties during the WebQuest	3.0
Working on computer	2.9
WebQuest too 'teacher-driven'	1.4
Other (e.g., 'I liked all of it...', 'the teacher was boring...', etc.)	7.3

were "I did not like making up my own words for the history facts" and "it was a little hard to design the format for the trading cards." This is an important finding. Dodge (1998) has described the task in the successful WebQuest as doable and interesting and these results indicate that nearly a quarter of students in the current study found the task less than interesting.

Slightly more than 6% of students identified the WebQuests' difficulty as their least favorite aspect. These students noted that the WebQuest was, in one students words, "hard and I did not like that" or as another put is "I got confused!!!!!!!!!!!!!!" One student wrote that "I did not like this sight (sic) because it was much harder than my teacher said." Another student summed up the consequences of this difficulty by stating "the thing I didn't like was being left behind. I didn't like it because it was hard and I got lost and then I got left behind."

Almost 6% of students felt that their WebQuest did not contain enough Internet resources or links to the information needed to successfully complete the WebQuest. While this is a small proportion of students, this result was still ironic given that the Internet's access to vast amounts of information is often cited as one of its most powerful benefits. Students noted that "it was hard to find some of the stuff," "sometimes you can't find all the information and you waste some of the hour," and "it was difficult to find information on my person." One must be careful when interpreting these results, however, as it may well be the case that students are pointing out a potential flaw in that the WebQuest model may not be the most convenient format for organizing the resources of the Internet. It is also possible, however, that these flaws students pointed out were specific to poorly-designed WebQuests—ones that *did not* have enough resources listed in its process section. In contrast to the students who thought their Webquests were lacking information, slightly more than 8% of students felt there was *too much* information in their WebQuest to work through in order to complete the task. One student complained that "there was so much information, it got sort of complicated." Others noted that there was "too much reading" or they disliked having to "read everything."

Each of the additional categories that emerged contained fewer than 5% of the responses (see Table 5.6). These remaining categories included student dislike of:

1. Searching for information as part of their WebQuest (e.g., "didn't like having to search many websites to find answers. I thought it would be better with only one page, but it wasn't.");
2. Specific design aspects of the WebQuest or multimedia resources used with it (e.g., "it was a very bad website, color wise. The colors made it hard to read and first impressions are important," and "I would have been happier using PowerPoint®.");
3. The time needed to complete the WebQuest was too great relative to the benefits.;
4. The technical difficulties incurred during the WebQuest activity (e.g., "some of the websites didn't work" and "I didn't like when we had to keep switching back and forth because it was getting irritating.");
5. The WebQuest being too teacher-driven;
6. Working on the computer or on the Internet (e.g., "I really don't like the Internet at all, so I don't like the fact that it was online.").

One final aspect of the WebQuest that students disliked warrants further discussion. Several students stated they disliked the fact that their WebQuest "didn't have any games in it." This raises an interesting question about a previously unquestioned assumption about Internet-based learning. Namely, can the medium (in this case the Internet) actually be detrimental to student learning because students' previous experience with the medium is overwhelmingly non-educational (i.e., PlayStation, X-box, etc.)? This question is considered in more detail in the discussion section of this report.

Student Learning Associated with the WebQuest

When asked to describe what they learned during the WebQuest, a large number of students indicated they, as one student put it, "learned a lot more than I thought I would." More than 90% of students identified some WebQuest-specific knowledge they had gained. Take, for example, one 5th grade class where one student noted that he had "learned a lot about the 1860 election," another 5th grader stated he learned "about pyrite and other minerals," a third learned "Washington had size 13 boots." A more reflective student from the same class noted she learned "quite a bit actually, besides discovering a lot of information on my person, I learned about the spy business, slavery, and how many slaves were put to work in the American Revolution." Another student in the same class noted that "I learned about different acts, and why the rebels were rebels and why the loyalists were loyalists. I learned that not everyone is good at debating!" One final student from this class represented these types of responses by stating "I learned a lot more information than I probably would have if I hadn't done the WebQuest, a lot more than I know from a book."

Despite these findings, less than 10% of the students indicated that they had learned something, or some skill, that was applicable beyond their respective WebQuest task. Only a few students expressed their satisfaction with the work. One 7th grade student did state that "there was a lot more information in the WebQuest then (sic) there is in books and (it was) somewhat easier to find." Given that proponents of the WebQuest model advocate the carryover of important inquiry skills such as these, however, it was somewhat surprising that more students did not identify this type of learning explicitly.

Aspects of the WebQuest Model Teachers Enjoyed Most

As of this report, 24 of the 32 Project EnTICE teachers had completed the online instrument. One of the open-ended questions on the teacher instrument asked participants what they liked best about using their WebQuest with students. The teachers' responses fell into three categories. The majority of the teachers indicated that they liked that the WebQuest required students to be self-directed and take responsibility for their own learning. One 7th grade teacher noted she enjoyed "not having to explain what needed to be done, that students were doing self-directed learning." A 5th grade teacher noted that she enjoyed "seeing them take responsibility for their own learning, many of them seemed excited by what they found."

A second theme focused around the creativity students were afforded by the WebQuest model. As one teacher noted, the WebQuest gave students "an opportunity to conduct research and present their learning in a creative manner." According to another teacher, the WebQuest "was different than a typical lecture or question/answer format, it enabled them to use their creativity." This opportunity to tap into student creativity appeared to have very positive results for several of the teachers: "I enjoyed observing the students going to different sites; they were having so much fun LEARNING [emphasis in original]!"

The third category of teacher response focused on the WebQuest as a specific vehicle for harnessing the Internet. As one teacher put it, "it gave the students 'ready-made' avenues to explore facts about the Holocaust." Another teacher wrote that "its fun and you learn a lot about the topics and I think you can learn more on the WebQuest than in a classroom because the WebQuest has information that the teacher may not have down." A third teacher indicated that the best part of the WebQuest project was:

> The experience my students had using the Internet. Most of my students do not have computers at home, but they do have playstations (sic). They viewed a computer as a place to play games. The WebQuest with the authoring tools used in conjunction with it gave them the opportunity to see the computer in a different light.

Aspects of the WebQuest Model Teachers Enjoyed Least

Many respondents indicated that they (much like some of their students) liked all aspects of the WebQuest model. For example, one teacher stated that there was "really nothing about it I did not like." Other respondents, however, did have some concerns about the use of the WebQuest with their students. These respondents expressed two main concerns with the WebQuest model and with their experience using it. First, some teachers noted that they had to endure technical problems that often plagued their efforts. For example, one teacher noted "links are always a problem" and "pop-ups [pop-up advertising screens] on a couple of links interfered with our research." Another respondent stated that "the trouble with links is always a pain." Still, another had initial difficulty getting her WebQuest to load at all.

The final teacher concern had less to do with the WebQuest model than with students' reaction to using it. Several teachers were frustrated by their students' unwillingness to engage in the self-directed learning promoted by WebQuest use: "some didn't take initiative—they wanted me to walk them through it step-by-step." This issue was summarized by one respondent as:

Students also do not take the time to read directions. They love using the search engines even though you give them all the information they need. They simply do not want to take the time to read through all the information they need. They want a quick and easy fix.

DISCUSSION AND CONCLUSIONS

As noted previously, very few studies have examined the impact of the WebQuest model on student learning and motivation. The current study represented a modest effort at collecting very preliminary data on these questions. In spite of the relatively large sample size, this was a preliminary study with no attempt at randomized treatment and no attempt to compare students to those who had not participated in a WebQuest. Given these issues, any conclusions must, of course, be interpreted with some degree of caution. Despite this caveat, however, there are some noteworthy conclusions that can be drawn from the study.

Student and Teacher Perception of the WebQuest Model

On the surface, the results of the current study seem to support the overwhelmingly positive claims of WebQuest advocates. However, closer examination of these data seems to more closely support Milson's (2002) "cautious optimism" for the WebQuest's value as an instructional approach rather than the "zealous support" found in many of the previously cited reports of WebQuest use (p. 348). For example, a majority of students indicated that they felt more involved in their own learning while using the WebQuest and they felt they learned more than they would have had the material been introduced in a traditional, textbook-based lesson. While these are indeed very positive results, it must be noted that while nearly half of the respondents indicated that they enjoyed learning using the WebQuest model 'more' or 'much more' than a traditional lesson, the other half enjoyed the model 'about the same' or 'less.'

It was interesting to note that some of the additional benefits claimed by advocates of the WebQuest model were not necessarily perceived as such by students. One such example was the belief that the WebQuest model provided an efficient mechanism for organizing and utilizing Internet resources. Only about 4% of student respondents identified this as their favorite aspect of the model. Another claim made by WebQuest advocates is that the use of the model—in and of itself—is motivating to students, presumably, in part, because it provides access to multimedia resources not found in textbooks, and represents something new and different for students. Results of the current study indicated that this 'motivating effect' was not necessarily present for all students. Indeed, a number of students indicated that they did not enjoy being online, nor did they enjoy working on the Internet, and less than 5% of students identified the interactive multimedia elements of the WebQuest as their favorite aspect. In addition, the students disliked a wide range of aspects of the WebQuest model; from the task itself to the time needed to complete the WebQuest. In these findings, the current study echoes Strickland (2005) who cautioned that use of the Internet may not be as intrinsically motivating to students as previously believed, particularly for those students who already have Internet access at home and may use it on a daily basis.

Milson (2002) concluded that not all students had the same reaction to the WebQuest model, and this conclusion was supported in the current study. Quite a few students indicated that the WebQuest model allowed them to use their preferred mode of learning. However, while some indicated that this was due to the individualized nature of their respective WebQuest, others students indicated this was due to cooperative grouping in their WebQuests. This would appear to be a problem for teachers developing WebQuests—should they be individualized or should they use, as Dodge (1998) suggested, a cooperative group structure?

Other results were mixed as well. A number of teachers indicated that the creativity of the WebQuest tasks (e.g., "making the poems or raps") was a positive aspect of the model. Students were more divided in their opinions, however: while approximately 19% indicated the creativity the WebQuests tasks afforded them was their most favorite aspect, nearly 22% of students indicated that a specific task associated with a WebQuest was their *least* favorite aspect.

Final Discussion

Clearly, one important finding of the current study is that simply implementing the WebQuest model does not necessarily ensure success with all students, and this is especially true with poorly designed, or ill-conceived WebQuests. This is an important finding because it reminds teachers that technology integration—in and of itself—is no guarantee of success, and that the poor application of any curriculum model is likely to be unsuccessful. Results of the current study confirm those of Milson (2002) in that WebQuests were perceived differently by different students. Moreover, the results suggest that not all topics lend themselves to the WebQuest model. Dodge (1998) noted that WebQuests are "inquiry-oriented activities" and should not simply be Internet-based scavenger hunts. Indeed, some topics may lend themselves to other types of educational technology; recall the student who stated "I would have been happier using PowerPoint®." These are both issues that teachers and curriculum developers should keep in mind when exploring WebQuest use and development.

Several students noted that they did not like the WebQuest because it "didn't have any games on it." This reaction seemed closely related to the teacher who noted "most (of my) students see the computer as a place to play games." This raises the interesting question of whether some students may be predisposed to have difficulty with the WebQuest model because their experience with computers is limited to gaming. Becker (2000) found that "playing games has always been the primary use of home computers for children . . . only about half as many parents reported their children used home computers for educational programs as reported their use for playing games (p. 60)." Unfortunately, this question remains beyond the scope of the current study. However, in this current study not all students respond to WebQuests in the same ways and future studies should investigate variables (such as previous experience with gaming) that may influence student success with the model.

While the results of the current study do to some degree confirm advocates' claims for the WebQuest model, it is important to note that 'a WebQuest is not a WebQuest is not a WebQuest.' That is, the model may not be uniformly accepted by all students and should not be promoted as such. These preliminary results indicated that several factors appeared to impact student perception of the WebQuest model. For example, students in third and eighth grades were more likely—relative to students in other grades—to feel they 'learned less' using the WebQuest model. It was also clear that not all students were motivated by, nor enjoyed completing, certain WebQuest tasks. In addition, these results imply that the design of the WebQuest and its use of Internet and multimedia resources appear to impact student reaction to the model. Recall the student who noted, about the WebQuest he participated in: "it was a very bad website, color wise. The colors made it hard to read and first impressions are important." Teachers seeking to maximize the positive aspects of the model should design and implement WebQuests based on the needs and interests of students and not assume that employing the WebQuest model will necessarily result in increased student learning or motivation.

This report provided preliminary data on student and teacher perceptions of the WebQuest model. These data came from students and teachers who participated in WebQuests related to citizenship education and the social studies. Much more research in a variety of settings and contexts (e.g., other content areas) needs to be conducted in order to fully demonstrate the benefits of the WebQuest model. Future research should focus on measuring impact of the WebQuest model on student learning and motivation and should include both quasi-experimental designs (comparing matched, intact, classes of students who employ the WebQuest model with classes who do not) as well as deep narratives describing the kind of learning that WebQuests do (or do not) foster. In the current study, teachers designed WebQuests to fit their specific curricular needs, and rightly so. If more systematic study of the impact of the WebQuest model is to be accomplished, however, it would require having the same teachers use the same WebQuest to cover the same content—a standardized treatment, if you will. In addition, such a study would utilize standardized assessment that would measure content learning as well. Regardless of the methodology, however, if we are to expand the scant research literature in this area, we must begin to ask questions about how the use of WebQuests impacts student outcomes beyond attitude and engagement.

NOTES

1. These figures represent computational estimates based on algorithmic calculations from raw data and, in the case of the secondary estimate, may have been rounded up (from 99.5% to 100%). See http://nces.ed.gov/programs/digest/d04/tables/dt04_424.asp.
2. For more information about the James F. Ackerman Center for Democratic Citizenship, please see http://ackerman.education.purdue.edu.
3. For more information, please see http://research.soe.purdue.edu/ackerman/participant_webquests_frame.html.
4. For peer review process see http://research.education.purdue.edu/ackerman/webquest_peer_review_template.html.
5. For the full WebQuest, see http://research.soe.purdue.edu/ackerman2/webquest1/webquest1_frame.htm.
6. See the online instruments at https://discovery.education.purdue.edu/surveys/survey.asp?survey_id=SI_2005_ST and https://discovery.education.purdue.edu/surveys/survey.asp?survey_id=SI_2005_TEACHER

REFERENCES

Becker, H. J. (2001, April 10–14). *How are teachers using computers in instruction?* Paper presented at the annual meeting of the American Educational Research Association, Seattle, WA.

Becker, H. (2000). Who's wired and who's not: Children's access to and use of computer technology. *Children and Computer Technology*, 10 (2), 44–75.

Becker, H. J. (1999). *Internet use by teachers: Conditions of professional use and student-directed use.* Irvine, CA: Center for Research on Information Technology and Organizations. Retrieved September 7, 1999, from: http://www.crito.uci.edu/TLC/findings/Internet-Use/startpage.htm

Braun, J., Fernlund, P., & White, C. (1998). *Technology tools in the social studies classroom.* Wilsonville, OR: Franklin, Beedle and Associates.

Brucklacher, B., & Gimbert, B. (1999). Role-palying software and webquests: What's possible with cooperative learning and computers. *Computers in the Schools, 15*(2), 37–48.

Diem, R. (2000). Can it make a difference? Technology and the social studies. *Theory and Research in Social Education, 28*(4), 493–501.

Dodge, B. (1998). *Some thoughts about Webquests.* San Diego State University. 3 pages. Retrieved September 15, 2006, from: http://edweb.sdsu.edu/courses/edtec596/about_webquests.html

Follansbee, S., Hughes, B., Pisha, B., & Stahl, S. (1997). Can online communications improve student performance? Results of a controlled study. *ERS Spectrum, 15*(1), 15–26.

Hack, L. and Smey, S. (1997). A survey of Internet use by teachers in three urban Connecticut schools. *School Library Media Quarterly, 25*(3), 151–155.

Hicks, D., Doolittle, P., & Lee, J. K. (2004). History and social studies teachers' use of classroom and Web-based historical primary sources. *Theory and Research in Social Education, 32*(2), 213–247.

Information Please. (2005). *Internet statistics and resources.* Retrieved September 6, 2005, from: http://www.infoplease.com/ipa/A0778256.html

Lipscomb, G. (2003). 'I guess it was pretty fun': Using webquests in the middle school classroom. *The Clearing House, 76*(3), 152–155.

Mathison, C., & Pohan, C. (1999). An internet-based exploration of democratic schooling within pluralistic learning environments. *Educational Technology, 39,* 53–58.

McGlinn, M., & McGlinn, J. (2004). The effects of webquests in the social studies classroom: A review of research. *Society for Information Technology and Teacher Education International Conference, 2004*(1), 4833–4839.

Milson, A. (2002). Theinternet and inquiry learning: Intergrating medium and method in a sixth grade social studies classroom. *Theory and Research in Social Education, 30*(3), 330–353.

National Center for Educational Statistics. (2003). *Digest of education statistics, 2004.* Washington, DC: Author. Retrieved October 23, 2005 from: http://nces.ed.gov/programs/digest/d04/tables/dt04_424.asp

Parsad, B., & Jones, J. (2003). *Internet access in U.S. public schools and classrooms: 1994–2003* (NCES 2005015). U.S. Department of Education. Washington, DC: National Center for Education Statistics.

Patton, M. (1990). *Qualitative evaluation and research methods.* London: Sage.

Santavenere, A. (2003). *The effects of educational technology upon the critical thinking and analytical skills of below grade-level and or non-college bound high school students.* ERIC document number ED476469.

Shiveley, J. M., & VanFossen, P. J. (2001). *Using Internet primary sources to teach critical thinking in government, economics, and contemporary world issues.* Westport, CT: Greenwood Press.

Strickland, J. (2005). Using webquests to teach content: Comparing instructional strategies. *Contemporary Issues in Technology and Teacher Education, 5*(2), 138–148.

VanFossen, P. J. (2005). Reading and math take up so much of the time . . . : An overview of social studies instruction in elementary classrooms in Indiana. *Theory and Research in Social Education, 33*(3), 376–403.

VanFossen, P. J. (2000). An analysis of the use of the internet and world wide web by secondary social studies teachers in Indiana. *International Journal of Social Education, 14*(2), 87–109.

Vidoni, K., & Maddux, C. (2002). Webquests: Can they be used to improve critical thinking skills in students? *Computers in Schools, 19*(1/2), 101–117.

Wiesenmayer, R., & Meadows, G. (1997). Addressing science teacher's initial perceptions of the classroom uses of Internet and World Wide Web-based resource materials. *Journal of Science Education and Technology, 6*(4), 329–335.

Wilson, J. (1995). Social studies online resources. *Social Studies and the Young Learner, 7*(3), 24–26.

Yoder, M. (1999). The student webquest: A productive and thought provoking use of the internet. *Learning and Leading with Technology, 26*(7), 6–9.

Zenanko, M., King, F., & Nelson, J. (1996). *A survey of Internet access and usage in a selected sample of northeast Alabama schools.* Paper presented at the annual meeting of the Mid-South Educational Research Association, Tuscaloosa, AL.

WEBSITE RESOURCES

The WebQuest Page: http://webquest.sdsu.edu/

CHAPTER 6

MULTIMEDIA-BASED HISTORICAL INQUIRY STRATEGY INSTRUCTION

Do Size and Form Really Matter?

David Hicks and Peter E. Doolittle

ABSTRACT

This chapter examines how the integration of a multimedia tool (SCIM Historical Inquiry Tutorial) can support the teaching of history. Specifically, we report on the results of an experiment that asks: To what extent does the level of strategic engagement (superficial or comprehensive) and the nature of the multimedia presentation (animation (A), narration (N), and on-screen text (T)) impact students' understandings of historical inquiry and the strategic knowledge required to engage in source analysis? Participants included 195 male and 209 female undergraduate students ($n = 404$). While the superficial/comprehensive instructional strategy results provided evidence that sustained engagement is necessary for the development of strategic thinking, the multimedia group (i.e., AN, AT, ANT) results surprisingly yielded no significant or meaningful findings. This study joins a growing body of empiri-

Research on Technology in Social Studies Education, pages 127–152

cal research designed to examine how digital technologies can support the teaching and learning of the doing of history.

INTRODUCTION

It is only when students understand that historians can ask questions about historical sources that those sources were not designed to answer, and that much of the evidence used by historians was not intended to report anything, that they are freed from dependence on truthful testimony. Much of what holds interest for historians... could not have been "eyewitnessed" by anyone, not even by us if we could return by time machine. Once students begin to operate with a concept of evidence as something inferential and see eyewitnesses not as handing down history but as providing evidence, history can resume once again; it becomes intelligible, even a powerful, way of thinking about the past. (Lee, 2005, pp. 36–37)

Progression in the discipline of history begins with a recognition that there is more to teaching history than the simple "aggregation" of historical facts, whereby success is simply quantitatively gauged by "an increase in the amount of information pupils could recall" (Lee & Shemilt, 2003, p. 113). Learning history, as the opening quote illuminates, requires learners to engage in the process of historical inquiry in terms of "the use of analysis to identify connections, relationships, and structures that tie together individual events or pieces of evidence" (Barton & Levstik, 2004, p. 69). The importance of preparing students to unpack historical sources as part of answering historical questions has long been advocated (see Osbourne, 2003) and remains prominent in the current benchmarks and standards of the American Historical Association (AHA, 2003), the National Center for History in the Schools (NCHS, 1996), and the National Council for the Social Studies (NCSS, 1994). While such an "analytic stance," in terms of teaching historical inquiry and analysis, is often identified as the 'ideal' approach for teaching and learning history, the shift from theory to practical application within today's classrooms can be difficult and time consuming (see Bain, 2000; Barton, 1997, 2005; Barton & Levstik, 2004; Hicks, Doolittle, & Lee, 2004; Levstik & Barton, 2001a,b; VanSledright, 2002b,c).

However, over the last 30 years a growing body of research clearly indicates that given careful and appropriate instruction students as young as seven can begin to engage critically with historical sources as part of the process of historical inquiry (see Ashby, Lee, & Dickinson, 1997; Barton, 1997; Barton & Levstik, 2004; Lee, 2005; VanSledright & Limón, 2006). As Barton (1998) notes, it is important to see a student's abilities to comprehend history and think historically as "a set of skills educators can nurture, not an ability whose development they must wait for or whose absence they must lament" (p. 80). Nurturing such abilities, Riley (1999) contends, requires teachers to engage in "systematic and sophisticated literacy work" with their students (p. 8). Such work itself necessitates that teachers provide students with scaffolds to support the development of procedural/strategic and metacognitive knowledge.

Set within and through such a disciplinary understanding of the purpose of history, which recognizes that the acquisition of historical knowledge is "both the servant and the result of enquiry" (Counsell, 2000, p. 70), this chapter examines how the integration of multimedia can support the teaching of history, and specifically scaffold such distinguishable slices of the inquiry process as the analysis of historical sources. Our research is explicitly designed to extend the literature that examines the extent to which the use of multimedia impacts student learning in history. Within the study we build on our previous work that sought to develop and evaluate the impact of one specific multimedia supported strategy to teach historical inquiry by taking into consideration the extent to which teacher concerns with limited class and preparation time can serve as stumbling blocks to (1) engaging students in the learning of the doing of history and, specifically, source analysis; and (2) integrating digital technologies into the social studies classroom (Hicks & Doolittle, 2007; Hicks, Doolittle & Ewing, 2004). Specifically, we report on the results of an experiment that asks: To what extent does the level of strategic engagement (superficial or comprehensive) and the nature of the multimedia presentation (animation, narration, and on-screen text) impact students' understandings of historical inquiry and the strategic knowledge required to engage in source analysis? Before introducing and explaining the multimedia tool (SCIM Historical Inquiry Tutorial) and reporting on the experiment at hand, we briefly situate our work within the field of multimedia learning in the social studies.

MULTIMEDIA LEARNING IN THE SOCIAL STUDIES

Literature reviews focusing on the integration of digital technologies in the social studies continue to reveal that the field is still in its "adolescence" (Berson & Balyta, 2004, p. 148) and to a great extent "research lite" (Friedman & Hicks, 2006, p. 251) in terms of studies examining the impact of digital technologies on the teaching and learning of social studies (Berson, 1996; Ehman & Glenn, 1991; Friedman & Hicks, 2006; Whitworth & Berson, 2003). Interestingly however, a small number of researchers, informed by empirical research examining how students' learn history (for overviews see Barton & Levstik, 2004; VanSledright & Limón, 2006), have used such findings to inform, develop, and investigate the utility of multimedia tools to support the teaching and learning of the doing of history. The research of Wiley and Voss on writing historical accounts (Voss & Wiley, 1997, 2000; Wiley, 2001), Britt and her colleagues working with the Sorcerers Apprentice (Britt & Aglinskas, 2002; Britt et al., 2000; Britt, Rouet, & Perfetti, 1996; Rouet et al., 1996), Spoehr and her colleague working with *American Culture in Context: Enrichment for Secondary Schools* (Spoehr & Spoehr, 1994); and Saye and Brush working with their problem-based inquiry tool *Decision Point!* (Brush & Saye, 2000, 2001, 2002, 2004; Saye & Brush, 2002, 2004, 2005, 2006, 2007; Wolf, Brush, & Saye, 2003) have all examined the extent to which multimedia environments can be effective for supporting the teaching and learning of working with multiple sources as part of the doing of history. What is clear from these studies as Wiley and Ash (2005) note is that "simply giving students access to multiple sources or multimedia learning environments will not guarantee any meaningful learning. This type of knowledge needs to be acquired through participation in highly structured guided activities with clear problem-solving and inquiry goals" (p. 385). The programmatic series of studies conducted by Saye and Brush have gone a long way to aid our understanding of the nature and utility of the type of structures, what they call soft and hard scaffolding, to support the teaching of history when working in a multimedia environment. Saye and Brush have consistently and explicitly identified the potentials, pitfalls, and provisos facing teachers and students as they worked with a multimedia historical inquiry tool they developed called *Decision Point! (DP!)* as part of the process of engaging in an authentic and meaningful historical inquiry on the Civil Rights era. In discussing their work, Saye and Brush are quick to acknowledge how issues of time, and the difficulty and breadth of the task assigned clearly impact students' abilities to learn to work with multiple sources and engage in the doing of history. They note:

> Despite additional scaffolding in *DP!* students continued to have difficulty acquiring deep, broad views of the civil rights knowledge base. These difficulties may be related to the breadth of the problem presented to the students in the unit. We hypothesize that the problem landscape for the *DP!* unit is too expansive for students to gain mastery in the time they have been given. In most classrooms, resources such as those available in *DP!* might be used more effectively if initial problems explored by students were smaller and more bounded. Students participating in both *DP!* 1 and *DP!* 2 had virtually no experience in participating in problem-based curriculum units in their social studies classes. (Saye & Brush, 2002, pp. 92–93)

In a recent review of their work Saye and Brush (2007) again recognize the limits to student learning and engagement because of class time, the scope of work expected, and the difficulty inherent in working with multiple sources. They explain:

Our investigations have led us to believe that more tightly bounded problems are necessary to produce optimal improvement in student performances. We created the expansive *DP: Civil Rights*...in the hope that students could follow their curiosity to construct knowledge about their own questions as they arose as part of their investigations. However, we must balance this potential against the disorientation and superficiality that such an embarrassment of riches seemed to engender. We are currently developing much smaller defined sets of source documents. Smaller document sets will allow us to attend more closely to student conceptual and metacognitive needs by embedding supporting information and questions directly into the documents, a level of support that was impractical in the more open-ended *DP* event investigations. (pp. 216–217)

In recognition of such insights, our work has sought to re-scale the nature and use of multimedia to support the teaching and learning of history in terms of more closely scaffolding and also examining the impact of multimedia environments on more discrete slices of the inquiry process across different instructional contexts. Specifically, we developed a tool—the SCIM Historical Inquiry Tutorial—to explain the historical inquiry process and model how to examine and unpack individual sources. The SCIM historical Inquiry Tutorial derives from the SCIM-C strategy that is made up of five key phases that are designed to serve as scaffold to support student analysis of multiple historical sources in order to develop a historical account (Summarizing, Contextualizing, Inferring, Monitoring, and Corroborating). Such specific fine-grained research not only acknowledges the difficulties inherent in developing evidential understanding in working with various and multiple historical sources, but also provides the opportunity to "systematically investigate the effects of the content and design of multimedia environments on history learning... [while also identifying] which aspects of multimedia inquiry tasks are responsible for better learning outcomes" (Wiley & Ash, 2005. p. 386).

MULTIMEDIA AND HISTORICAL INQUIRY: THE SCIM HISTORICAL INQUIRY TUTORIAL

The SCIM Historical Inquiry Tutorial is an example of a multimedia instructional environment that focuses on the social studies domain and is designed to foster a deeper understanding of the doing of history in terms of understanding the concept of historical inquiry and the analysis of individual historical sources. The following sections describe the SCIM-C strategy for historical inquiry, upon which the multimedia tutorial is based, and the two versions of the SCIM Historical Inquiry Tutorial designed to examine the impact of superficial and comprehensive engagement on strategic knowledge development. It is important to point out that the SCIM Historical Inquiry Tutorial that we used for this study was deliberately designed to examine the participants' abilities to analyze a single historical source rather than multiple sources, therefore only the first four phases of the SCIM-C process were taught and assessed. In doing this, our goal was to acknowledge the difficulties inherent in teaching how to analyze one historical source as part of the historical inquiry process, never mind teaching how to develop accounts based on multiple sources.

The SCIM-C Strategy for Historical Inquiry

Historical inquiry is not a process that students tend to understand and adopt naturally. Fortunately, however, historical inquiry *is* a process that can be entered into in at various levels of sophistication. This entering, or engagement, into historical inquiry is often quite daunting for students at all levels and requires careful scaffolding. One method of scaffolding the historical inquiry process is to use the SCIM-C strategy. The SCIM-C strategy provides students with the structural and conceptual help they need in interpreting historical primary source documents, in negotiating the spaces between fact-based and perspectival historical understanding, and in reconciling various accounts of the past, as they try to make sense of evidence from the past in order to answer historical questions (Hicks, Doolittle, & Ewing, 2004).

The SCIM-C model is founded upon a belief that a central goal of doing history is to gain a critical understanding of the broad picture of the past. This broad picture is constructed from traces or sources of information from and about the past. These historical sources are then analyzed as part of the process of historical interpretation. History in this sense is not everything that happened in the past, but is a way of organizing and explaining the past. To actually engage in this process of doing history means that we have to ask and answer historically relevant questions. In order to answer historically relevant questions, students need to understand how to (a) evaluate sources in order to use them as historical evidence, and (b) reconcile conflicting evidence to create an interpretive account of the past. Ultimately the final narrative is an interpretation of the past based on an analysis of the available evidence.

Grounded within ongoing research on teaching and learning history (Barton & Levstik, 2001a,b, 2004; Wineburg, 1991a,b, 2001; VanSledgright, 2002a–c) and building upon and Riley's (1999) layers of inference models to support teaching evidential understanding, the SCIM-C model utilizes a five-phase process to teach students how to analyze historical primary sources in pursuit of answering historical questions. While there are many questions that can be asked of a historical source, the SCIM-C strategy focuses on five broad questioning phases: Summarizing, Contextualizing, Inferring, Monitoring, and Corroborating. Specifically, when students examine an individual source, they move through the first four phases—summarizing, contextualizing, inferring, and monitoring—and then, after analyzing several individual sources, they contrast the sources collectively in the fifth phase, corroboration.

Within each phase there exists a series of four spiraling and analyzing questions that serve to scaffold critical engagement with each source so that students may interact and transact with the source in light of the historical question being asked. More guiding questions can be asked within each phase as teachers rework the model to support the contexts within which they teach. The model should be viewed as an initiating device through which to nurture and support students' abilities to begin to engage in source analysis.

The model's utility lies in the recognition that SCIM-C simply provides a point of entry through which to teach historical analysis. The model, like any scaffold, is a support to "build other things with, and should be erected with an eye to taking them down" (Goffman, 1959, p. 254). The overall process of moving through the phases of the SCIM-C strategy should be viewed as a precise, recursive, and thoughtful approach to historical inquiry. It is an approach that requires a concerted level of engagement with each source whereby teachers allow students the time necessary to question, reflect, and comprehend the source in order to develop and write a historical interpretation. The following section addresses each of the five phases of SCIM-C, including the four spiraling analyzing questions for each phase.

Summarizing. Summarizing is the first phase of the SCIM-C strategy and begins with having students quickly examine the documentary aspects of the historical source, in order to find any information or evidence that is explicitly available from the source. Within this phase students identify the source's subject, author, purpose, and audience, as well as the type of historical source (e.g., letter, photograph, cartoon). In addition, the student looks for key facts, dates, ideas, opinions, and perspectives that are immediately apparent within the source. The four analyzing questions associated with the summarizing phase include:

1. What type of historical document is the source?
2. What specific information, details and/or perspectives does the source provide?
3. What are the subject and purpose of the source?
4. Who were the author and/or audience of the source?

Contextualizing. Contextualizing begins the process of students spending more time with the source in order to explore the authentic aspects of the source in terms of locating the source within time and space. One of the main problems people have when analyzing historical sources is making sense of the source within the context or time period in which the source was produced. That is, sources are remains of the past and were produced during a specific time and period for specific purposes by specific individuals or groups. Failing to pay attention to the importance of the historical context(s) from which the source originates leaves both students and teachers open to the risk of treating the source as a product of today and succumbing to the sin of historical anachronism (Berkhofer, 1995).

Students must recognize that it is important to understand that archaic words and/or images from the period may be in a source. These words and/or images may no longer be used today or they may be used differently, and these differences should be noted and defined. In addition, the meanings, values, habits, and/or customs of the period may be very different from those today. Students and teachers must be careful to avoid treating the source as a product of today as they pursue their guiding historical question. The four analyzing questions associated with the contextualizing phase include:

1. When and where was the source produced?
2. Why was the source produced?
3. What was happening within the immediate and broader context at the time the source was produced?
4. What summarizing information can place the source in time and place?

Inferring. Inferring is designed to provide students with the opportunity to revisit initial facts gleaned from the source and begin to read subtexts and make inferences based upon a developing understanding of the context and continued examination of the source. In answering a historical question and working with the primary source, sometimes the evidence is not explicitly stated or obvious in the source, but rather, the evidence is hinted at within the source and needs to be drawn out. As part of inferring, it becomes important to revisit initial facts gleaned from the two earlier phases and begin to draw conclusions. In addition, by leaving out certain details and highlighting others, the author/creator of a source can influence the reader. The inferring stage provides room for students to explore the source and examine the source's perspective in the light of the historical questions being asked. The four analyzing questions associated with the inferring phase include:

1. What is suggested by the source?
2. What interpretations may be drawn from the source?
3. What perspectives/points of view are indicated in the source?
4. What inferences may be drawn from absences or omissions in the source?

Monitoring. Monitoring is the capstone stage in examining individual sources. Here students are expected to question and reflect upon their initial assumptions in terms of the overall focus on the historical questions being studied. At this point in the analysis, students will have garnished a fair amount of information through summarizing and contextualizing the source, as well as inferring from the source. This reflective monitoring is essential in making sure that students have asked the key questions from each of the previous phases. Such a process requires students to examine the usefulness or significance of the source for answering the historical questions at hand. By doing this, students are double-checking and demonstrating their own awareness of the necessity to carefully and thoughtfully analyze the historical source.

An additional aspect of monitoring, beyond monitoring the execution of the SCIM-C strategy itself, is to examine the credibility of the source. The "information value" of certain documents may in some cases be exaggerated, offering perspectives or images that are clearly inconsistent with similar sources. Sometimes people have lied about their experiences. Sometimes historical sources are produced a long time after the events it portrays, telling us more about recollections in old age, for example, than the events themselves. Finally, the source may have been produced with a specific purpose in mind that is no longer relevant.

Ultimately, monitoring is about reflection—reflection upon the use of the SCIM-C strategy and reflection upon the source itself. The SCIM-C strategy is recursive in nature and thus revisiting phases and questions is essential as one begins to create a historical interpretation of a source in light of one's historical questions. The four analyzing questions associated with the monitoring phase include:

1. What additional evidence beyond the source is necessary to answer the historical question?
2. What ideas, images, or terms need further defining from the source?
3. How useful or significant is the source for its intended purpose in answering the historical question?
4. What questions from the previous stages need to be revisited in order to analyze the source satisfactorily?

Corroborating. Corroborating involves comparing the developed evidence from each source based on the initial topic of investigation and the guiding historical questions. What similarities and differences in ideas, information, and perspectives exist between the analyzed sources? Students should also look for gaps in their evidence that may hinder their interpretations and the answering of their guiding historical questions. When they find contradictions between sources, they must investigate further, including the checking of the credibility of the source. Once the sources have been compared, the student then begins to draw conclusions based upon the synthesis of the evidence. The four analyzing questions associated with the corroborating phase include:

1. What similarities and differences between the sources exist?
2. What factors could account for these similarities and differences?
3. What conclusions can be drawn from the accumulated interpretations?
4. What additional information or sources are necessary to answer more fully the guiding historical question?

The SCIM-C strategy for historical inquiry served as the foundation for the SCIM historical inquiry multimedia tutorial, which was created in both a superficial and comprehensive strategy instruction version. Since the SCIM Historical Inquiry Tutorial was designed to focus on the analysis of individual sources, corroboration is not included within the tutorial.

SCIM Historical Inquiry Tutorial: Comprehensive Strategy Instruction Version

The SCIM Historical Inquiry Tutorial, a multimedia instructional scaffold, was designed to assist teachers and students in the development of historical inquiry knowledge and skills (see http://www.historicalinquiry. com for an example of the tutorial). That is, the tool was *not* designed to replace teacher–student interaction, nor was it designed to subsume the teacher's instructional role. The SCIM multimedia instructional scaffold seeks to engage students in inquiry, critical thinking, and critical reflexivity through an extensive and systematic engagement with historical sources.

This systematic engagement was designed based on research addressing (a) historical inquiry (see Levstik & Barton, 2001a, b; Riley, 1999; Wineburg, 2001); (b) cognitive strategy instruction (see Collins, Block, & Pressley, 2002; Reid & Lienemann, 2006); (c) instructional multimedia development (see Mayer, 2001, 2005); (d) scaffolding in technologically-rich instructional environments (see Quintana, et al., 2004; Reiser, 2004; Saye &

Brush, 2006); and (e) classroom-based history teaching at the elementary, middle, secondary and college levels (see Booth, 2003; Doolittle & Hicks, 2003; Hadyn, Arthur, & Hunt, 2001; Levstik & Barton, 2001a; VanSledright, 2002a–c). The tutorial itself was created using Adobe's Flash™ and is a combination of animation, explanatory narration, and optional on-screen text mirroring the explanatory narration.

At the macro level, the SCIM Historical Inquiry Tutorial was designed as four instructional episodes lasting 30–45 minutes each (for a detailed account of the SCIM strategy, see Hicks & Doolittle, 2007). At the micro level, each instructional episode comprised a combination of *strategy explanation*, *strategy demonstration*, and *strategy participation* (see Figure 6.1). Specifically, during the first instructional episode students engaged in approximately 15 minutes of explicit SCIM strategy instruction, 15 minutes of expert demonstration (modeling), and no strategy participation. However, as the student progressed from the first to the fourth instructional episode the amount of time engaged in explicit strategy explanation and strategy demonstration decreased while the amount of time engaged in strategy participation increased. Indeed, during the fourth instructional episode the students were entirely engaged in strategy participation.

The *strategy explanation* sections of the instruction were designed to explicitly address a general approach to historical inquiry and introduce the specific phases and questions of the SCIM strategy. The section on the general approach to historical inquiry begins with the asking of historical questions and continues with the idea that historical sources must be obtained and analyzed as historical evidence. This historical evidence is then used to create a historical interpretation that addresses the original historical

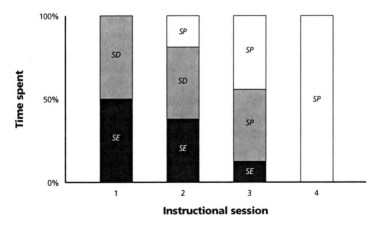

Figure 6.1 The distribution of time spent within the SCIM Historical Inquiry Tutorial on strategy explanation (SE), strategy demonstration (SD), and strategy participation (SP) across four days of instruction.

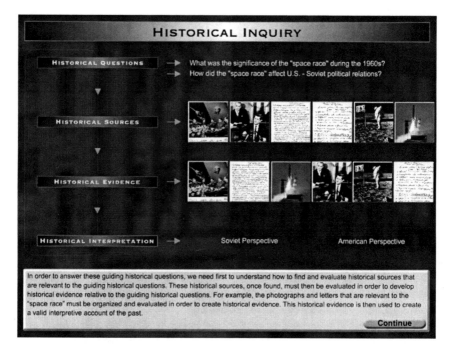

Figure 6.2   The SCIM tutorial and the historical inquiry process.

questions (see Figure 6.2). Following this discussion of the general historical inquiry approach, an explanation of the SCIM strategy is provided that focuses on explicit instruction in the use of the strategy (i.e., summarizing, contextualizing, inferring, and monitoring) with authentic sources (see Figure 6.3). Metacognitive knowledge of when, where, and why to use the strategy and examples of the strategy in use is also provided.

The *strategy demonstration* sections of the instruction are based on the think aloud protocols of historians as they analyzed various sources relative to specific guiding historical questions. This modeling of the SCIM strategy by experts is necessary for students to develop both the skills to use the strategy and the metacognition necessary to know when, where, and why to use the strategy. Specifically, these expert-based demonstrations model the iterative nature of the SCIM phases, the process of source analysis and evidence generation, and the creation of historical interpretations.

The *strategy participation* sections involve the students in making decisions relative to the analysis and interpretation of sources under study. Questioning, decision-making, and feedback dominate the strategy participation sections. Specifically, students are provided with a historical source to read and then are asked to answer identification and interpretation questions. Identification questions are surface level questions that focus on identify-

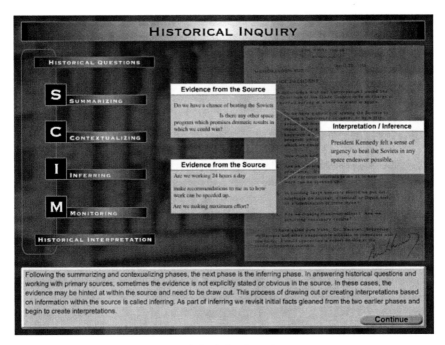

Figure 6.3   The SCIM strategy and the inferring phase.

ing explicit summary statements, simple contextualizing statements, obvious inferential statements, and basic monitoring questions. Interpretation questions, however, require students to read complex interpretive statements and determine the most accurate statements relative to the source under analysis. In addition, after students answer each question, they are provided with explicit feedback related to the correctness of their answer and guidance on how to analyze and interpret the source given the question asked. These identification and interpretation questions encourage students to self-regulate and control their use of the strategy.

SCIM Historical Inquiry Tutorial: Superficial Strategy Instruction Version

In addition to the comprehensive version of the SCIM Historical Inquiry Tutorial, lasting four sessions of 30–45 minutes, a superficial version of the tutorial was created, lasting only 3.5 minutes. The superficial version of the tutorial included an explanation of historical inquiry—comprising historical questions, historical sources, historical evidence, and historical interpretations—and a basic explanation of the SCIM strategy. The explanation of the SCIM strategy included a discussion of the four phases of the SCIM strategy and the analyzing questions associated with each phase. The superficial version of the SCIM tutorial does not include any of the source analysis examples, expert-modeled demonstrations, or source analysis practice opportunities.

RESEARCH QUESTIONS

It is hypothesized that the development of historical inquiry requires extensive engagement with historical sources and the application of specific cognitive and metacognitive strategies. The SCIM-C historical inquiry strategy and the SCIM Historical Inquiry Tutorial were designed with this purpose in mind. The development of the strategy and tutorial raise the issue of whether or not the strategy and tutorial create an effective instructional environment. In addition, given that the tutorial is multimedia-based, another question of interest is whether or not the tutorial's efficacy is affected by its presentation format, specifically, whether or not the tutorial is subject to the modality and redundancy multimedia effects (Ginns, 2005; Kalyuga, Chandler, & Sweller, 1999; Mayer, Heiser, & Lonn, 2001; Mayer & Moreno, 1998). Therefore, a study was designed to answer the following questions:

1. Is student recall and application of the SCIM strategy affected by the comprehensiveness (superficial versus comprehensive) of the SCIM tutorial multimedia instructional environment?
2. Is student recall and application of the SCIM historical inquiry strategy affected by the multimedia format (modality and redundancy principles) of the instruction?

METHODOLOGY

The purpose of this study was to determine the effects of (a) superficial and comprehensive strategy instruction in a multimedia instructional environment, and (b) instructional presentation format (animation, narration, and/or on-screen text), on the development of historical inquiry knowledge (recall) and skills (application). Specifically, students engaged in the SCIM Historical Inquiry Tutorial for either one 3-minute instructional session (superficial) or four 40-minute instructional sessions (comprehensive). In addition, students experienced the multimedia tutorial in one of three multimedia instructional environments—animation with concurrent narration (AN), animation with concurrent on-screen text (AT), or animation with concurrent narration and on-screen text (ANT). According to previous studies, students should recall and transfer more from multimedia tutorials comprising animation and narration (AN) than animation and on-screen text (AT), which is known as the modality principle (Mayer & Moreno, 1998; Moreno & Mayer, 1999), and students should recall and transfer more from multimedia tutorials comprising animation and narration (AN) than animation, narration, and on-screen text (ANT), which is known as the redundancy principle (Kalyuga et al., 1999; Mayer et al., 2001). The modality and redundancy effects are based on the premise that the presentation of multiple sources of information within one perceptual and/or processing channel (e.g., an animation with on-screen text, both visual stimuli) can split one's attention and overload the perceptual/processing channel and lead to decreased cognitive performance.

Participants

Participants included 195 male and 209 female undergraduate students ($n = 404$), with a mean age of 20.4 years (SD = 2.1), enrolled in a health education course at Virginia Tech. The sample was ethnically reflective of the U.S. population with 72.5% White, 14.6% Black, 6.7% Asian, 2.5% Hispanic, and 2.0% Multiracial.

Participants' prior knowledge of historical inquiry was assessed using a five-item self-rating scale and a seven-item checklist. The self-rating scale asked participants "Please rate your knowledge of historical inquiry" from 1 (*very low*) to 5 (*very high*), while the checklist asked participants to indicate which statements applied to them: (a) I have an undergraduate degree in history, or a history related field; (b) I have an advanced degree in history, or a history related field; (c) I like to watch the History Channel or BBC on television; (d) I like to read historical novels; (e) I can explain the differences between primary and secondary historical sources; (f) I can explain historiography or presentism; and (g) I can explain why history is always less than the past. The historical inquiry prior knowledge assessment had a maximum score of 12; specifically, 1 to 5 points on the self-rating scale and one point for each checklist item checked. Since the current study addressed the development of historical inquiry knowledge and skills, participants that scored 7 points or higher on the historical inquiry assessment were not included in the data analysis. Using this procedure, 9 participants were excluded.

Design

The experimental design was a 2×3 factorial design with instructional group (superficial, comprehensive) and multimedia group (AN, AT, ANT) as between-subject variables. Participants were randomly assigned to either the superficial ($n = 189$) or comprehensive ($n = 215$) instructional group, and the AN ($n = 124$), AT ($n = 140$), or ANT ($n = 140$) multimedia group.

Materials and Apparatus

The SCIM Historical Inquiry Tutorial. The tutorials created a multimedia instructional environment based on an interactive program designed to scaffold students' learning of the SCIM strategy for historical inquiry (see Hicks & Doolittle, 2007; Hicks, Doolittle, & Ewing, 2004). The comprehensive instructional strategy tutorial consisted of three main sections, strategy explanation, strategy demonstration, and strategy participation, and was distributed across four 40-minute segments (see previous discussion). The superficial strategy instruction tutorial consisted of one main section, strategy description, and comprised one 3.5-minute segment (see previous discussion).

Strategy recall test and scoring. Participants' recall of the historical inquiry process and the SCIM strategy was assessed using a single open-ended question: "Write down everything you know about the process of engaging in historical inquiry (i.e., analyzing primary historical sources)." Two trained scorers evaluated each response such that a response (inter-rater reliability, $r = .93$) received one point each for describing the four phases of historical inquiry—asking historical questions, finding and evaluating historical sources, creating historical evidence from historical sources, and writing historical interpretations—and one point each for describing the four phases of the SCIM strategy—summarizing, contextualizing, inferring, and monitoring. Thus, the maximum score for each recall test was 8.

Strategy application test and scoring. Participants' ability to analyze historical source letters, and write an interpretation based on a specific historical question, was assessed by two trained scorers (inter-rater reliability, $r = .84$). Each strategy application test consisted of participants reading a historical letter on the computer screen and then writing a historical interpretation to a historical question based on the letter in a text box on the computer screen. The strategy application test letter was written in 1865 by Thomas Christie, a soldier in the U.S. Civil War, to his brother (see Appendix A). Each response was scored such that four points were possible for each of the four SCIM phases, for a maximum score of 16 points. Within the summarizing phase, participants received one point each for including the letter's subject, author, audience, and purpose. In addition, within the contextualizing phase, participants received one point each for including in the response when, where, and why the letter was written, as well as what was happening within the immediate and/or broader context in which the letter was written. While evaluating the inferring phase, participants received one point each for including explicit inferences, implicit inferences, inferences based on omissions from the letter, and inferences based on perspectives. Finally, while evaluating the monitoring phase, participants received one point each for including in the response the need to define terms, the need for information beyond the source, the usefulness or significance of the source, and the need to revisit questions addressed previously in the analysis.

Procedure

All data collection and media presentations were completed on wireless laptop computers. Participants in the superficial and comprehensive strategy instruction groups were studied separately. Those participants in the superficial strategy instruction group were required only to attend one experimental session. These participants, upon entering the computer lab and being assigned to a laptop computer, completed a demographics questionnaire and the prior knowledge of historical inquiry assessment. Participants were then provided brief instructions regarding the superficial version of the SCIM historical inquiry tutorial. Participants then engaged in their specific version (i.e., An, AT, ANT) of the tutorial. Following the engagement in the tutorial, participants were given 10 minutes to complete the strategy recall test and 20 minutes to complete the strategy application test.

Those participants in the comprehensive strategy instruction group were required to attend four experimental sessions on different days during a single week. On the first day, upon entering the computer lab and being assigned to a laptop computer, participants completed a demographics questionnaire and the prior knowledge of historical inquiry assessment. Participants were then provided brief instructions regarding the comprehensive version of the SCIM historical inquiry tutorial. Students then engaged in the first 40-minute segment of their specific version (i.e., AN, AT, ANT) of the tutorial. On the second and third days of the study, participants were again given brief instructions and then completed the second and third 40-minute segments of their specific version of the tutorial, respectively. On the fourth day, participants were again given brief instructions and then completed the final 40-minute segment of their specific version of the tutorial. Following engagement in the final tutorial segment, participants were given 10 minutes to complete the strategy recall test and 20 minutes to complete the strategy application test.

RESULTS

The purpose of this study was to determine the effects of (a) superficial and comprehensive strategy instruction in a multimedia instructional environment, and (b) instructional presentation format (i.e., AN, AT, ANT), on the development of historical inquiry knowledge (recall) and skills (application). These two questions were analyzed using a 2 (superficial, comprehensive) × 3 (AN, AT, ANT) ANOVA with both the recall and application data. All post-hoc comparisons involved Tukey analyses with an alpha criterion of 0.05 and all effect size calculations involved Cohen's d (Cohen, 1988).

Superficial versus Comprehensive Strategy Instruction

According to the cognitive strategy instruction literature (see Pressley & Harris, 1990; Pressley & Woloshyn, 1995; Weinstein & Mayer, 1986), participants that engaged in comprehensive strategy instruction involving explicit explanations, expert modeling, extensive examples, and practice with feedback should learn to understand and apply the strategy more readily than participants that engaged in superficial strategy instruction that included general explanations only. This superficial versus comprehensive strategy instruction effect was confirmed for recall of the strategy (see Table 6.1), $F(1,398) = 177.36$, $d = 1.35$, $p = .00$. In addition, the superficial versus comprehensive strategy instruction effect were confirmed for application of the strategy, $F(1,398) = 552.11$, $d = 2.43$, $p = .00$. These results indicate that a more sustained instructional experience significantly increased both recall and application of the SCIM historical inquiry strategy.

TABLE 6.1   Means and Standard Deviations for Recall and Application Scores for the SCIM Strategy for Students Engaging in Superficial and Comprehensive Strategy Instruction

	Recall		Application	
	M	**SD**	**M**	**SD**
Superficial	3.58	1.70	3.70	1.50
Comprehensive	5.83*	1.63	10.50*	3.66

Note: Max recall score = 8. Max transfer score = 16.
* $p < .05$

TABLE 6.2   Means and Standard Deviations for Recall and Application Scores for the SCIM Strategy for Students in Differing Multimedia Groups

	Recall		Application	
	M	**SD**	**M**	**SD**
AN	4.85	2.02	7.36	4.39
AT	4.53	2.05	6.74	4.32
ANT	4.96	1.92	7.86	4.55

Note: Max recall score = 8; Max transfer score = 16; AN = animation + narration; AT = animation + on-screen text; ANT = animation + narration + on-screen text.
* $p < .05$

Modality and Redundancy Effects

According to the cognitive theory of multimedia (see Mayer, 2001, 2005a), participants that engaged in a multimedia tutorial that include animation with concurrent narration (AN) should learn more than participants who engaged in a multimedia tutorial that provided animation with on-screen text (AT) (known as the modality effect), and more than participants who engaged in a multimedia tutorial that provided animation with both concurrent narration and on-screen text (ANT) (known as the redundancy effect). Results of the analysis indicated a non-significant main effect for recall (see Table 6.2), $F(2,398) = 0.50$, $p = .60$. The analysis of the strategy application data also demonstrated a non-significant main effect, $F(2,398) = 0.36$, $p = .69$. These results indicate that there was neither a modality (AN vs. AT) nor a redundancy (AN vs. ANT) effect. These results are in contrast to prior research (Kalyuga et al., 1999; Mayer & Moreno, 1998; Moreno & Mayer, 1999) that found significant modality and redundancy effect. In addition, there were no interaction effects within the recall, $F(2,398) = 0.19$, $p = .82$, or application, $F(2,398) = 0.27$, $p = .75$, ANOVAs.

DISCUSSION

The findings clearly illustrate that the quality of instructional engagement, superficial versus comprehensive, significantly affected both the recall and application of the SCIM strategy. While superficial engagement is beneficial for introducing the strategy, the findings reflect the importance and necessity of sustained engagement in learning and utilizing the SCIM- Historical Inquiry Tutorial to prepare students to engage in the cognitively sophisticated task of analyzing a historical source. Throughout the research we never expected the participants to learn to become expert historians, rather our hope was that the design and evaluation of the different versions of the multimedia tool would provide insights into the impact of the tool on scaffolding the teaching and learning of source analysis as part of preparing students for the overall process of historical inquiry.

If students are to acquire and use their strategic knowledge to engage in the doing of history, initially learning such a simple strategy as SCIM as part of the process of historical inquiry is an important first step. However, such a first step to facilitating complex thinking cannot occur overnight, rather teachers and students must be ready, willing and able to spend time, work with and maintain such scaffolds as the SCIM Historical Inquiry Tutorial within and through their teaching. Sustained engagement of 2.5 hours did provide students with the initial support to begin to recall and apply the SCIM strategy to source analysis; however it is not clear that 2.5 hours was enough time for students to be ready to have the scaffolding, or intellectual training wheels, removed. If the ability to work with historical sources is as important as Lee (2005, p. 36) in the opening quote contends it is for understanding and learning history—"once students begin to operate with a concept of evidence as something inferential and see eyewitnesses not as handing down history but as providing evidence, history can resume once again"—then it would seem that in the big picture, 2.5 hours of initial sustained engagement is time well spent for establishing a strong foundation from which a teacher would continue throughout the year to invest in, nurture and build upon the students' abilities to use their strategic knowledge to develop their source analysis skills, and learn to more fully engage in the authentic process of the doing of history.

While the superficial/comprehensive instructional strategy results provided evidence that sustained engagement is necessary for the development of strategic thinking, the multimedia group (i.e., AN, AT, ANT) results yielded no significant or meaningful findings (Table 6.2). The lack of a modality effect is somewhat surprising given Ginns' (2005) meta-analysis of the modality effect, in which he examined 43 relevant studies, yielding an overall weighted mean effect size (Cohen's d) of 0.72. One explanation may be that the vast majority of Ginns' 43 studies used cause-and-effect multimedia tutorials (e.g., what causes lightning), while the current study used a strategy-based multimedia tutorial. This reason, cause-and-effect tutorials versus strategy-based tutorials, may also be the cause of the lack of a redundancy effect. Ultimately, the lack of modality and redundancy effects calls into question the generalizability of the effects.

Finally, while the SCIM Historical Inquiry Tutorial is no panacea for preparing teachers and students to engage in source analysis, the tutorial does appear to provide a potentially worthwhile example of (a) a hard scaffold within a technology enhanced learning environment for teachers and students to engage in the type of sustained metacognitive strategic engagement required to develop a knowledge and understanding of the power and purpose of history; and (b) the type of design-based research needed within the field of social studies to examine the impact of digital technologies and tight technology enhanced learning environments on clear cut student learning outcomes.

APPENDIXA
Strategy Application Test Letter

My dear Sandy,
Savannah, Ga., Jan. 5th 1865

While we were in position on the lines outside the city we had several very exciting duals with the Rebel Batteries of 32 pdrs, & 10 pound Rifles. On the 15th Nov. they opened fiercely on us and our Cannoniers rushed to their posts, while I looked out a position from which I could observe the fire of my Gun. On the flank of our work was an old Rice mill, of which you have heard before. I thought this would be a good spot from whence to get a view of the Rebel position. On going inside however I found the stairs had been taken down by the men for firewood, so I had to give up the project. I had scarcely got to my piece again when a 32 pound shell from one of the Guns in front of us struck the old window blind & burst just inside the mill. I could not but think that if those stairs had been all right in their place, I would have had a hard time of it at that old window.

A day or two after that close call of mine, a shot from the same flank Gun, dashed through an Embrasure of the 15th Ohio, in the same fort with us, & tore a man's shoulder & arm all to pieces. He has since died. When we passed through the line of Rebel forts on our way to the city on the morning of the 21st, we had a good chance to see the effect of our shots. Their embrasures were completely torn to pieces, & two of their Guns had been dismounted by our Rodmans. I don't think you have much idea of the terrible accuracy of our kind of Guns, which the Rebels confess they dread far more than any other kind.

If you enlist under the new call Sandy, and if no persuasions will keep you at home you must come to us. Never think of joining any other Company than ours.

Yours hurriedly,
Th. D. Christie.

REFERENCES

American Historical Association. (2003). *Benchmarks for professional development in teaching history as a discipline.* Retrieved June 20, 2002, from: http://www.theaha.org/teaching/benchmarks.htm

Ashby, R., Lee, P., & Dickinson, A. (1997). How children explain the "why" of history: The Chata research project on teaching history. *Social Education, 61*(1), 17–21.

Bain, R. (2000). Into the breach: Using research and theory to shape history instruction. In P. Stearns, P. Seixas, & S. Wineburg. (Eds.). *Knowing, teaching, and learning history: National and international perspectives* (pp. 331–352). New York: New York University Press.

Barton, K. (1997). I just kinda know: Elementary students' ideas about historical evidence. *Theory and Research in Social Education, 25,* 407–430.

Barton, K. (1998, April). *That's a tricky piece: Children's understanding of historical time in Northern Ireland.* Paper presented at the Annual Meeting of the American Educational Research Association, San Diego, CA.

Barton, K. (2005). Teaching history: Primary sources in history: Breaking through the myths. *Phi Delta Kappan, 86*(10), 745–751.

Barton, K., & Levstik, L. (2004). *Teaching history for the common good.* Mahwah, NJ: Erlbaum.

Berkhofer, R. F. (1995). *Beyond the great story: History as text and discourse.* Cambridge, MA: Harvard/Belknap.

Berson. M. J. (1996). Effectiveness of computer technology in social studies: A review of the literature. *Journal of Research on Computing in Education, 28*(4), 486–499.

Berson, M. J., & Balyta, P. (2004). Technological thinking and practice in the social studies: Transcending the tumultuous adolescence of reform. *Journal of Computing in Teacher Education, 20*(4), 141–150.

Booth, A. (2003). *Teaching history at university.* London: Routledge.

Britt, M. A., & Aglinskas, C. (2002). Improving students' ability to identify and use source information. *Cognition and Instruction. 20*(4), 485–522.

Britt, M. A., Rouet, J., & Perfetti, C. (1996). Using hypertext to study and reason about historical evidence. In J. Rouet, J. Levonen, A. Dillon, & R. Spiro (Eds.), *Hypertext and cognition* (pp. 43–72). Mahwah, NJ: Lawrence Erlbaum.

Britt, M. A., Perfetti, C., Van Dyke, J., & Gabrys, G. (2000). The sorcerer's apprentice: A tool for document supported history instruction. In P. Stearns, P. Seixas, & S. Wineburg. (Eds.). *Knowing, teaching, and learning history: National and international perspectives* (pp. 437–470). New York: New York University Press.

Brush, T., & Saye, J. (2000). Implementation and evaluation of a student-centered learning unit. A case study. *Educational Technology Research and Development 48*(3), 79–100.

Brush, T., & Saye, J. (2001). The use of embedded scaffolds in a technology-enhanced student-centered learning activity. *Journal of Educational Multimedia and Hypermedia, 10*(4), 333–356.

Brush, T., & Saye, J. (2002). A summary of research exploring hard and soft scaffolding for teachers and students using a multimedia supported learning environment. *Journal of Interactive Online Learning, 1*(2). Retrieved January 1, 2006, from: http://www.ncolr.com/jiol/issues/PDF/1.2.3.pdf

Brush, T. & Saye, J. (2004). Supporting learners in technology-enhanced student-centered learning environments. *International Journal of Learning Technology, 1*(2), 191–202.

Cohen, J. (1988). *Statistical Power analysis for the behavioural sciences,* 2nd edition. Hillsdale, NJ: Erlbaum.

Collins Block, C., & Pressley, M. (2002). *Comprehension instruction: Research-based best practices.* New York: Guildford.

Counsell, C. (2000). Historical knowledge and historical skills: A distracting dichotomy. In J. Arthur & R. Phillips (Eds.), *Issues in history teaching* (pp. 54–71)., London: Routledge.

Doolittle, P. E., & Hicks, D. (2003). Constructivism as a theoretical foundation for the use of technology in Social Studies. *Theory and Research in Social Education, 31*(1), 72–104.

Ehman, L. H., & Glenn, A. D. (1991). Interactive technology in the social studies. In J. P. Shaver (Ed.), *Handbook of research on social studies teaching and learning* (pp. 513–522). New York: Macmillan.

Friedman, A. M., & Hicks, D. (2006). The state of the field: Technology, social studies, and teacher education. *Contemporary Issues in Technology and Teacher Education* [Online serial], *6*(2). Retrieved online May 22, 2007, from: http://www.citejournal.org/vol6/iss2/socialstudies/article1.cfm

Ginns, P. (2005). Meta-analysis of the modality effect. *Learning and Instruction, 15,* 313–331.

Goffman, E (1959). *The presentation of self in everyday life.* London: Allen Lane/Penguin Press.

Hadyn, T., Arthur, J., & Hunt, M. (2001). *Learning to teach history in the secondary school: A companion to school experience.* London: Routledge.

Hicks, D., & Doolittle, P. E. (2008). Fostering analysis in historical inquiry through multimedia embedded scaffolding. *Theory and Research in Social Education, 36*(3), 206–232.

Hicks, D., Doolittle, P. E., Ewing, T. (2004). The SCIM-C strategy: Fostering historical inquiry in a multimedia environment. *Social Education, 68*(3), 221–225.

Hicks, D., Doolittle, P., & Lee, J. (2004) Social studies teachers' use of classroom-based and web-based historical primary sources. *Theory and Research in Social Education, 32*(2), 213–247.

Kalyuga, S., Chandler, P., & Sweller, J. (1999). Managing split-attention and redundancy in multimedia instruction. *Applied Cognitive Psychology, 13,* 351–371.

Lee, P. (2005) Putting principles into practice: Understanding history. In M. S. Donovan, M. S., & J. D. Bransford (Eds.), *How students learn: History in the classroom: Committee on how people learn: A targeted report for teachers* (pp. 31–77). Washington, DC: The National Academies Press.

Lee, P., & Ashby, R. (2000) Progression in historical understanding among students ages 7–14. In P. Stearns, P. Seixas, & S. Wineburg, (Eds.), *Knowing, teaching and learning history: National and international perspectives* (pp. 199–223). New York: New York University Press.

Lee, P., & Shemilt, D. (2003). A scaffold is not a cage: Progression and progression models in history. *Teaching History, 113,* 13–24.

Levstik, L., & Barton, K. (2001a). *Doing history: Investigating with children in elementary and middle schools.* Mahwah, NJ: Erlbaum.

Levstik, L., & Barton, K. (2001b). Committing acts of history: Mediated action, humanistic education, and participatory democracy. In W. B. Stanley (Ed.), *Critical issues in social studies research for the 21st century* (pp. 119–147). Greenwich, CT: Information Age.

Mayer, R. (2001). *Multimedia learning.* Cambridge: Cambridge University Press.

Mayer, R. (Ed.). (2005). *The Cambridge handbook of multimedia learning.* Cambridge: Cambridge University Press.

Mayer, R. E., Heiser, J., & Lonn, S. (2001). Cognitive constraints on multimedia learning: When presenting more material results in less understanding. *Journal of Educational Psychology, 93*(1), 187–198.

Mayer, R. E., & Moreno, R. (1998). A split-attention effect in multimedia learning: Evidence for dual processing systems in working memory. *Journal of Educational Psychology, 90*(2), 312–320.

Moreno, R., & Mayer, R. E. (1999). Cognitive principles of multimedia learning: The role of modality and contiguity. *Journal of Educational Psychology, 91*(2), 358–368.

National Center for History in the Schools. (1996). *National History Standards.* Los Angeles: Author.

National Council for the Social Studies. (1994). *Expectations for excellence: Curriculum standards for social studies.* Washington, DC: Author.

Osborne, K. (2003). Fred Morrow Fling and the source-method of teaching history. *Theory and Research in Social Education, 31*(4), 466–501.

Pressley, M., & Harris, K. (1990). What we really know about strategy instruction. *Educational Leadership, 48,* 31–34.

Pressley, M., & Woloshyn, V. (Eds.). (1995). *Cognitive strategy instruction that really improves children's academic performance.* Cambridge: Brookline.

Quintana, C., Reiser, B., Davis, E., Krajcik, J., Fretz, E., Duncan, R., Kyza, E., Edelson, E., & Solowya, E. (2004). A scaffolding design framework for software to support science inquiry. *Journal of the Learning Sciences, 13*(3), 337–386.

Reid, R., & Lienemann, T. (2006). *Strategy instruction for students with learning disabilities.* New York: Guilford Press.

Reiser, B., (2004). Scaffolding complex learning: The mechanisms of structuring and problematizing student work. *Journal of the Learning Sciences, 13*(3), 273–304.

Riley, C. (1999). Evidential understanding, period, knowledge and the development of literacy: A practical approach to 'layers of inference' for key stage 3. *Teaching History, 97,* 6–12.

Rouet, J., Britt, M. A., Mason, R. A., & Perfetti, C. (1996). Using multiple sources of evidence to reason about history. *Journal of Educational Psychology, 88*(3), 478–493.

Saye, J., & Brush, T. (2002). Scaffolding critical reasoning about history and social issues in multimedia-supported learning environments. *Educational Technology Research and Development, 50*(3), 77–96.

Saye, J., & Brush, T. (2004). Scaffolding problem-based teaching in a traditional social studies classroom. *Theory and Research in Social Education, 32*(3), 349–378.

Saye, J., & Brush, T. (2005). The persistent issues in history network: Using technology to support historical inquiry and civic reasoning. *Social Education, 69*(3), 168–171.

Saye, J., & Brush, T. (2006) Comparing teachers' strategies for supporting student inquiry in a problem-based multimedia-enhanced history unit. *Theory and Research in Social Education, 34*(2), 183–212.

Saye, J., & Brush, T. (2007) Using technology-enhanced learning environments to support problem-based historical inquiry in secondary school classrooms. *Theory and Research in Social Education, 35*(2), 196–230.

Spoehr, K. T., & Spoehr, L. W. (1994) Learning to think historically. *Educational Psychologist, 29*(2), 71–77.

VanSledright, B. (2002a). Fifth graders investigating history in the classroom: Results from a researcher-practitioner design experiment. *Elementary Education Journal, 103*(2), 131–160.

VanSledright, B. (2002b) Confronting history's interpretive paradox while teaching fifth graders to investigate the past. *American Educational Research Journal, 39*(4), 1089–1115.

VanSledright, B. (2002c). *In search of America's past: Learning to read history in elementary school.* New York: Teachers College Press.

VanSledright, B., & Limón, M. (2006). Learning and teaching social studies: A review of cognitive research in history and geography. In P. Alexander & P. Winne (Eds.). *Handbook of educational psychology* (pp. 545–570). Mahwah, NJ: Erlbaum.

Voss, J. F., & Wiley, J. (1997). Developing understanding while writing essays in history. *International Journal of Educational Research, 27*, 255–265.

Voss, J. F., & Wiley, J. (2000). A case study of developing historical understanding via instruction. The importance of integrating text components and constructing arguments. In P. Stearns, P. Seixas, & S. Wineburg, (Eds.), *Knowing, teaching and learning history: National and international perspectives* (pp. 375–389). New York: New York University Press.

Weinstein, C. E., & Mayer, R. E. (1986). The teaching of learning strategies. In M. Wittrock (Ed.), *Handbook of research on teaching* (pp. 315–327). New York: Macmillan.

Whitworth, S., & Berson, M. (2003). Computer technology in the social studies: An examination of the effectiveness literature (1996–2001). *Contemporary Issues in Technology and Teacher Education, 2*(4). Retrieved June 20, 2003, from: http://www.citejournal.org/vol2/iss4/socialstudies/article1.cfm

Wiley, J., & Ash, I. K. (2005) Multimedia learning in history. In R. E. Mayer (Ed.), *The Cambridge handbook of multimedia learning* (pp. 375–392). Cambridge: Cambridge University Press.

Wiley, J. (2001). Supporting understanding through task and browser design. *Proceedings of the 23rd Annual Conference of the Cognitive Science Society.* Hillsdale, NJ: Erlbaum.

Wineburg, S. (1991a). Historical problem solving: A study of the cognitive processes used in the evaluation of documentary and pictorial evidence. *Journal of Educational Psychology, 83,* 73–87.

Wineburg, S. (1991b). On the reading of historical texts: Notes on the breach between school and academy. *American Educational Research Journal, 28,* 495–519.

Wineburg, S. (2001) *Historical thinking and other unnatural acts.* Philadelphia, PA: Temple University.

Wolfe, S., Brush, T., & Saye, J. (2003). Using an information problem-solving model as a metacognitive scaffold for multimedia-supported information-based problem. *Journal of Research on Technology in Education, 35*(1), 321–341.

SECTION 3

RESEARCH ON TEACHERS USING TECHNOLOGY IN SOCIAL STUDIES

CHAPTER 7

IF YOU BUILD IT, SHOULD I RUN?

A Teacher's Perspective on Implementing a Student-Centered, Digital Technology Project in His Ninth-Grade Geography Classroom

Sonja Heer Yow and Kathleen Owings Swan

ABSTRACT

While a growing body of literature advocates the use of new technologies in social studies education, many teachers have yet to jump on the technology bandwagon (Becker, 1999; Cuban, 2001; Pew Institute, 2002). For instance, Yow (2005) posits that middle and high school geography teachers in the central region of a state in the upper south rarely employ instructional technologies due to issues of access and reliability. Moreover, these teachers report that poor access to technology prevents them from implementing Internet research projects, as well as utilizing other types of technology in their geographic instruction. In an effort to further investigate this phenomenon, we designed this study so that we could explore teacher use of digital technologies in a geography classroom where certain instructional technologies

Research on Technology in Social Studies Education, pages 155–172
Copyright © 2009 by Information Age Publishing

were readily available. Using money from a small university grant, we "built" a technology-rich environment in a ninth-grade geography classroom, complete with digital cameras, computers, and Windows Moviemaker software. Interestingly, findings from our study indicate that even with easy access to instructional technology, teachers may still struggle to use digital technologies effectively because such use deviates from typical teaching practices.

I had no intention of photographing prostitutes until a friend took me to the red light district in Calcutta. From the moment I stepped foot inside that maze of alleyways, I knew that this was the reason I had come to India. I spent months trying to gain access to this impenetrable place . . . It was the children who accepted me immediately. I thought it would be great to see this world through their eyes. (Director of the documentary, *Born into Brothels*, Zana Briski, New York, January 2004)

I want to show in pictures how people live in this city. I want to put across the behavior of man. (Gour, a child photographer in *Born into Brothels*)

When I have a camera in my hands I feel happy. I feel like I am learning something . . . I can be someone. (Suchitra, a child photographer in *Born into Brothels*)

Born into Brothels (Briski, 2004), *Shootback* (Wong, 1999), *Kids with Cameras* (Eskenazi, 2004) and other student-centered photojournalism projects have inspired children around the world to document their own physical and cultural environments. Through these captured images, impenetrable places such as the brothels of Calcutta, the slums of Nairobi, and Muslim and Jewish communities in Jerusalem are made real to us through the eyes of those that live there and through the unique 'voice' of children. In fact, the National Geographic Society has experienced more than 110 years of success at doing just this—feeding our insatiable curiosity about the world with images from places both near and far. Allowing children the opportunity to participate in the same sort of work of professional photographers, as with Gour and Suchitra, not only provides an empowering learning opportunity, but can deeply touch those who experience the indelible images. As fourteen-year-old Suchitra, so eloquently states in response to her experience with the Academy Award winning *Born into Brothels* project (2004), "When I have a camera in my hands, I feel happy. I feel like I am learning something . . . I can be someone."

Borrowing from the work of these photojournalists, we set out to work alongside a classroom teacher who wanted to craft a photojournalism project for his geography students. Specifically, this chapter documents an exercise in which one ninth-grade geography class in the central region of a state in the upper south explored the use of digital photography and documentaries to better understand geographic skills and concepts. We sought to document the students' use of the digital tools, as well as the teacher's experiences in both creating and executing a project which employed instructional technology to facilitate a student-centered geographic inquiry project.

The National Geography Standards (1994) state that students should know and understand how to ask geographic questions; acquire, organize, and analyze geographic information; and answer geographic questions by the end of twelfth grade. Likewise, Stoltman (1990) asserts that "geography skills are essential if citizens are to preserve rights, accept responsibilities, and determine the necessary tasks related to the natural environment and human dimensions of a shrinking planet"—the foundations of global citizenship (p. 1). Without geographic skills and knowledge, Drake (1987) warns that students in the United States will act like "ostriches with their heads in the sand" and remain unprepared to make reasoned decisions about their local, national, and global environments (p. 300). Biddulph and Adey (2004) suggest that teachers can help students overcome this geographical handicap by explicating the why of geography in the classroom and providing students with opportunities to satisfy their curiosities and delve into the study of the world using a repertoire of technological tools that a real geographer might use.

Fortunately, some of the resources necessary to support geographic inquiry and learning within the K–12 classroom have been made accessible through modern tools (e.g., maps, images, graphs, sketches, diagrams, and photos, etc.) and technologies (e.g., computers, global positioning satellite units, geographic information systems, software applications, presentation machines, digital cameras, etc.). These tools and technologies allow students to build competencies in applying geographic skills to geographic inquiry (National Geography Standards, 1994, p. 45). In addition, some state and local school districts are beginning to require a computer literacy component in their graduation requirements. Thus, graduating seniors in school systems that require geography courses and that provide access to emerging technologies should possess a high level of geographic literacy and a strong facility with digital technologies, but these situations are not the norm.

CONCEPTUAL FRAMEWORK

The research reported in this chapter looks at two phenomena, student learning with technology and teacher dispositions about using technology. This conceptual framework thus addresses both of these areas.

Recent research in geographic education advocates instructional approaches that engage students in the processes of learning geography, including conducting geographic inquiry, using geographic tools and technologies, and encouraging students to become global citizens (Bednarz &

Bednarz, 2004; Donaldson, 1999; Drake, 1987; Hertzog & Leible, 1996; Lyman & Foyle, 1991; Stoltman, 1990). Despite research and legislation advocating the use of technologies in the field of social studies education, most researchers report little technology usage between social studies educators and their students (Ehman & Glenn, 1991; Hofer & Swan, 2006; Martorella, 1997). Researchers looking at K–12 instruction across in social studies consistently suggest time, training, and access as issues that teachers face when incorporating technology into instruction (Doppen, 2004; Hicks, Doolittle, & Lee, 2004). Further, Yow's (2005) research indicates that many K–12 educators believe in the power of new technologies to foster a rich learning environment and bridge the acquisition of geographic skills; however, these same teachers report limited and unreliable technology in their schools and classrooms. In fact, the teachers in Yow's (2005) study perceive limited and unreliable technology as primary obstacles to its regular incorporation in their classrooms.

Beyond classroom computers, some studies have explored the connection between photography and geography in the K–12 classroom (Lantz, 1996; Mustoe, 1994). Lantz (1996) investigated the mutability and power of expression possible with new digital photography and its impact on instruction. He asserts that digital photography can provide "new avenues of expression," as well as images that are easily transmitted and much more readily accessible (p. 197). Similarly, other educators report that digital photography has great potential to stimulate and motivate students and teachers alike, allowing for enhanced learning and an energized curriculum (Berson & Swan, 2005; Clark, Hosticka, & Bedell, 2000; Hofer & Swan, 2005a,b; Lantz, 1996). However, while the expense of these technologies has declined rapidly over the past few years, cost is another reason pinpointed as a primary hindrance to using digital cameras in the classroom (Clark et al., 2000).

This research is also framed by existing research and theory focusing on why teachers do not more readily embrace technology as a teaching tool (Becker, 1999; Cuban, 2001; Hofer & Swan, 2006). Existing theory suggests that a process of conceptual change is necessary if teachers are to consistently and effectively use technology tools. In this book, Molebash, Capps, and Glassett describe a model for such conceptual change as reflexive and recursive. They describe the conceptual change process as including four stages, orientation, understanding, feasibility, and, progression. This model extends the long-standing work of Posner, Strike, Hewson, and Gertzog (1982) which also suggested four stages for conceptual change: dissatisfaction, intelligibility, plausibility, and fruitfulness.

Conceptual change is perhaps necessary, but not always immediately visible. In this age of technology innovation, if a new technology emerges that theoretically require some lengthy conceptual change and the technology's shelf life is shorter that the span of time required for conceptual change, the technology may not be adapted. However, some disposition or transferable understanding may be developed through a conceptual change process that could make future effective technology use more likely. Given these potential limitations and possibilities, we wanted to explore what would happen when we removed certain variables that may affect the speed of conceptual change such as cost and accessibility and provided a teacher with ample, dependable technology to conduct a student-centered, inquiry-based, digital photography project in his ninth-grade geography classroom. To this end, we received a small grant to provide a local geography teacher with technology (e.g., digital cameras, rechargeable batteries, and Windows Moviemaker software) so that he could involve his students in creating digital geographic documentaries. We called this work the *Capturing Geography* project. These documentaries allowed the students to explore a geographic question by fusing pictures, narration and music.

Because research suggests that teachers often face frustrations when implementing technology into instruction (Doppen, 2004; Hicks et al., 2004; Yow, 2005), our hope was to minimize these frustrations by providing training and technical support to the teacher, as well as free, reliable access to requisite technologies to complete the project as a way of finding out what other issues teachers face when implementing student-centered technology projects in the geography classroom. The research questions that frame our study are:

1. In what ways do student-created, digital, geographic documentaries support students in the process of geographic inquiry?
2. How does the teacher respond to a student-centered, technology-focused approach to geographic instruction?

METHODOLOGY

Because naturalistic inquiry can provide insight into how new digital technologies are incorporated into the classroom, as well as illuminate student and teacher impressions of phenomenon, we employed a qualitative, case study approach (Stake, 1995). In the case study design, we selected one geography teacher, Henry, for a collaborative study. The purpose was to better understand this teacher's attitude and perceptions of using digital technologies in a collaborative inquiry project in his ninth-grade geography classroom.

Henry, the teacher participant, was in his fourth year of teaching. His first three years of teaching were spent teaching social studies at the middle school level and the year of this study marked Henry's first year as a high school geography teacher. Specifically, Henry taught ninth-grade state geography and world geography when this study was conducted in the central region of a state in the upper south. Henry volunteered his classroom for the study after learning of the opportunity in a graduate level *Geography for Teachers* course—a course Henry was taking to earn credit toward his master's degree. During the class, Henry gained knowledge about the physical and cultural aspects of world geography, as well as strategies for teaching and integrating technology into the geography curriculum. The culminating project for the class required Henry and his peers to create digital movies pertaining to a geographic issue. Henry was especially enthusiastic with the digital movie project and its potential with his ninth-grade students.

Having used predominantly traditional approaches to teaching in the past (e.g., textbook, lecture, videos, and worksheets), Henry felt that the *Capturing Geography* project would help "energize his classroom." In fact, during one conversation after class, Henry said that "he would love to be able to do more innovative projects with his students, if he just had the resources to do so" (Personal communication, July 2005). Therefore, because of Henry's willingness to move away from a teacher-centered, passive-learning approach, and to try new technologies and pedagogical practices in his geography classroom, we chose Henry as the teacher participant for the *Capturing Geography* project.

We designed the *Capturing Geography* project in collaboration with Henry, and in an effort to implement the project within a naturalistic setting, Henry taught and assessed the student projects on his own. Our role as researchers was relatively unobtrusive so that we could collect data without disruption of a naturally occurring event (McMillan & Schumacher, 2001). Data for this study were collected both formally and informally. Formal data consisted of student pre- and post-surveys, a daily audio journal Henry kept, and students' digital movies and assignments. The pre- and post-surveys contained both open- and closed-ended responses and explored students' familiarity with geographic concepts and technology skills. Henry's daily audio journal kept track of logistical issues related to the project, as well as his daily thoughts and impressions. Informal data consisted of our regularly occurring conversations and e-mail correspondences with Henry.

Specifically, we used Reissman's (1993) narrative analysis to reveal Henry's stories of teaching, as well as stories of and by his students. The use of multiple data sources (e.g., students' pre- and post-surveys, students' conversations about the project, students' assignments and digital movies, Henry's daily audio journal, and phone/e-mail correspondence with Henry) allowed for qualitative cross validation, a process known as triangulation (McMillan & Schumacher, 2001). Other strategies used to enhance the design validity of our study included: prolonged fieldwork, participant language and verbatim accounts, low-inference descriptors, multiple research-ers, and mechanically recorded data (McMillan & Schumacher, 2001).

Overview of the Class Project

A primary curricular goal of the *Capturing Geography* project was to help students with the process of geographic inquiry—asking geographic ques-tions, gathering, organizing, and analyzing data, and finally using the data to answer a geographic question. Therefore, we provided Henry with the digital technology and training that would enable him to conduct this type of inquiry project with his students. After meeting with Henry for several one-on-one sessions in which we explored the digital cameras and Moviemaker software, we provided Henry with twelve new digital cameras with 156mb memory sticks and rechargeable batteries bought with money from the aforementioned grant. Because Henry's students worked in col-laborative groups of two to three, only seven of the twelve digital cameras were used. Further, the instructional technology specialist at Henry's high school helped Henry download the digital camera software onto comput-ers in the school lab and made sure that the school computers contained Windows Moviemaker software—a standard program with all Windows op-erating systems.

On the first day of classroom instruction for the *Capturing Geography* project, Henry's students posed questions about their own hometown, they acquired images by using digital cameras, they organized and ana-lyzed images and information by creating digital movies, and finally, they used their finished movies as a means to answer their posed geo-graphic questions. At the end of the project, students made "geographic generalizations"—the culmination of the process of inquiry (National Ge-ography Standards, 1994).

The *Capturing Geography* project took place during the last three weeks of the school's first nine-week session. Using a lecture and guided notes approach, Henry spent the first part of the nine-weeks teaching his stu-dents about geography's five themes—location, place, movement, human-environment interaction, and region. Because most of Henry's instruction before the project occurred in a traditional setting and with more didactic instructional methods, students were unfamiliar with the student-centered, active learning approach required by the *Capturing Geography* project. In-stead of asking the questions, Henry's students, like many others, have had few, if any, opportunities to participate in authentic inquiry (Levstik & Barton, 2001); therefore his students were more accustomed to answering questions posed by the teacher or textbook rather than asking questions themselves. Having never used a disciplined inquiry approach to learning in his classroom, Henry had to use several instructional days just to help students learn to ask meaningful geographic questions. After three class days of working with students on the first stage of geographic inquiry, Henry allowed students to work collaboratively to develop researchable geographic questions pertaining to their hometown. Following teacher approval, students created storyboards and plans as for how, when, and where they would take digital photos that would help them answer their posed geographic questions.

At the end of the project's first week, students checked out digital cameras and took them home over the weekend in order to take photographs for their movies. After acquiring images and downloading them onto a main station in the classroom, Henry spent one full class period leading students through the Windows Moviemaker tutorial. Following the tutorial, students began research. Most students used the computers to conduct Internet research, while some used print sources to gather information that would accompany their images. Students spent six class periods conducting research in the computer lab, gathering information for their digital movies, and creating movies. Henry facilitated students in dealing with technology issues, finding information, editing content, and organizing the content and images for their movies. Henry repeatedly emphasized that movies should be organized in a way that would answer their original geographic questions.

On the final day of the nine-weeks, Henry held a digital movie premiere in the high school auditorium. Although difficulties with audio-equipment arose, the show went on and students showed their movies to music played on a boom box. Following the premiere, students completed self and group assessments and Henry collected copies of all student movies in order to assess them according to a 100-point rubric that gauged whether or not the students were successful in using their digital movies to answer their posed geographic questions.

FINDINGS

As stated earlier, the purpose of this study was to document the ways in which student-created digital geographic documentaries support students' geographic understanding and to better understand how a teacher might respond to a student-centered, technology-focused approach to geographic instruction. Through the analysis of the data, we found that while students enthusiastically and successfully used new digital technologies in conjunction with a student-centered approach in the geography classroom, the teacher experienced formidable challenges with managing both disciplined inquiry and new digital technologies in the classroom.

Students Doing Geographic Inquiry

With instructional guidance from their teacher, the ninth-grade students demonstrated their abilities to develop and write their own geographic questions. Specifically, student success with the process of geographic inquiry was evidenced by the fact that sixteen of the nineteen students were able to develop and answer geographic questions through the process of gathering and organizing text and images for storyboards and digital movies. To begin, students wrote questions about their hometown such as "Why would people want to move to B-town?" and "What makes B-town unique?" Next, students brainstormed and participated in dialogue to help them generate answers to their questions. Once students had created a storyboard or outline for the images and information needed to create their movies, students went out after school and collected the digital photos needed to make their digital movies.

After groups had collected their photographs, Henry helped each group download their photographs in the computer lab onto each group's shared folder. Once downloaded, students were able to work in their collaborative groups to fuse their digital images and information with music and narration. Finally, students made "geographic generalizations"—the culmination of the process of inquiry (National Geography Standards, 1994) and answered their posed geographic questions through the information presented in their finished digital movies.

Beyond the positive learning outcomes associated with the *Capturing Geography* project, it became clear from the data that students enjoyed the opportunity to use digital technologies, such as cameras, computers, Windows Moviemaker, and the Internet during class time. While twelve of the nineteen students reported no prior use of digital technologies at school, this opportunity seemed to be an extraordinary experience for the students. On the final day of the nine-week grading period, rather than sitting quietly and taking a culminating exam, students enthusiastically reflected on the project in the school auditorium and discussed learning outcomes, as well as likes and dislikes of the project. One student, Miles replied, "I really liked Moviemaker, working with computers, and being able to get on the Internet! I also thought that adding effects to the movie was fun." Similarly, Taylor, Seth and Bonita had many positive comments to add. Taylor remarked that he "liked learning to use a camera. We had fun learning about the history of our town and doing research. It was fun working with Moviemaker too. This was a great experience." In a similar vain, Seth said that he taught the project was "really cool . . . we should do things like this more often. I really liked taking pictures, making the movie as a group, and doing the effects. I had fun with my group." Bonita said, "I liked the freedom of the project. It was interesting and taught us how to do and learn things we didn't already know. Going around town and taking pictures was cool too." The student-centered approach and the opportunity to use new digital technologies provided students with a freedom for learning that they had not often experienced in school. Student comments on the project's post-survey indicate that they were thankful for the opportunity to participate in a student-centered, technology-oriented project.

In his audio journal, Henry also commented on the level of student enjoyment with the project. He wrote:

> Overall, the students seemed to like the project. They liked being able to work with technology, create a movie, and use cool transitions and effects . . . so that was fun for them. I got several responses that they liked the freedom of the project and the ability to be able to create their own guidelines. They liked being able to see their end product and they actually enjoyed being able to see each others. The competition worked well for them.

Henry acknowledged that while difficulties arose throughout the project, most of the students (16/19) succeeded in the process of geographic inquiry (asking geographic questions, gathering, organizing, and analyzing data, and finally using the data to answer a geographic question). One group of students however, struggled with the project. A group of three male students, Larry, Jason, and Mark, were able to pose a geographic question, but had difficulty gathering, organizing, and analyzing images and information in a way that provided a complete and coherent response to their question. Moreover, their group movie contained a mere six images and no text or information. In an attempt to ascertain why these students were unsuccessful while the rest of the class demonstrated an ability to progress through the steps of geographic inquiry, we asked the three boys to talk to us individually about what would have allowed them to be more successful with the project. Interestingly enough, all three of the students stated that they should have "stayed on task, concentrated more, and looked up more information." Even though these students did not perform well on the assigned task, they reported liking the project, especially "being able to get on the Internet."

One group of students who experienced success with the project spent their time delving into the geographic theme of region. In an effort to answer their inquiry question, "What makes our hometown unique?" the students spent a weekend visiting landmarks and special places in their town. Specifically, this group of students photographed the town's cathedral, historic tavern, museum, dinner train, and downtown mansion, as well as natural landscapes and popular restaurants. To accompany their digital photographs, the students integrated historic, cultural, and geographical information into their digital movie. Complete with transitions and video effects, the group presented a unique geographic view and perspective of what makes their hometown unique through their eyes—a clear demonstration that these three students, in particular, were able to do geographic inquiry.

In demonstrating their geographic understandings, another group of students focused on the geographic theme of movement. The conversation below, which was reconstructed from field notes, highlights the students' thinking processes as they organized images and information for their digital movie.

Tenley: Why would people would want to move to B-town?
Brenda: I'd say that jobs are a major reason why people would want to come here.
Tenley: Yep, we have companies like Jideco and Fuji.
Marty: And aren't those Japanese, so people from Japan might come here.
Tenley: We also have some important historical features like the old tavern and My Old Kentucky Home.
Brenda: And Old Jailer's Inn and the historic dinner train.
Marty: What about our Stephen Foster musical and the Bourbon festival? Those are also important events here.
Brenda: Definitely.
Marty: You know, the historic cathedral and Catholic school were other reasons why some people might have moved to town.
Tenley: So, should we take pictures of all of these things?
Brenda: I think so . . .
Tenley: Well, we should probably take a picture of the "Welcome to B-town" sign for our first image.
Marty: And I'd be willing to go take pictures of the Japanese companies. Oh, and what about a map? We could use a map of B-town in the documentary.
Tenley: Good! So, let's divvy up the historical places and decide who is going to take each of the photos.

This conversation provides insight into how this particular group of students worked collaboratively while brainstorming their storyboard and organizing the collection of their data. Moreover, this group's finished product—the digital movie—demonstrated that the group's ideas came to fruition and they were able to effectively synthesize their own digital camera images with photographs found online, information gathered from the Internet, and print sources made available to them in the classroom.

While web-based inquiry can be difficult, as evidenced by other recent empirical studies (e.g., Lipscomb, 2002; Milson, 2002); the majority of students in this study were able to pursue their own investigations and reach their own conclusions in a creative digital format. The use of new digital technologies and disciplined inquiry as tools for learning geography allowed the majority of Henry's students to gain a deeper understanding of the geographic factors associated with their town.

A Teacher's Struggle with a New Style

In the second component of our investigation, we looked at how the teacher responded to a student-centered, technology-focused approach to geographic instruction. Interestingly, while Henry's students responded positively to the project, Henry himself experienced "an uphill battle" with the implementation of the project. During summer 2005, when the *Capturing Geography* project was in the planning stages, Henry, showed a great deal of enthusiasm and excitement about the opportunity to connect geography, technology, and student involvement in his classroom (e-mail correspondence, June, 10, 2005). However, as Henry noted in a later correspondence, his "ole gung ho attitude dwindled rapidly" once the project began (e-mail correspondence, September 28, 2005). Henry's change in attitude can most likely be attributed to the problems that Henry experienced with the technology, as well as his perceived relinquishment of classroom control when moving to student-centered approach. In fact, Henry's attitude evolved through four distinct phases during the planning and implementation of the project (see Table 7.1).

Stage one of the project planning process occurred during June and July, before Henry had met his students. During the months of June and July, Henry exhibited a high level of enthusiasm for the project. While planning the project in collaboration, Henry repeatedly expressed his "excitement" for having the "opportunity" to allow all of his classes to participate in the *Capturing Geography* project. He was thrilled to have the opportunity to use cutting edge technologies in his classroom and he even spoke of how he had "WOWed" other teachers in a summer class when he used Windows

TABLE 7.1   The Four Distinct Stages of Henry's Attitude throughout the *Capturing Geography* Project

Stage One	June 10–July 29 (Prior to start of school)	Enthusiasm
Stage Two	August 2–September 20 (School/project begin)	Skepticism
Stage Three	September 21–September 28 (Final Week of Project)	Survival
Stage Four	Post September 28 (Post-project)	Flight

Moviemaker software as a presentation tool (July 15, 2005). Overall, Henry was positive about and eager to begin the *Capturing Geography* project in his new ninth-grade classroom.

In August, however, at the beginning of the school year, Henry's disposition toward the project changed from enthusiasm to what we have characterized as skepticism. The following correspondence with Henry indicates this initial change:

> With all the new stuff and everything new to me, I'm a bit on edge and have entered freak-out mode. Just to forewarn you when you talk to me or see me next, you may not recognize me. (E-mail correspondence, August 2, 2005)

With his worries about the school year surfacing, Henry decided to pull back from the initial idea of implementing the project with all of his geography classes and instead, only allow his third period class to conduct the project. Henry's vocabulary also suggested a pronounced shift in attitude toward the project. For instance, the phrase, "being excited" was replaced with "being nervous," and "awaiting the opportunity" became "I'll try to keep the ball rolling" (E-mail correspondence, September 12, 2005). Hence, it seems likely that the pressures of a new school year initiated Henry's conceptual change from the "ideal classroom" to the "real classroom."

Once the project was underway, stage two unfolded into stage three—survival. On September 21, 2005, Henry explained that the project was a "live and learn experience . . . that is if I live through it!" Henry complained of multiple technology problems (e.g., lab scheduling problems, having students in too many locations at once, and audio difficulties associated with the Windows Moviemaker software), as well as a number of pedagogical problems (e.g., moving away from his traditional textbook and lecture approach, and affording students the freedom associated with inquiry learning). For instance, in his audio-journal, Henry recorded that the audio trouble with the Moviemaker software was "a major struggle that never got fixed" (September 28, 2005) and that when he encountered such frustrations with the technology, he was "tempted to revert back to a more traditional, textbook and lecture approach to teaching geography." Beyond the technology issues, Henry also struggled with his perceived relinquishment of classroom control. During the final week of the project, Henry said that he would have rather done a scavenger hunt activity and told students what to take pictures of instead of allowing them the freedom to choose. Henry also rebuked the use of disciplined inquiry with his students, saying that his ninth-grade students needed more structure because "they struggled with the concept of creating a question" and some of the more immature students used the freedom as an opportunity to "get off task" (September 28, 2005). In general, it seems that taking on new instructional technologies, combined with a new pedagogical approach, proved to be too intensive and stressful for Henry.

At the conclusion of the nine-weeks and the *Capturing Geography* project, Henry moved from stage three—survival to stage four—flight. In an interview with Henry, he said,

> To be honest, this was rather like waking up in the morning and taking a beating. I tried to have a positive attitude but it dwindled rapidly, largely because I bit off more than I could chew. I would even say that I was a hindrance to the project myself. I didn't do a good job of escorting the students through the baby steps. At this point, I don't believe I'll attempt the project again. Inquiry was too tough to tackle in conjunction with the technology project. (Personal contact, September 28, 2005)

Henry acknowledged that he was not only unsure about using technology and inquiry in the geography classroom, but he even questioned whether or not he wanted to remain in the teaching profession after his first nine-weeks of teaching at the high school level. Despite Henry's past teaching experience at the middle school level, his new ninth-grade teaching position, coupled with new pedagogy and technology, overwhelmed him so much that he even doubted his ability to be an effective teacher, at least within this new type of teaching and learning environment. Moreover, Henry's enthusiastic summer plan of "finding a way to write a grant to secure funds to purchase his own classroom cameras" (June 10, 2005), turned into "Thanks, but no thanks, you can have the cameras!" by the culminating movie premier (September 28, 2005).

Although the majority of Henry's students remained engaged, interested, and on-task throughout the project, Henry's perceived lack of classroom control and his frustrations with the management of the technology were enough to send him running, not only from a student-centered, technology-driven approach to teaching and learning, but perhaps from teaching as a profession.

DISCUSSION AND CONCLUSIONS

We recognize that this study represents the viewpoint and instructional context of a single classroom teacher which cannot be generalized. However, case studies such as this help illuminate issues for further research and exploration in other settings (Hofer & Swan, 2006; Swan, Hofer & Levstik, 2006). In our first research question, we asked, "In what ways do student-created, digital, geographic documentaries support students in doing geographic inquiry?" Through the analysis of students' storyboards and digital documentaries, we found that students were able to learn and successfully participate in the various steps of geographic inquiry. Student success with the inquiry project was evidenced through their digital documentaries in which students included photographs of images and researched text to answer geographic questions about their town. Student responses on the post-survey also indicated their enthusiasm with being able to go into the field to take photographs of their town. Many students expressed thanks for the opportunity to participate in real life geographic tasks and hands-on, collaborative field work using digital technologies.

The second research questions asked, "How does the teacher respond to a student-centered, technology-focused approach to geographic instruction?" While the students appeared to enjoy and learn from this exercise in geographic inquiry, the teacher's experience was ultimately frustrating. The findings of this study parallel the findings from Hofer and Swan's (2006) study in which the teacher participant, Jenny, lost enthusiasm for future technology implementations after completing a digital documentary project with her fifth grade students. While Jenny, like Henry, was pleased with the digital documentaries produced in the study, the introduction of technology in combination with a thematic, rather than a textbook-based approach, proved contradictory to Jenny's pedagogical orientation. And like Henry, the student-directed nature of the project contrasted with the teacher's perception of being at the core of the teaching and learning process. The bottom line for both of these teachers was that the digital documentary projects presented overwhelming technology and an uncomfortable overhaul of existing practice.

Photography and geography are clearly linked and the results of this study demonstrate that digital photography and digital movie-making can improve student attitudes toward learning. However, we cannot ignore the glaring challenges that teachers face in rethinking their own approaches to teaching and learning. So, the question is, what can we do to scaffold teachers in their enthusiasm to energize their classroom with geographic tools and technologies without overwhelming them? In others words, how can we prolong a teacher's enthusiastic stage and avoid a return to textbook-based, teacher-centered, passive-learning instruction? Perhaps a first step is to work collaboratively with teachers to design projects that are realistic for the classroom while still using technology as a catalyst for students' critical and conceptual thinking. Despite the challenges found in this case study, it is important that we do not give up on our vision for active, student-centered learning in geography.

Follow-up studies that seek to further examine the incorporation of new digital technologies into the geography classroom are warranted. More extensive classroom observation, as well as in-depth observations could also allow for a deeper understanding of this classroom phenomenon. It is also important to realize that when we as researchers become enthusiastic and ambitious about a classroom project, we must keep in mind the realities of the classroom (e.g., time constraints, a teacher's preferred style, and existing technology support) and work to ensure that if technologically advanced geography classrooms are built, teachers like Henry will not run from innovative teaching and learning opportunities.

REFERENCES

Becker, H. J. (1999). *Internet use by teachers: Conditions of professional use and teacher directed student use.* Retrieved November 5, 2008 from: from http://www.crito.uci.edu/TLC/findings/Internet-Use/startpage.htm

Bednarz, R. S., & Bednarz, S. W. (2004). Geography education: The glass is half full and it's getting fuller. *The Professional Geographer, 56*(1), 22–27.

Berson, M., & Swan, K. O. (2005). Digital images in the social studies classroom. In G. Bull & L. Bell (Eds.), *Digital images in the school curriculum* (pp. 147–172). Eugene, OR: International Society for Technology in Education.

Biddulph, M., & Adey, K. (2004). Pupil perceptions of effective teaching and subject relevance in history and geography at key stage 3. *Research in Education, 71,* 1–8.

Briski, Z. (Producer). (2004). *Born into brothels.* Retrieved November 4, 2008 from: http://www.kids-with-cameras.org/bornintobrothels/

Clark, K., Hosticka, A., & Bedell, J. (2000, February). *Digital cameras in the K–12 classroom.* Paper presented at the Society for Information Technology & Teacher Education International Conference, San Diego, CA.

Crocco, M. S. (2001). Leveraging constructivist learning in the social studies classroom: A response to Mason, Berson, Diem, Hicks, Lee, and Dralle. *Contemporary Issues in Technology and Teacher Education, 3*(1). Retrieved November 4, 2008 from: http://www.citejournal.org/vol1/iss3/currentissues/socialstudies.article2.htm

Cuban, L. (2001). *Oversold & underused: Computers in the classroom.* Cambridge, MA: Harvard University Press.

Dewey, J. (1933). *How we think: A restatement of the reflection of reflective thinking to the educative process.* New York: D.C. Heath.

Dewey, J. (1956). *The child and the curriculum and the school and society.* Chicago: University of Chicago Press.

Donaldson, D. P. (1999). *An Evaluation of multimedia technology in geography education: A case study of two sixth-grade classes in Ohio.* Unpublished doctoral dissertation, Kent State University, Kent, OH.

Doppen, F. (2004). Beginning social studies teachers' integration of technology in the history classroom. *Theory and Research in Social Education, 32*(2), 248–279.

Drake, C. (1987). Educating for a responsible global citizenship. *Journal of Geography, 86*(6), 300–306.

Ehman, L. H., & Glenn, A. D. (1991). Interactive technology in the social studies. In J. P. Shaver (Ed.), *Handbook of research on social studies teaching and learning* (pp. 513–522). New York: Macmillan.

Erickson, F. (1986). Qualitative methods in research on teaching. In M. C. Wittrock (Ed.) *Handbook of research on teaching* (pp. 119–161). New York: Macmillan.

Eskenazi, J. (2004). Kids with cameras–Jerusalem. Retrieved August 4, 2009, from http://www.jasoneskenazi.com/kwc/kwc01.html.

Gerber, R. (1996). Interpretative approaches to geographical and environmental education. *Understanding Geographical and Environmental Education: The Role of Research,* 12–25.

Hertzog, C., & Leible, C. (1996). A study of two techniques for teaching introductory geography: A traditional approach versus cooperative learning in the university classroom. *Journal of Geography, 95*(3), 274–280.

Hicks, D., Doolittle, P., & Lee, J. (2004). Social studies teachers' use of classroom-based and web-based historical primary sources. *Theory and Research in Social Education, 32*(2), 213–247.

Hicks, D., Tlou, J., Lee, J. K., Parry, L., & Doolittle, P. (2002). Global connections: Using the Internet to support citizenship education. *International Journal of Social Education, 17*(1), 93–102.

Hofer, M., & Swan, K. O. (2005). Digital image manipulation: A compelling means to engage students in discussion of point of view and perspective. *Contemporary Issues in Technology and Teacher Education, 5*(3).

Hofer, M., & Swan, K. O. (2005). Digital moviemaking—The harmonization of technology, pedagogy, and content. *International Journal of Technology in Teaching and Learning, 1*(2), 102–110.

Hofer, M., & Swan, K. O. (2006). Standards, firewalls, and general classroom mayhem: Implementing student-centered technology projects in the elementary classroom. *Social Studies Research and Practice, 1*(1), 120–144.

Kist, W. (2005). *New literacies in action: Teaching and learning in multiple media.* New York: Teachers College Press.

Lantz, C. (1996). Digital photography and its impact on instruction. *Eyes on the future: Converging images, ideas, and instruction.* Selected readings from the Annual Conference of the International Visual Literacy Association, Chicago, IL.

Levstik, L., & Barton, K. (2001). *Doing history: Investigating with children in elementary and middle schools* (2nd ed.). Mahwah, NJ: Lawrence Erlbaum.

Levstik, L., & Barton, K. (2004). *Teaching history for the common good.* Mahwah, NJ: Lawrence Erlbaum.

Lipscomb, G. (2002). Eighth graders' impressions of the Civil War: Using technology in the history classroom. *Education Communication and Information, 2,* 51–67.

Lyman, L., & Foyle, H. (1991). Teaching geography using cooperative learning. *Journal of Geography, 90*(2), 223–226.

Martorella, P. (1997). Technology and social studies: Which way to the sleeping giant? *Theory and Research in Social Education, 25*(4), 511–514.

McMillan, J. H., & Schumacher, S. (2001). *Research in education* (5th ed.). New York: Longman.

Milson, A. J. (2002). The internet and inquiry learning: Integrating medium and method in a sixth grade social studies classroom. *Theory and Research in Social Education, 30,* 330–353.

Mustoe, M. (1994). *The versatility of Photo CD technology in the classroom.* Paper presented at the Annual Conference of the League for Innovation in the Community College. Houston, TX, November 13, 1994.

National Center for Education Statistics. (2001). *NAEP geography press release presentation.* Retrieved October 28, 2008 from: http://nces.ed.gov/nationsreportcard/geography/results.

National Geography Standards. (1994). *Geography for life: What every young American should know and be able to do in geography.* Washington, DC: National Geographic Research and Exploration.

Natoli, S. J. (1994). *Strengthening geography in the social studies.* Washington, DC: National Council for the Social Studies.

Pew Institute. (2002). *The digital disconnect: The widening gap between internet savvy students and their schools.* Washington, DC. Retrieved November 5, 2008 from: http://www.pewInternet.org/reports/toc.asp?Report=67

Posner, G. J., Strike, K. A.. Hewson. P. W., & Gertzog, W. A. (1982). Accommodation of a scientific conception: Towards a theory of conceptual change. *Science Education, 66*(2), 211–227.

Reissman, C. K. (1993). *Narrative analysis.* Newbury Park: Sage.

Sandholtz, J. H., Ringstaff, C., & Dwyer, D. (1997). *Teaching with technology: Creating student-centered classrooms.* New York: Teachers College Press.

Stake, R. E. (1995). *The art of case study research.* Thousand Oak, CA: Sage.

Stoltman, J. P. (1990). *Geography education and citizenship.* Bloomington, IN: Social Studies Development Center.

Stoltman, J. P. (1991). Research on geography teaching. In J. Shaver (Ed.), *Handbook of research on social studies teaching and learning* (pp. 437–447). New York: Macmillan.

Swan, K. O., Hofer, M., & Levstik, L. (2006). And...action! Students collaborating in the Digital Directors Guild. *Social Studies and the Young Learner, 19*(4), 17–20.

Wong, L. (1999). *Shootback.* London: Booth-Clibborn.

Yin, R. K. (1994). *Case study research: Design and methods.* Thousand Oaks, CA: Sage.

Yow, S.H. (2005, November). *A window to the world: Teachers' conceptions of geography and technology.* Paper presented at the College and University Faculty Assembly of the National Council for the Social Studies, Kansas City, MO.

CHAPTER 8

TECHNOLOGY INTEGRATION

The Trojan Horse for School Reform

Cheryl Mason Bolick

ABSTRACT

A primary focus of technology research has been on technology integration (Casson et al., n.d.; Sandholtz, Ringstaff, & Dwyer, 1997; U.S. Department of Education, 2002). The literature focused on both technology integration in teacher education and technology integration in K–12 education. Whether the focus is teacher education or K–12 education, many educational technology researchers and developers claim that technology integration is a "Trojan horse" that will lead to educational reform (Harris, 2005, p. 120). There is, however, no substantive basis in the literature that proves that technology integration will lead to school reform. This chapter will explore the contradicting agendas of technology integration and a framework for technology in teaching and learning. It will then outline a study that was conducted to learn about technology integration into a graduate social studies teacher education program and conclude with recommendations for future research.

Research on Technology in Social Studies Education, pages 173–187
Copyright © 2009 by Information Age Publishing

INTRODUCTION

A primary focus of recent technology research has been on technology integration (Casson et al., n.d.; Sandholtz, Ringstaff, & Dwyer, 1997; U. S. Department of Education, 2002). This research has focused on technology integration in teacher education and technology integration in K–12 education. Whether the focus is teacher education or K–12 education, many educational technology researchers and developers claim that technology integration is a "Trojan horse" that will lead to educational reform (Harris, 2005, p. 120). This metaphor of the Trojan horse suggests that hidden within technology integration programs are measures that will covertly lead to educational reform. There is, however, no substantive basis in the literature that proves that technology integration will lead to school reform. This chapter will explore the contradicting agendas of technology integration and a framework for technology in teaching and learning. It will then outline a study that was conducted to learn about technology integration into a graduate social studies teacher education program and conclude with recommendations for future research.

TECHNOLOGY INTEGRATION

There is a void in the literature about how technology integration impacts teaching and learning. Harris (2005) claims there are two reasons why past efforts to integrate technologies into the curriculum have failed: *technocentrism* and *pedagogical dogmatism*. She draws upon Papert's work in which he explained the concept of technocentrism as egocentrism. That is, educational technology researchers erroneously focus on technology itself rather than on content. Papert originally coined the term as an adaptation of Piaget's notion of egocentrism.

Harris (2005) cites pedagogical dogmatism as the second reason we are failing at technology integration. Pedagogical dogmatism refers to the changing role of students and learners in the technology-rich learning environment. She describes efforts over the past twenty-five years to use technology to promote educational reform. Educators who have led efforts to use technology for educational reform most often were seeking to reform education around constructivist aims (Spivey, 1997). She argues that:

> Though many educational technology leaders may prefer to teach and learn in constructivist ways, it is time to question whether professional, political, or personal penchants should dictate large-scale educational policy—especially in democratic societies that value ideological diversity. (p. 119)

Researchers such as Becker (2001) have discussed correlation between an educator's teaching philosophy and the nature of technology integration. Becker's research that was based on the Teaching Learning Computing (TLC) survey data set do present the case that teachers with a constructivist philosophy are more prone to use technology in constructivist methods in the classroom is an exception to the argument that there is scant recent technology research that objectively presents technology through a constructivist lens. Culp, Honey, and Mandinach (2003) also reflect upon the focus on educational technology and school reform this time through the review of government policy reports.

> During this period, policy reports begin to present education technology as a *driver* of school reform, rather than as a class of tools and resources that, to varying extents, could be matched to educational challenges already recognized by educators. In these reports technology becomes a tool of *transformation*, which promised, simply by its presence and capabilities, to cause changes in how teachers teach, how schools are organized, and how students work together and learn. (p. 20)

Responding to the current status of the field, Harris sets a challenge for educators to "consider seriously whether it is more appropriate to try to change the nature of teaching and learning through the integration of educational technologies—or to help teachers and learners use appropriate curriculum-based technological applications more pervasively in all of their varied forms" (p. 121). She concludes that now is the time for the field to choose an agenda in terms of researching technology integration.

Technology in Schools Framework

It is helpful to use a framework as a lens to conceptualize the role and purpose of technology in schools. Bull et al. (2002) present a framework to define the goals and objectives of technology integration in teaching and learning. This framework seeks to establish a common language for the role and purpose of technology in schools. The technology in school's framework identifies two main goals for the use of technology in schools: to improve efficiency (to teach as we teach now but more efficiently, e.g., transmissive pedagogy) or to reconceptualize the curriculum (to teach in an entirely different way promoting a new vision of excellence in education, e.g., constructivist pedagogies). In each of these situations, the use of technology is considered to either be in the background or foreground with the focus of student learning either on content (technology in the background) or the focus of student learning is on technology (technology in the foreground). This framework is helpful in establishing a common

TABLE 8.1   Technology in Schools Framework

Use of Technology	Improve Efficiency	Reconceptualize Curriculum
Foreground	Computer Literacy	School Reform
Background	Computer Assisted Instruction (CAI)	Discipline-based Reforms

Source: Bull et al., 2002

language for the role and purpose of technology in education and also provides a lens to examine the momentum behind technology integration efforts. The framework is divided into four quadrants (Table 8.1). The table categorizes the background and foreground uses of technology as either to improve efficiency or to reconceptualize the curriculum. The section below will define each of the quadrants below. It is important to note that this cited table does not distinguish between transmissive pedagogy and student-centered pedagogies, however one may consider that to improve efficiency is transmissive, while receonptualization is student centered.

Technology in the foreground to promote computer literacy.   The term "computer literacy" was coined in the early 1980s for the purpose of entrenching the field of information technology into the school curriculum (Bull et al., 2002). When technology is in the foreground to promote computer literacy, instructional emphasis is on mastering technology skills to become a more efficient learner and worker. An example of this might be a stand-alone technology course in which pre-service teachers are required to master technology skills such as recording grades in a spreadsheet or creating a PowerPoint presentation. Teachers are often introduced to these skills outside of the context of academic content. Rather, computer literacy instruction is focused on ensuring students master the skills to complete a task that will make them more efficient.

Technology in the background to promote computer-assisted instruction (CAI).   CAI is computer-based software program designed to support students as the learner specific content. The aim of CAI is for students to learn more efficiently. CAI is focused on student learning, rather than the development of computer literacy skills. Examples of CAI software include simulations, drill and practice, and tutorials. Teacher education programs may use CAI to help pre-service teachers learn about topics such as creating Individual Evaluation Plans (IEP) for special education students. CAI software may be used to guide students through the process of creating an IEP in a more efficient way than having an instructor teach the lesson.

Technology in the foreground to promote school reform.   When technology is used in the foreground to promote school reform, pre-service teachers are intentionally introduced to technology tools and expected to master the skills required to use them effectively. Effective use of technology tools is defined as seamlessly using technology to promote a more constructivist learning environment (Bolick, 2004). In such environments, technology is introduced within the context of the content to be learned. However, the focus of the lesson will be more on the technical aspects of learning with technology. For example pre-service social studies teachers might use technology in the foreground when learning to design a web page so that they can develop and implement a WebQuest project in a classroom.

Technology in the background to promote discipline-based reforms. When technology is used in the background to reconceptualize the curriculum, the result is discipline-based reforms. Content area experts, such as historians, lead discipline-based reforms. As scholars in the content areas use technology to reform teaching and learning within their discipline, they generate pedagogical changes which impact teaching and learning within their field. For example, as historians make use of online primary sources within their own teaching and researching, they impact how university students learn the discipline of history.

The technology in schools framework discussed below provides a conceptual map to understand how technology is emphasized when it is integrated into the curriculum. The messages pre-service teachers receive about these emphases on technology from their teacher education program is an important part of the success of their training. Situating the role of technology in the learning experience helps to frame how technology is used to enhance learning. This framework will be used to analyze the experiences of social studies teachers in a technology-rich graduate program.

METHODOLOGY

The purpose of the study was to investigate how technology was integrated into a social studies teacher education program. Specifically, this study sought to examine the role and purpose of technology. A qualitative design was employed to present a rich picture of the many layers of technology integration in a social studies teacher education course. Multiple pieces of data were collected over a period of time to tell a complex story of how technology was used in one group of teachers' graduate school experience. The research question that framed this study was: *What are the role and purpose of technology in one social studies graduate education program?*

From 2003–2005, data were collected from a cohort of experienced teachers enrolled in a graduate social studies education program. The fourteen teachers in the cohort represented a variety of technology interest levels and technology skills. They also represented diverse educational and professional backgrounds. This study closely examined the teachers' beliefs and practices related to technology throughout the 2½ years that they were enrolled in the graduate program.

Participants

Participants of the study were fourteen classroom social studies teachers enrolled in a part-time Master's of Education (M.Ed.) program at a large, public university. Six of the teachers were middle school social studies teachers and eight were high school social studies teachers. The M.Ed. program was specifically designed for practicing teachers, as all of the courses were held during the summer or during after-school hours. The program is a cohort-based program focused on content areas. Of the 31 credit hours taken by the teachers, 15 of the credit hours were social studies specific courses and 16 credit hours were courses taken by all students in the M.Ed. program, regardless of content area (Table 8.2).

Technology played a significant role in both the delivery and content of the five social studies courses. These courses were designed as hybrid courses. That is, 50% of the coursework was face-to-face and 50% of the coursework was online. Blackboard was used as a web interface for the online components. The two primary uses of the Blackboard site were the dissemination of class reading materials and the asynchronous discussion

TABLE 8.2   M.Ed. Curriculum

	Core Courses	Specialty Area Courses
Spring 2002		Social Studies and Humanities for Teaching and Learning
Summer 2003	Reinventing Teaching	
Fall 2003	Teaching & Differentiation A	Contemporary Research for Social Studies Teaching
Spring 2004	Ways of Knowing	Disciplinary StudiesA: Informing Social Studies Pedagogy & Learning
Summer 2004	Assessment & Accountability	Cultural Diversity & Global Education in the Social Studies
Fall 2004	Action Research I Teaching & Differentiation B	
Spring 2005	Action Research II	Disciplinary StudiesB: Informing Social Studies Pedagogy & Learning
Summer 2005	Restructuring Schools and Teaching for a Democratic Society	

within the discussion page. Technology was also a focus of the content of social studies courses. The students worked extensively with digital history archives and were introduced to a variety of technology tools.

For example, the students were introduced to digital history archives in the first social studies course, *Social Studies and Humanities for Teaching and Learning*. In this course, the students were introduced to the concept of digital history archives. They met with designers of a digital library to learn about content and design of one digital history collection. They designed a curriculum project to accompany the specified collection. The students built on this initial exposure to digital history archives in the subsequent course, *Disciplinary Studies B: Informing Social Studies Pedagogy & Learning*. In this course, the students studied historical thinking in hypertext learning environments. The students designed and developed hypertext learning Web Inquiry Projects (WIPs).

Data Sources

A variety of data related to technology integration were collected throughout the students' 2½ years in the program. Data were categorized into three categories: student coursework, emails and outside course communication, and interviews (Table 8.3).

Student coursework data included samples of students' work such as on-line postings within Blackboard, course papers, and course projects. Many of the course assignments were targeted specifically at technology in the forefront. For example, students wrote personal narratives at the beginning and end of the program reflecting on their beliefs about technology and their practices using technology. Students also created web-based digital history projects in one course and wrote a reflection paper on their experiences writing hypertext.

Emails and outside course communication data included emails sent from students to the instructor as well as emails posted to the cohort class

TABLE 8.3 Data Sources

Category	Sample Data Source
Student Coursework	Online postings
	Course papers
	Course projects
	Course evaluations
Emails & Course Communication	Emails from students to instructor
	Emails posted on cohort listserv
Interviews	Individual interviews with teachers

listserv. The substance of this data covered a variety of topics. For example participants used the listserv to share exciting new web pages or to ask for technical assistance.

Interviews were conducted with each of the participants at the end of the program. The interviews were structured around three issues: overall experiences in the M.Ed. program, beliefs and practices related to technology, growth since entering the M.Ed. program and post-graduation plans. A graduate research assistant conducted interviews. Each interview lasted approximately 30 minutes. Interviews were recorded and transcribed.

Data Analysis

The constant comparative method was used to analyze the data collected from the various sources. Glaser's (1978) six steps for analyzing the data in the constant comparative method guided the data analysis:

1. Collect preliminary data.
2. Identify categories of focus.
3. Continue data collection.
4. Begin writing about the emerging themes, while continually searching for new themes.
5. Work with the data and the preliminary analysis to reveal basic social processes and relationships.
6. Code and write, while focusing on the core categories.

Goetz and LeCompte (1981) refer to this method as one that "combines inductive category coding with a simultaneous comparison of all social incidents observed (p. 58). Data undergoes repeated review throughout the data collection and analysis process, leading to the refinement of categories. "As events are constantly compared with previous events, new topological dimension, as well as new relationships, may be discovered" (Goetz & LeCompte, p. 58). The research team began by collecting all course materials, emails and outside communication, and interview transcripts. Individual researchers then categorized the data. Each research team member then read through sets of data to identify themes.

As the research evolved, a running list of emerging themes was maintained; new patterns were added to the list and revisions made. From this iterative process, themes gradually developed. The following section highlights the themes that emerged from the data analysis.

FINDINGS

The research question that guided this study was, *What are the role and purpose of technology in one social studies graduate education program?* Analysis of the data revealed that the teachers in the M.Ed. program had a variety of experiences with technology. All of the 14 teachers self-reported that technology played a significant role in what they learned and how they learned throughout the program. Data analysis revealed changes in the participants' thinking over time. Each of their experiences was interpreted individually, revealing multiple perspectives on the integration of technology into the graduate program.

Davis et al.'s (2001) framework for implementation of new technology in teacher education can be used to categorize the factors that seem to explain changes in the teachers' beliefs and practices related to technology during the span of time the teachers were enrolled in the M.Ed. program. This framework is helpful in understanding the findings because it situates technology integration within teacher beliefs ad practices. The data that was collected from this study provided insightful information related to participants' technology beliefs and practices. Many of these factors are well documented in the literature, but these findings contextualize them within the field of social studies education. The findings are framed within these factors: Human factors: Changing roles, Human factors: Substitution to transformation, Human factors: New teaching skills, Human factors: New learning skills, Curricular issues: Openness of the curriculum.

Human Factors: Changing Roles

The structure of the hybrid courses presented the participants with changing roles that were different from the traditional teacher-centered instruction to which they were accustomed. The online components of the courses allowed the teachers to be more in control of what they learned and how they learned. One teacher commented in a written reflection on this factor:

> The online discussions were a lot to keep up with. It was like class was always "there." But, I liked that we could take the readings and go different ways with them. Sometimes, we'd have four different "conversations" going about the same article. It gave us an opportunity to learn more about the things we wanted to learn about. There wasn't a right or wrong answer about the main point of an article.

The participants' experiences were consistent with the literature that open and flexible learning situations are more constructivist in nature. These situations require students to be more independent learners who are curious, rather than be dependent learners who are seeking right or wrong answers.

Human Factors: Substitution to Transformation

The changing roles discussed above occurred over the 2½ years participants were enrolled in the program. The first technology course experience for participants was very structured compared to their last courses. For example, in the first course, the instructor gave detailed prompts for the online discussions and dictated how many responses each teacher should post. By the final course, the students were creating the prompts themselves and were not given detailed instructions on how many responses to post. Rather, the students were encouraged to follow their own line of inquiry to engage in the discussion.

Human Factors: New Teaching Skills

Davis et al. (2001) identified online readings and communication as crucial new learning contexts, which in turn require new teaching skills. There were a number of online readings for the courses in this program. The participants noted that their interactions with the text were directly related to the format of the text and the instructors' teaching skills. For example, some online readings, such as pdfs, can be as straightforward as traditional readings. They are linear, with a beginning and an end. However, hypertext documents are much more open-ended. Hypertext is nonlinear, allowing the reader to control how they read material. When an instructor prepares or assigns a hypertext document, they are never quite sure what the students will read and how they will read. One student commented on the unique nature of working with hypertext readings,

> It can be really confusing, because you click on one link and it takes you off somewhere else. You can do just a few links and all of a sudden you're five pages away from the assigned reading. The whole class could read the same assignment, but each one of us could end up somewhere different.

Methods of promoting effective dialogue or communication are another essential new teaching skill that had to be taught and practiced throughout the program. The teachers used primarily email, whole class discussions, and small class discussions to facilitate their communication. The participants' communication was either professional or personal. Professional conversation was focused on class assignments, while personal communication tended to focus on the participants' personal lives and on supporting one another throughout the program.

Human Factors: New Learning Skills

It was clear to the teachers in this study that learning with technology was different from previous learning experiences as they had as students before the Internet. The teachers in this research adopted new learning skills at different increments. One teacher commented, "I can't believe how much class work I can do online! I can sit at home and read almost any article in the library. If I'd had the Internet when I was in undergrad, I probably never would have gone to the library!" Another teacher who described himself as a technology novice both at the beginning of the program and at the end of the program moved toward developing new learning skills at a much slower pace than his cohort members. For example, by the end of the program, he still printed out each online article before reading. Yet, he had developed new learning skills such as online searching techniques and he learned how to manage documents on his computer. Another teacher, who described herself as technology savvy at the beginning of the program, acquired new learning skills that assisted her in reading articles on her computer screen. She would open another window and type notes as she read.

Curricular Issues: Openness of the Curriculum

Developing courses that provided students opportunities to explore new learning environments was an investment on the part of the instructors and the administration in the M.Ed. program. Instructors were called upon to invest time to develop new courses and to learn the technology required to effectively teach online courses. The administration supported these efforts by appointing a graduate assistant to each course. One teacher noted the openness of the graduate curriculum by commenting, "This is not what I expected in graduate school. I expected a lot of book reading and paper writing. Instead we have spent hours learning about new technology and writing web pages instead of papers."

Examining the data through the lens of Davis et al.'s (2001) factors that affect implementation in teacher education, reveals that the teachers in the M.Ed. program had a variety of experiences with technology. Technology was used in the forefront of instruction and in the background of instruction. It also was used to improve efficiency and to reconceptualize the curriculum. Earlier Bull et al.'s (2002) framework was used to categorize technology usage. Table 8.4 highlights examples from this research in three of the four categories.

Technology was introduced in the foreground to improve efficiency. Throughout the program, class sessions devoted specifically to mastery of technology skills. One example of this was a class session in which the teachers learned to use Blackboard. The class session was a lab-based class meeting in which a user's guide was distributed. The teacher led the students through the mechanics of using Blackboard and allowed the students time to practice using the different functions. Blackboard was seen as a technology tool to improve efficiency because web interface used throughout the program to facilitate class discussions and to conduct administrative tasks in an online environment.

No evidence emerged in this research study of technology being used in the form of Computer-Assisted Instruction (CAI). At no point during the period of the study was technology used in the form of a tutorial or simulation. The most frequent use of technology was to promote school reform particularly as it was used in the foreground to reconceptualize the curriculum. One of the most obvious cases of this was an assignment in which teacher participants created a web page to teach a digital history lesson. This required the teachers to learn how to create and post a web page, yet the class sessions focused on using digital history resources to promote inquiry-based learning. One student commented on the seamless nature of this process by saying, "I'm so proud of myself for making this web page. I can't wait to use it in class. We just kinda learned how to do it along the way. I almost didn't realize what we were learning."

The most infrequent, yet the most transformative use of technology in this research study was technological use within the discipline. Technology was at the background of the class sessions in which the teachers used online primary sources to investigate historical inquiry questions. This is an example of discipline-based reforms as noted in the technology in schools

TABLE 8.4   Technology in Schools Framework with Sample Data

Use of Technology	Improve Efficiency	Reconceptualize Curriculum
Foreground	Computer Literacy	School Reform
	Teachers used Blackboard to engage in online professional discussions	*Teachers created a web page to teach a digital history lesson.*
Background	Computer Assisted Instruction (CAI)	Discipline-Based Reforms
	No evidence	*Teachers used online primary sources to investigate a historical inquiry question.*

framework. The teachers selected a line of inquiry and were required to use digitized primary sources to conduct their inquiry. The focus of the class sessions was on the historical inquiry process, yet the teachers could not have completed the assignment without the technology.

DISCUSSION

By focusing on the factors that influence technology integration into teacher education and on the uses of technology in teaching and learning, this study provides us with a more focused view of technology in social studies teacher education. It is evident that technology integration did occur in the graduate education experience of these social studies teachers. There were instances in which there was a technocentric approach to integration, such as the instruction on how to use Blackboard. There were also instances of pedagogical dogmatism, such as the activities using digital history resources. The participants in the study all cited experiences that and situations that decidedly changed their views of teaching and learning with technology. These perceptions, however, were limited to the teachers' experiences as students in the graduate program.

It is not evident from the data if the teachers' experiences translated into technology integration into their own classrooms. Although technology integration into teacher education is necessary, technology integration in the K–12 classroom is the tipping point that is the most essential to student learning. Results of this study do not clarify Harris' (2005) rhetorical question about choosing our agenda:

> Still, I urge us to consider seriously whether it is more appropriate to try to change the nature of teaching and learning through the integration of educational technologies—or to help teachers and learners use appropriate curriculum-based technological applications more pervasively in all of their varied forms. (p. 121)

CONCLUSION

This qualitative study tells the story of one cohort of social studies teachers' engagement with technology through a graduate education program. The data collected included interviews, course materials, and student work over a 2½ year period. The Bull et al. (2002) framework provided a lens to understand the purpose of technology integration in education. The Davis et al. (2001) framework helped to situate the data within the contextual frame of the unique nature of this particular graduate education program.

This study focused on technology in the graduate education experience. Therefore, the data extended the original framework by providing subject specific examples in graduate teacher education.

The findings from this study accentuate Harris' notion that technology integration is still highly unsuccessful in schools because the field wavers between technocentrism and pedagogical dogmatism. The implications of these findings for teacher education are important. So long as education at the K–12 level reinforces these technocentric and dogmatic stances, teacher education students will likely be limited in their ability to integrate technology in their teaching practices in a manner that is similar to the experiences they may have in teacher education programs. Analysis of the data in the study described in this chapter demonstrates that it is possible to integrate technology with a dual purpose, both technocentrism and school reform. Yet, to reach the results the field expects from "technology as a Trojan horse," we should pursue a line of inquiry that investigates technology integration through the lens of instructional strategies, rather than studying technology integration through innovative technologies.

REFERENCES

Becker, H. (2001). *How are teachers using computers in instruction?* Paper presented at the 2001 Meetings of the American Educational Research Association, Seattle, WA.

Bolick, C. M. (2004). Technology and social studies in teacher education: A framework. In S. Adler (Ed.), *Critical issues in social studies and teacher education* (pp. 131–144). Greenwich, CT: Information Age Publishing.

Bull, G., Bell, R., Mason, C. L., & Garofalo, J. (2002). Information technology and elementary/secondary education. In J. M. Pawlowski (Ed.), *Handbook on information technologies for education and training*. New York: Springer.

Casson, L., Bauman, J., Fisher, E., Lindlad, M., Sumpter, J. R., Tornatzky, L. G., et al. (n.d.). *Making technology happen: Best practices and policies from exemplary K–12 schools for teachers, principals, parents, policymakers and industry*. Southern Growth Policies Board.

Culp, K. M., Honey, M., & Mandinach, E. (2003). *A retrospective on twenty years of education technology policy*. Washington, DC: U.S. Department of Education, Office of Educational Technology. Retrieved March 16, 2006 from: http://www.nationaledtechplan.org/participate/20years.pdf

Davis, N., Hawkwa, M., Heinecke, W., & Veen. W. (2001). Evaluating educational technology: Four perspectives. In W. Heinecke & L. Blasi (Eds.), *Methods of evaluating educational technology*. Greenwich, CT: Information Age Publishing.

Goetz, J. P., & LeCompte, M. D. (1981). Ethnographic research and the problem of data reduction. *Anthropology and Education Quarterly, 12*, 51–70.

Harris, J. (2005). Our agenda for technology integration: It's time to choose. *Contemporary Issues in Technology and Teacher Education, 5*(2), 116–122.

Sandholtz, J. H., Ringstaff, C., & Dwyer, D. (1997). *Teaching with technology: Creating student-centered classrooms.* New York: Teachers College Press.

Spivey, N. N. (1997). *The constructivist metaphor: Reading, writing, and the making of meaning.* New York: Academic Press.

U.S. Department of Education. (2002). *Exemplary and promising educational technology programs: 2000* (No. ORAD 2002-1005). Washington, D.C.: Office of Educational Research and Improvement.

CHAPTER 9

THE EFFECT OF TEACHERS' CONCEPTIONS OF STUDENT ABILITIES AND HISTORICAL THINKING ON DIGITAL PRIMARY SOURCE USE

Adam M. Friedman

ABSTRACT

A digital primary source is a firsthand account of a historical event in electronic format, and can be used to engage students in historical thinking. In this qualitative study, six world history teachers were asked about their beliefs regarding student achievement and abilities in terms of how these characteristics impacted the teachers' willingness to use digital primary historical sources. Student achievement level served as a determining factor in terms of how the teacher participants viewed their students' ability to think historically. The extent to which these teachers believed that their students were capable of engaging in historical thinking subsequently influenced their desire to use digital primary historical sources. These views also influenced the type of digital primary sources participants were willing to use in their classroom as well as the manner by which the participants used them. These findings as well as related implications are discussed.

Research on Technology in Social Studies Education, pages 189–204
Copyright © 2009 by Information Age Publishing
All rights of reproduction in any form reserved.

INTRODUCTION

Primary sources, as traces from the past, offer social studies students the opportunity to study history by analyzing evidence and taking perspective. These processes require historical thinking skills in which students "evaluate evidence, develop comparative and causal analyses, interpret the historical record, and construct sound historical arguments and perspectives on which informed decisions in contemporary life can be based" (National Center for History in the Schools, n.d. given, online). This study was focused on the extent to which digital primary historical source use was compatible with world history teachers' current practices. To contextualize this study, in the section below I briefly consider how uses of technology are diffused throughout the social studies community and then review some specific uses of digital primary historical sources.

TECHNOLOGY DIFFUSION AND DIGITAL
PRIMARY HISTORICAL SOURCES

In his 1995 work *Diffusion of Innovations*, Rogers describes the process by which an innovation is spread throughout a culture or community. Rogers emphasizes that the adoption of an innovation by a particular group of people is not an overnight decision; rather it is the result of individuals adopting the innovation over time until it is ubiquitous in a particular society or culture. Rogers (1995) maintains that there is a higher likelihood of an innovation being adopted if, (1) it provides an improved method of attaining a goal, (2) it is inversely proportional to the degree to which an innovation is perceived of as complex, and (3) it is compatible with current practices. Rogers (1995) defines an innovation's compatibility as "the degree to which an innovation is perceived as consistent with the existing values, past experiences, and needs of potential adopters" (p. 224). If Rogers' (1995) theory is accurate, technological innovations such as those related to using digital primary historical sources would need to be viewed by teachers as activities that are compatible, or in other words would fit seamlessly into their current practice.

Social studies educators' use of primary historical sources has been encouraged by scholars as enabling a deeper historical understanding than what is offered in their textbook (Singleton & Giese, 1999). At the same time primary historical source use can help students draw their own conclusions (Shiroma, 2000). Further, by studying the traces of the past left by primary sources, students are enabled to construct their own interpretations (Seixas, 1998). Although Barton (2005) warns that primary historical sources can at times be misused, he nevertheless encourages "open-ended investigation" from multiple sources in order for students to determine the validity of the viewpoints that are presented (p. 751).

The use of digital primary historical sources can be an invaluable tool for social studies instruction (Braun & Risinger, 1999; Hicks & Ewing, 2003). Such use can satisfy two of the conditions of technology integration in social studies set forth by Mason et al. (2000), namely that such uses are within the context of social studies content and that these uses offer teachers and students the opportunity to engage in an activity that they otherwise might not be able to. Although the Internet provides an opportunity for access to primary historical sources, merely having an Internet connection does not ensure their use, nor does it ensure that they are used in a manner consistent with student ability.

The use of primary historical sources in the secondary social studies classroom was once reserved only for classes where teachers undertook the often cumbersome process of physically acquiring the primary sources. With thousands of web sites hosting a variety of digital primary historical sources, teachers and students now have access to a wide array of primary historical sources (Cohen & Rosenzweig, 2006). As of 2003, "93% of public school instructional rooms" had accessibility to primary historical sources and with this access has come a sea change in what is possible (Parsad & Jones, 2005, p. 4). Cohen and Rosenzweig (2006) have posited that the preponderance of primary (as well as secondary) historical sources on the Internet not only offers "instantaneous access" to historical materials that were previously difficult to obtain, but simultaneously "open[s] locked doors" (p. 4). Anyone with an Internet connection, from a "high school student...to senior historian," can enter the archive, a result of which "will likely alter historical research and writing in ways we haven't yet imagined" (Cohen & Rosenzweig, 2006, p. 4).

While the use of primary historical sources offers students the opportunity to engage in historical thinking by "examin[ing] the historical record for themselves," this is not necessarily an easy task (National Center for History in the Schools, 2005, online). Rather, as VanSledright (2002) observes, the process of historical thinking "demands some fairly sophisticated thinking processes" in which it is necessary to "recapture and recount a reality that is no longer available" (pp. 5–6). Lévesque (2008) elaborates on the higher-order thinking (and thus presumed difficulty) involved in historical thinking, noting "to think historically is thus to understand how knowledge has been constructed and what it means" (p. 27). Stemming from his study of student teachers designing instructional activities with primary historical source documents, Seixas (1998) outlines how challenging it can be to find appropriate sources and develop suitable questions. Further, students have to engage in activities and thought processes that may contradict their previous experiences in the history classroom (Greene, 1994). Despite these difficulties, studies have shown that children are capable of engaging in historical thinking (Kobrin, 1996; VanSledright, 2002).

Researchers argue that teachers' historical thinking skills have some bearing on their students' ability to engage in this type of discourse (VanSledright & Frankes, 2000; Yeager & Wilson, 1997). Pre-service teachers generally take one or more methods courses in their content area, and it is in this course that particular strategies for teaching content are presented. However, various studies have demonstrated that not only is the notion of historical thinking interpreted differently by different pre-service teachers, but when pre-service teachers from the same methods course student teach, they foster historical thinking in their students to varying degrees (Yeager & Wilson, 1997). In their study of three pre-service secondary teachers, Yeager and Davis (1995) noted that each had a range of abilities and familiarity with primary sources even though they had taken the same methods course.

Because historical thinking involves judgments based on interpretation of evidence, it is inherently subjective. While this subjectivity could very well be the root cause of why individuals conceive of historical thinking in different ways, it does not necessarily explain why teachers foster historical thinking skills at different rates, as was the case in Yeager and Wilson's (1997) study. Although Yeager and Wilson (1997) note that "the maturity level of their pupils" (para. 30) was a negative influence in their fostering of historical thinking skills, student "intellectual level...did not seem to be a major constraining factor" (1997, para. 28). Because primary historical sources come in various formats such as text, images, and political cartoons, the goal of this study was to examine whether and to what degree world history teachers' conceptions of historical thinking as well as student achievement level had an influence on the frequency and type of digital primary source use. In other words, were digital primary historical sources "compatible" with teacher beliefs and student abilities (Rogers, 1995, p. 224)?

METHODS

As part of a larger study that examined world history and world geography teachers' use of digital primary historical sources and the reasons behind their use or non-use (Friedman, 2004), six teachers were asked how the achievement level of their students influenced their uses of these sources. Participants were asked to define historical thinking in their own words, and whether their students were capable of thinking in this manner. Data from the study were analyzed using Erickson's (1986) method of analytic induction in which the researcher was the instrument for data collection. Erickson (1986) argues that the underlying epistemological assumptions of this type of research focuses on constructed meanings rather than measured findings. Therefore, the researcher, through his experiences in the field, is able to build a credible description of what is happening in a particular classroom. Erickson (1986) posits that no absolute or correct answer exists; rather, the researcher constructs findings as he interacts with participants in the research setting in the hopes of producing data with "plausibility" (p. 149).

At the core of qualitative research is a focused, in-depth study of the details of the activity of a small number of participants, with the goal of understanding what is happening, how a process unfolds, and why certain activities occur (Miles & Huberman, 1994). Findings from this larger study demonstrated that teachers' access to computer projectors was a more prominent explanation for their use of digital primary sources than the training that they received (Friedman, 2006a), and that state high stakes standards and testing policies negatively influenced digital primary source use (Friedman, 2006b). The goal of this study was to understand how and why world history teachers utilized primary sources at different rates.

In order to select participants, thirty-four world history teachers from five public high schools in Virginia (each of which varied in size and socioeconomic status) were given a survey that asked how often they used primary sources and how those primary sources were acquired. The surveys were based on the Virginia Standards of Learning (SOLs) and asked the teachers about the rate at which they used primary sources for each specific Standard of Learning. In this study, participants were selected using "theoretical" or "purposive" sampling, as these individuals were "chosen not for their representativeness but for their relevance to the research question" (Schwandt, 2001, p. 232). From this survey data, three high-frequency digital primary source users (those that used digital primary sources on at least 90% of the standards), two low-frequency (15% or less), and one middle-frequency (54%) participants consented to be interviewed and observed. Each of the six participants was a licensed social studies teacher; five of the six had been undergraduate history majors, and four of the six held Master's degrees (Table 9.1).

TABLE 9.1   Digital Primary Source Use, Teacher, and School

Digital Primary Source Use	Teacher	School	Type of School
High	Mr. Lukas	Mountainview HS	Suburban
High	Mr. Clark	Lakefront HS	Suburban
High	Ms. Pullen	Eastside HS	Urban
Middle	Ms. Lewin	Lakefront HS	Suburban
Low	Mr. Mitchell	Eastside HS	Urban
Low	Ms. Mather	Plains HS	Rural

Data collected included interviews, observations, field notes, and archival evidence such as lesson plans, student handouts, and specific web sites. Erickson (1986) maintains that the blending of different data sources will yield more precise answers to the research question. Each teacher participated in one formal (1.5 hours) interview based on Patton's (1990) general interview guide approach, of which a portion was focused on participants' conceptions of historical thinking and whether they believed their students were capable of engaging in historical thinking. Participants were also asked if they thought primary historical sources were useful in fostering historical thinking and they were asked about student achievement level in their world history courses. Each participant teacher was observed on one or two occasions for a full class period during which archival evidence was also collected. During these observations, the researcher did not interrupt the normal flow of the class and did not interact with the teacher or students. Immediately following an observation, analytic memos as described by Maxwell (1996) were written with the purpose of helping to monitor and analyze data.

In order to achieve validity in Erickson's (1986) interpretive mode, the most important task of the researcher is, quite literally, to interpret, or make meaning of what was observed in the field. The researcher needs to comprehend what happened and what those actions represent. In interpretive research, Erickson (1986) states that it is "difficult," but necessary "to probe analytically the significance of the concrete details reported" (p. 152). Therefore, the researcher should "establish an evidentiary warrant" for claims he has interpreted from the data; without which might give less credence to the findings (p. 146). To address these issues, data were analyzed all through the study. As the researcher commenced collecting data, assertions were made, and data were constantly reviewed to find confirming or disconfirming evidence. Simultaneous to this, data that were collected influenced subsequent interviews and observations in terms of what the researcher looked for.

RESULTS

After in-depth interviews and observations with the six teacher participants, it became apparent that each teacher desired to use digital primary historical sources of all types in their instruction. However, their beliefs about student abilities as well as their conceptions of historical thinking, served to influence their rate of digital primary source use as well as the type that they used.

Each of the six world history teachers interviewed and observed conveyed an interest in and enthusiasm for using primary historical sources (in digital and non-digital format) and expressed the belief that they add value to instruction. For example, Mr. Lukas was an advocate of using digital primary historical sources in his instruction, as he felt that their use not only increased student interest and engagement with the material, but provided his students with the opportunity to understand history rather than memorize it. As he explained, "I think there's an advantage to showing them something visual and having them write down what they see. I think it just makes more sense to them and they're just more engaged by the picture." Ms. Pullen was also enthusiastic about her use of digital primary sources, as she described making a conscious effort to include at least one in every lesson plan. During one observation, she showed her class original photographs of a World War I trench because, as she expressed immediately after class, her students "like getting grossed out."

This enthusiasm for primary historical source use was not limited to high-end users such as Mr. Lukas and Ms. Pullen. When asked about using digital primary sources in her world history class, Ms. Lewin, the middle-frequency user in this study, responded by stating "I think they're a great idea." Mr. Mitchell, who used digital primary historical sources at a lower rate, felt similarly saying, "I don't think you can teach [world history] well without [primary sources]."

Departmental Culture, Lack of Pressure

While each participant valued the use of primary historical sources in their instruction, no one indicated that their social studies department coordinator or another administrator required them to use primary sources in their teaching. However, there appeared to be awareness among the participants about the culture of primary historical source use in their schools. Each participant perceived unique implicit messages from their school. At one extreme was Plains High School's Ms. Mather, who stated that "I don't feel pressure that I have to use [digital primary sources] at all," and the same sentiment was echoed by Ms. Lewin and Mr. Clark at Lakefront High School. At the other extreme were Mr. Mitchell and Ms. Pullen, both of Central High School. Mr. Mitchell "feel[s] that we're encouraged to [use digital primary sources] by our peers," but he was quick to add that "I don't get extra points for using them." Ms. Pullen also stated that primary historical source use is something that is more personal than directive. "Our department head is definitely an advocate of using primary sources. We're under no pressure to do so, but just from conversation I know that she definitely uses a lot of primary sources in her classes." The overall feeling of teachers in terms of this was summarized by Mountainview High School's Mr. Lukas:

> Our department chair or school doesn't really come down and say you need
> to teach primary sources—I don't think that's a real big focus. We've talked

about it, and I think all teachers do to some degree use [both digital and non-digital] primary sources but I don't think there's anybody encouraging it or discouraging it.

Conceptions of Historical Thinking and Student Achievement Level

The inherent subjectivity of the historical thinking described above was evidenced when participants were asked to define the term and each participant provided a different definition. Though no two participants gave the same definition, each made note of the higher-order thinking processes which were involved. For example, Mr. Lukas defined historical thinking as "being able to break down the facts and information in order to assess change over time, to recognize how different themes or concepts are evolving or devolving." Mr. Clark described it as the "ability to see events that happen and their causes." Ms. Lewin conceived of it as "different perspectives on the same event." Ms. Mather made a clear distinction between knowing history and the ability to think historically. She thought of knowing history as being able to recall facts, but historical thinking as the ability to "take from the past and be able to use it in the future."

All of the schools where participants worked, students were grouped by ability level. This tracking and the resultant teacher perception of student ability influenced how teacher participants used digital primary sources. The achievement level of students had an effect on whether teachers viewed their students as capable of historical thinking, and as a result, influenced the type of digital primary sources that teachers used as well as the way in which they used them.

Enabling Students' Historical Thinking

Despite the overarching similarities in how they defined historical thinking, participants expressed a wide range of views about whether their students were capable of thinking historically. These perceptions were often related to the achievement level of their students, as an association emerged between whether participants believed that students were capable of engaging in historical thinking and their use of digital primary historical sources in their instruction. Four participants stated that their students were capable of thinking historically, while one did not believe this to be the case, and one said that they might be able to. The participants in this study that believed their students were capable of historical thinking were more prone to using digital primary historical sources in their instruction, while those

TABLE 9.2   Teacher, Belief Toward Students Thinking Historically, Student Achievement Level

Teacher	Belief Toward Students	Achievement Level
Mr. Lukas	Capable	High
Mr. Clark	Capable	Average
Ms. Pullen	Capable	Average
Ms. Lewin	Capable	Below Average
Mr. Mitchell	Not Capable	Low
Ms. Mather	Maybe	Heterogeneous

who did not believe that their students were capable of this type of thinking utilized digital primary historical sources less frequently (see Table 9.2).

Mr. Lukas taught classes designated as high student achievement levels (typically honors classes) at Mountainview High School. He believed that the majority of his students were capable of historical thinking. He explained while some of his students were more capable than others, they were all capable of doing some historical thinking, particularly given that he believed that historical thinking is a skill that can be taught. Mr. Lukas described an example of his students using a digital version of Karl Marx' *Communist Manifesto*. The class analyzed the document and in his words, "broke it down" in order to learn about what was happening in 19ᵗʰ century Europe. He described assigning both text-based and visual primary sources in the activity. Mr. Lukus described how he often gave his students an overriding theme or question and then directed them to one or two web sites that contained hyperlinks to various text and visual primary sources. Students could then search these sources in order to create an informed opinion on the cause of a certain event or its repercussions. Mr. Lukas noted that this approach to using digital primary historical sources worked well with his honors students, but would be much more difficult with his students that have a lower achievement level. As he put it,

> It's funny the difference between [lower student achievement level] and honors. With honors kids, they're *obsessed* with getting the answers, [but] the standards are like "ah, we'll move on."

Ms. Pullen also described student achievement level as having an influence on digital primary historical source use. She explained this as follows:

> When you teach an applied class, you're teaching students that are reading at a 3rd–5th grade level, which makes you very limited in how you can use them [digital primary sources]. You have to read it out loud or break it down with a guided reading.

Low frequency user Ms. Mather echoed this sentiment, stating that "because of their reading level, I think visual primary sources are better for 9th graders." This was reflected in observations of both of these teachers, as neither engaged their students in an activity that involved reading anything other than their textbook and related worksheets. However, Ms. Pullen felt that students were capable of thinking historically, and one way that historical thinking could be fostered was by using digital primary historical sources of all types, particularly images. Although her use of digital primary historical sources was limited in that it was generally teacher-centered, in her words the use of these resources, "put a name with a face." Ms. Lukus belief that students were capable of thinking historically may have led her to use digital primary historical sources at a higher rate.

Mr. Clark taught what he described as an "average" class at Lakefront High School. Although he used digital primary historical sources frequently in his instruction, the achievement level of his students influenced the type that he used. While he believed that digital primary historical source as "literature selections" could "carry a lot of weight," he said that he found it challenging to locate those that are the "right size [and] that [are at] the reading level for your kids." He also described less reading-intensive digital primary sources, such as images and political cartoons, as useful in his instruction. Similar to Ms. Pullen, Mr. Clark believed that students were capable of historical thinking. However, Mr. Clark thought that most of his students had not engaged in historical thinking prior to entering his class. He ultimately thought that social studies learning should be focused on historical facts. Nonetheless, he believed that historical thinking could be taught, and in his opinion, the best method of doing this was to "make use of primary sources as much as possible." Although he utilized digital primary historical sources (similarly to Ms. Pullen) in a teacher-centered format where, in his words, he would "shock" students rather than engage in their analysis, Mr. Clark felt that their use was beneficial in terms of helping to engage students in historical thinking.

Ms. Lewin stated that digital primary historical sources were an excellent means of encouraging historical thinking among her students, and that her students were "definitely capable" of engaging in these thought processes. However, she described her students as "low functioning." Because of this, Ms. Lewin said that she was limited in the type of digital primary source that she could use. She found that her students responded enthusiastically and excitedly to digital primary historical sources that were visual in nature, but frowned upon those that were text-based. She explained that students responded to opportunities to work with visual digital primary historical sources because many of her students read below their grade level and often found text-based sources to be frustrating. In her words:

They love doing the art—they love everything about primary sources minus the text and they hate that because it's really harder for them to decipher. Like we tried reading a little bit of Shakespeare and it was a disaster because they're so low functioning. Their reading's poor to begin with, and then, these sentences aren't making sense to them, and then their reading's so slow that nobody else is really even understanding what the sentence was to begin with ... I think they'd rather *not* do the text-based primary sources.

Ms. Lewin observed that reading was a "*huge* issue" for her students and she used her students' reading level as rational for using visual digital primary historical sources. As she said, "what I think is really hard, is to find things at their reading level." Students' limited reading ability was noted during the observation, as some students clearly had difficulty reading text from a twentieth-century historian's description of the fall of Rome. Guided reading questions that Ms. Lewin had provided seemed to help students navigate the text.

Avoiding Historical Thinking

Two of the teachers in this study, Ms. Mather and Mr. Mitchell, tended to avoid historical thinking activities with their students. Both of these teachers felt that their students lacked the necessary skills to engage in what they conceive of as historical thinking. Perhaps not coincidentally, both of these teachers reported using primary historical sources at low rates, and stated that they did not intend to utilize a primary historical source in the near future.

Although Ms. Mather claimed that her students might be able to do more advanced historical thinking activities if she put the time into it, she stated that the way that schools were organized limited opportunities to complete historical thinking activities. Ms. Mather believed that her students could "know the facts" in terms of dates, people, and places, but due to the curriculum and an emphasis on standardized tests has pushed students to memorize information, she did not think she had the instructional time to engage students in higher order thinking. Ms. Mather described an activity in which the class read Hammurabi's Code as piquing student interest and understanding, but said that because students were not necessarily able to engage in higher order thinking on their own. Ms. Mather described such activities as time-consuming and infrequent. Although the focus on low level information was not Ms. Mather's ideal pedagogy, it was typical particularly given what she viewed as time constraints and a broad curriculum. As a result, in Ms. Mather's words, "most of the things other than just lectures have to be skipped." Ms. Mather's two classroom observations reflected this teacher-centered focus. These classes consisted of a warm-up vocabulary activity followed by notes from an overhead projector and then a textbook-based map activity that was completed in groups.

Mr. Mitchell also limited the type of digital primary historical sources that he used, but instead of limiting these uses based on curriculum restraints, Mr. Mitchell claimed that the achievement levels of his students limited his ability to using primary historical sources. Mr. Mitchell's world history class was composed of low achieving students. When he did use primary historical sources, which was quite limited, Mr. Mitchell said that he preferred to use digital primary historical sources that were visual in nature, such as paintings and maps. He based the limited use of such resources to the low reading level of his students with numerous students reading below grade level and limited as English language learners. In his words, "if you're reading on a 3rd or 4th grade level in 10th grade, it's tough." He therefore portrayed himself as "limited" with regard to the types of digital primary historical sources that he could utilize. However, he used maps "all the time," and while studying the Renaissance, the class looked at paintings. While the class as a whole "occasionally" read excerpts of primary historical sources from different time periods such as the Enlightenment or Italian unification, Mr. Mitchell said that he found it difficult to do this because he often had trouble locating primary historical sources that were on the reading level of his students.

Mr. Mitchell defined historical thinking as "thinking about the ways we view the past." He expressed that his students were capable of doing this in a very basic, literal sense. In other words, they understood the idea that people may have dissimilar ways of looking at the past, but that they "struggle[d] when it comes to any kind of sophisticated reflection on why people think about the past the way they do." As a result of this, he said that he had to be "pretty limited" in the amount of both digital and non-digital primary historical sources that he uses. While he had tried to help his students understand the context of past events, he had difficulties because of the students' limited reading ability. Consequentially, he felt as if he must stick to what he referred to as the "basic facts" of a historical event, such as what occurred, when, where, and the participants.

It was clear from interviews, observations, and document analysis that each teacher participant was interested in utilizing primary sources in their instruction. Each participant defined historical thinking differently, but they all described it as a higher order thinking process. However, some participants perceived their students as incapable of historical thinking or perceived the curriculum as imposing constraints to using primary historical resources. These perceptions influenced the extent to which participants were willing to use digital primary historical sources in their classrooms.

DISCUSSION, IMPLICATIONS, AND CONCLUSIONS

Although most of the teachers in this study viewed their students as capable of historical thinking at different levels, each believed that the use of digital primary historical sources could help students develop higher-order thinking skills and they all had some interest in using digital primary sources in their instruction. Perceived student abilities and curriculum restraints limited some participants from actually using the digital primary historical sources in their classroom.

Findings in this study support Rogers' (1995) contention that an innovation's compatibility with existing pedagogical understandings has a strong influence on its adoption. Every teacher in this study had an Internet connection in their classroom and therefore the ability to acquire digital primary historical sources. However, participants utilized digital primary historical sources at different rates and used different types of sources based on their beliefs as to their compatibility with student abilities. For some, compatibility was a more important influence on the adoption of this innovation than availability.

Although primary historical sources can lead to historical thinking, in this study they were used mainly "to convey information about the past," and not necessarily to encourage higher order thinking (Barton, 2005, p. 752). Mr. Lukas (who taught an honors class) was the only exception, pursuing activities with his students that, as Seixas (1998) put it, enable students to "read historical texts in dynamic tension with their historical contexts" (p. 314). This is a similar approach to how Mason et al. (2000) advocate for technology use, namely that it should be integrated "seamlessly" into content (p. 109).

Teacher Educators

The results of this study have direct implications for teacher education. As digital primary historical sources are used in increasing numbers, teacher educators must prepare pre-service teachers for how to take advantage of these learning tools; not merely for the sake of using the technology itself, but in a way that extends social studies content and allows students to do something that they otherwise would not be able to.

It was apparent in this study that digital primary historical sources that were visual in nature were regarded by teachers as better suited for, or in the words of Rogers (1995), more "compatible" with teaching world history (p. 224). Teachers in this study made decisions about using text-based digital primary historical sources given the level of text complexity and their perceptions of the abilities of their students. The complexity of text served as a barrier to digital primary historical source use. One way to work through this barrier might be to have teachers develop pedagogically arranged electronic portfolios of digital primary historical sources. These portfolios would essentially be web-based, annotated bibliographies in which the digital source and teaching strategies that might go along with this are electronically stored. By deciding which sources to include (or exclude), teachers would be thinking about the content while simultaneously designing instructional strategies that they might use to teach it. This could then potentially foster the development of appropriate, context-specific questions. These portfolios could be arranged so that there are different categories for the different subjects within the social studies, such as United States history, world history, or local history.

Digital history teaching portfolios might include visual and text-based digital primary sources, but pre-service teachers should be made aware that text resources may require more scaffolding. Developing these scaffolds might present opportunities for pre-service teachers to engage in valuable learning, as they create reading guides and/or "translate" the text for their portfolio. This would once again allow pre-service teachers to engage in the content while pedagogically pondering how this content might be taught and simultaneously providing opportunities to research the effects of this on teaching and learning. Portfolios need not be limited to primary historical sources, as secondary sources could be included as well, reflecting Barton's (2005) contention that secondary sources "tend to be more reliable" than "any single primary source," as there is a greater likelihood that they are free from bias (p. 746).

CONCLUSION

This study demonstrated that teacher beliefs about historical thinking as well as student achievement level served as a mediating factor for teachers as they selected instructional approaches in their classrooms. Each teacher in this study had Internet access and, to some extent, a desire to use primary historical sources in their instruction. Although not every participant believed that their students were capable of historical thinking and curriculum constraints limited some participants with regard to the extent to which they thought primary historical sources could be used in their classes, there was a general belief among teachers in this study that digital primary historical source use could aid in higher-order thinking among students. Participants examined digital primary historical sources' compatibility (or lack thereof) through the filters of curriculum and student abilities as they determined the extent to which sources could be used and the type of source that was used. Some participants were reticent to use text-based primary historical sources for fear of students not being able to read the material, and thus often preferred sources that were visual in nature. The results of this study have implications for teachers and teacher educators, as they may design and construct different strategies to facilitate the process by which teachers engage their students in historical thinking through the use of digital primary historical sources.

REFERENCES

Barton, K. C. (2005). Primary sources in history: Breaking through the myths. *Phi Delta Kappan, 86*(10), 745–753.

Braun, J., & Risinger, F. (1999). *Surfing social studies.* Washington, DC: National Council for the Social Studies.

Cohen, D. J., & Rosenzweig, R. (2006). *Digital history: A guide to gathering, preserving, and presenting the past on the web.* Philadelphia: University of Pennsylvania Press.

Erickson, F. (1986). Qualitative methods in research on teaching. In M. C. Wittrock (Ed.), *Handbook of research on teaching* (pp. 119–161). New York: Macmillan.

Friedman, A. M. (2004). *Digital primary source use in world history and world geography* (Doctoral dissertation, University of Virginia, 2004). *Dissertation Abstracts International, 65,* 2958.

Friedman, A. M. (2006a). World history teachers' use of digital primary sources: The effect of training. *Theory and Research in Social Education, 34*(1), 124–141.

Friedman, A. M. (2006b). State standards and digital primary sources: A divergence. *Contemporary Issues in Technology and Teacher Education* [Online serial], *6*(3). Available: http://www.citejournal.org/vol6/iss3/socialstudies/article1.cfm

Hicks, D., & Ewing, E. (2003). Bringing the world into the classroom with online global newspapers. *Social Education, 67*(3), 134–139.

Kobrin, D. (1996). *Beyond the textbook-teaching history using documents and primary sources.* Portsmouth, NH: Heinemann.

Lévesque, S. (2008*). Thinking historically: Educating students for the twenty-first century.* Toronto, ON: University of Toronto Press.

Library of Congress. (2002). Library of Congress Learning Page. *The historians sources': Types of primary sources.* Retrieved on September 14, 2006 from: http://memory.loc.gov/learn/lessons/psources/types.html.

Mason, C., Berson, M., Diem, R., Hicks, D., Lee, J., & Dralle, T. (2000). Guidelines for using technology to prepare social studies teachers. *Contemporary Issues in Technology and Teacher Education* [Online serial], *1*(1). Available: http://www.citejournal.org/vol1/iss1/currentissues/socialstudies/article1.htm

Maxwell, J. (1996). *Qualitative research design: An interactive approach.* Thousand Oaks, CA: Sage.

Miles, M. B., & Huberman, A. M. (1994). *An expanded sourcebook: Qualitative data analysis.* Thousand Oaks, CA: Sage.

National Center for History in the Schools. (n.d.). *Definition of standards.* Retrieved on July 15, 2007 from: http://nchs.ucla.edu/standards/dev-5-12b.html.

National Center for History in the Schools. (2005). *Overview of standards in historical thinking.* Retrieved on March 7, 2006 from: http://nchs.ucla.edu/standards/thinking5-12.html.

National Council for the Social Studies. (1994). *Expectations for excellence: Curriculum standards for social studies.* Washington, DC: National Council for the Social Studies.

Parsad, B., & Jones, J. (2005). *Internet access in U.S. public schools and classrooms: 1994–2003.* (NCES 2005-015). U.S. Department of Education. Washington, DC: National Center for Education Statistics.

Patton, M. (1990). *Qualitative evaluation and research methods.* Newbury Park, CA: Sage.

Rogers, E. M. (1995). *Diffusion of innovations* (4th ed.). New York: The Free Press.

Schwandt, T. (2001). *Dictionary of qualitative inquiry.* Thousand Oaks, CA: Sage.

Seixas, P. (1998). Student teachers thinking historically. *Theory and Research in Social Education, 26*(3), 310–341.

Shiroma, D. (2000). *Using primary sources on the internet to teach and learn history.* Bloomington, IN: ERIC Clearinghouse for Social Studies/Social Science Education. ERIC Document 442 739.

Singleton, L. R., & Giese, J. R. (1999). Using online primary sources with students. *The Social Studies, 90*(4), 148–151.

VanSledright, B. A., & Frankes, L. (2000). Concept- and strategic- knowledge development in historical study: A comparative exploration in two fourth grade classrooms. *Cognition and Instruction, 18*(2), 239–283.

VanSledright, B. (2002). *In search of America's past.* New York: Teachers College Press.

Yeager, E. A., & Davis, O. L. (1995). Between campus and classroom: Secondary student-teachers' thinking about historical texts. *Journal of Research and Development in Education, 29*(1), 1–8.

Yeager, E. A., & Wilson, E. K. (1997). Teaching historical thinking in the social studies methods course: A case study. *The Social Studies, 88*(3), 121–126.

SECTION 4

RESEARCH REVIEWS

CHAPTER 10

UTILIZING THE POWER OF TECHNOLOGY FOR TEACHING WITH GEOGRAPHY

Tina L. Heafner

ABSTRACT

Geography provides a lens for understanding interaction between humans and the environment, explaining location and the physical nature of the Earth, and defining differences between places and the people who occupy them. These interactions characterize cultures, communities, and the global society, and provide valuable insights into life and learning. Geography is an integral part of human development and education, however it sits on the periphery of the K–12 curriculum. This secondary role results from the perception of geography as a static and isolated content area as well as from the utilization of static and one-dimensional geographic resources. Rethinking geography as a visually-based, integrative, interactive, and engaging subject area through the use of technology can enliven the field and can lead to more active and interesting student experiences. Meaningful technology use in geography instruction can shift the field from its current mostly static focus on geographic concepts to more dynamic experiences focused on patterns, relationships, and change over time. This chapter presents a purposeful literature

Research on Technology in Social Studies Education, pages 207–230
Copyright © 2009 by Information Age Publishing

review focused on a conceptual overview of geography teaching and learning that are constructivist, active, technology-supported, and integrative.

INTRODUCTION

Geography is a framework that can be used to organize our understanding of people and the environment, thus, making the study of geography essential knowledge for all citizens in an ever-increasing interdependent global community. Geography fundamentally influences and connects cultures, societies, and ways of life (ESRI, 2007). Geography also provides a lens for explaining and comprehending why things are located where they are on Earth, differences between places and people, and human interaction with the environment (Association of American Geographers, 2007b). Despite its recognized value in understanding current global climates and societies, geography instruction in the K–12 curriculum fails to live up to its potential. This chapter presents a purposeful literature review focused on supporting a conceptual framework about geography teaching and learning that are constructivist, active, technology-supported, and integrative and captures the value of geographic knowledge in shaping tomorrow's citizens as an emphasis within social studies education.

Social studies educators are expected to provide their students with opportunities to learn geographic content in active and engaging ways. Consider the following vignette that describes an instructional lesson in a ninth grade honors world history class in an urban high school in North Carolina.

Students are studying a unit on environmental geography. The teacher's learning goal for this unit of study was to help students understand the direct relationship between economic, political, and social decision-making and the environment. The teacher also expected students to understand the importance of becoming well-informed decision-makers in a globally interdependent society. On the first day of the unit, the teacher provided a focus for class discussion by reading the following dialogue that she had created from an actual conversation with a friend.

> At lunch the two adults are discussing the progress in their town. Let's join in their conversation. . . .
>
> Scott, grabbing a piece of bread, asks Kim, "Have you seen the new construction over by Lowes' Hardware?"
>
> Kim responds, "Yes, I think they are building a new Target. That will be great. Now we'll have more variety in shopping. We'll have Target to go along with Walmart, Kohls, and Staples." She adds, "There's a new Lowes Food down the road and there are renovations being made to the Food Lion next door. That should give Harris Teeter some competition."

After a brief pause to consume a bite of soup, Kim continues, "Did you know that the city is planning to build a new road through town connecting to the main highway? I'm sure it will bring in many more fast food restaurants. It will be nice to have different choices of restaurants. I remember when we moved to Mapleville just seven years ago, there were only four restaurants in town and they all served the same country cooking. I like variety and having options of restaurants will make this town more attractive and I'm sure it will continue to grow. You know competition is good."

Scott, who is much older than Kim, comments, "I remember when there was nothing in Mapleville," reminiscing about what life was like when he moved here sixty years ago. Scott continued, "Things have really changed. The convenience is nice but the town has really changed and I'm not sure that it's for the better."

Once the dialogue was presented, the teacher then directed student thinking by stating, "Americans claim that progress is our most important product. It is our contribution to the global community and builds a mentality that more is always better." The teacher asked, "Is economic progress always good? What are the costs and benefits of decisions made for economic gain?" Student opinions flowed and most seemed to favor convenience and prosperity without much consideration of potential cost or tradeoffs. Students responded with a variety of examples from their own experiences in their city and neighborhood as they noted many similar changes and greater choice options as described in the vignette. The mentality of more is better was the prevailing majority student opinion in the discussion.

The teacher continued the class discussion by encouraging students to "contemplate the historical and current impact of economically driven decisions on people, cultures, and the environment." Students were asked to share their initial thoughts and to address the following questions: "Who does not benefit from economic progress? and, How is the environment affected?" These questions set the stage for the inquiry-based task students were assigned. The teacher explained that students would be working through a case study to evaluate the environmental changes to the Aral Sea.

To begin the case study analysis, students were presented with some contextual information about the Aral Sea. Soviet propaganda posters and images of the great agricultural nation diverting water from the Aral Sea to irrigate rice fields were shown to capture student interest. The teacher displayed interactive and visually intuitive animated locational maps of the Aral Sea using GPS and mapping software [e.g., Google Earth] supported by static photos to document the environmental and physical changes in the Aral Sea over the last fifty years. Images included dry sea beds, stranded and decaying ships, abandoned fishing villages and towns no longer located near water, animations of the shrinking of the Aral Sea, and the current topography of the Aral Sea. The teacher then posed these questions:

"What is happening to the Aral Sea and why? What are the economical, environmental, social, cultural, political, and historical consequences of these changes?" Students were then given a resource handout providing directions for a problem-based learning experience, as well as Internet resources for researching the problem. The teacher described the dilemma of the Aral Sea as "a conflict among economic, social, political, and environmental issues" and the teacher provided multilevel map analysis using Geographic Information System (GIS) databases that visualize population trends in density, migration, mortality statistics, and health issues; environmental shifts in climate, precipitation, vegetation, and land use; and infrastructural changes in streets, roads, settlements, and industry. The students analyzed these maps, defined relationships between and among the data, and interpreted these findings. The learning process required students to formulate research questions, evaluate maps and visual representations for interpreting, analyzing and synthesizing data, and use spatial patterns and relationships in investigating a real-life problem.

RETHINKING GEOGRAPHY INSTRUCTION

The mode of instruction presented in the vignette just presented was grounded in a constructivist pedagogy that promotes higher order thinking through inquiry. Geography was at the forefront of the content analysis suggested by the teacher and technology was the medium for conceptualizing, contextualizing, and evaluating changes in the Aral Sea region. This classroom activity demonstrated a pedagogical approach of teaching with geography through the use of technology in contrast to traditional forms of teaching geography in isolation using only maps and static images.

Regretfully, this classroom is the exception on many levels to what occurs in K–12 classrooms across the nation. With the increased pressures imposed by high stakes accountability as well as fear of sanctions and punishments, schools systems and teachers have shied away from utilizing methodologies such as those described in the vignette above for emphases on behaviorist-based pedagogy and test preparation strategies (Hargrove et al., 2000; Heafner, Lipscomb, & Rock, 2006; Lintner, 2006; Neill & Guisbond, 2005). Even more disconcerting is that geography is rarely recognized as a core subject within state curriculum standards (Gildersleeve, 2004; Howarth & Mountain, 2004; Kenney, 2004; Lewis, 2004; Morrill, 2004); thus, geography instruction is often left to the discretion of individual schools or teachers (Howarth & Mountain, 2004; Sharma, 2007). Unless students are enrolled in an elective or Advanced Placement (AP) geography course, there is no guarantee that they will have the opportunity to learn geography.

This subordinate role of geography within the public school curriculum seems contradictory as curriculum designers have turned their attention to standards for educating the global citizen. Many states have begun to revise their standards for students and for teacher education candidates to include preparation for 21st century skills, which emphasize core academic knowledge of history and geography, global awareness, financial and civic literacy (Partnership for 21st Century Skills, 2007). Geography as an afterthought or a common indulgence will not suffice in the age of globalization. Perceptions of geography and geography instruction need to change. This process begins by reshaping opinions about geography and with an understanding of the limitations of existing approaches to teaching geography while rethinking current practices through the lens of new technologies that can enhance both student learning and the value of geography.

Even within the current emphasis on curriculum streamlining (i.e., limiting the curriculum to core tested subjects such as writing, reading, and mathematics), geography should be valued as a central part of K–12 curricula. Geography enables students to build spatial, relational, and environmental understanding, encourages openness and responsiveness to diverse cultures and perspectives, promotes knowledge and evaluation of population growth patterns and impacts on local, national and global communities, and supports comparative understanding of world regions and political systems. Geography serves a broader purpose of promoting global understanding (Lidstrone & Stoltman, 2004) and global mindedness (Merryfield et al., 2008) that is integral to life and learning (ESRI, 2002; GESP, 1994; Kenny, 2004; Morrill, 2004). Rather than being in conflict with or absent from existing curriculum, geography can support the achievement of multidisciplinary curriculum (Hinde & Ekiss, 2005; Howarth & Mountain, 2004). The curriculum streamlining movement should be viewed not as a barrier to teaching geography, but as an invitation to rethink the role of geography for improving teaching and learning (Kerski, Linn, & Gindele, 2005; Lewis, 2004) and as a model for promoting 21st knowledge and skills (Partnership for 21st Century Skills, 2007).

This chapter presents a literature review in support of teaching with geography. Specifically, the chapter includes research support for why geography and technology are a good fit, how technology can enhance the geography instruction, the effectiveness of technology integration in geography, the impact of technology integration on K–12 student learning, and applications of geo-technologies. This purposeful literature review is focused on supporting a conceptual framework about geography teaching and learning that are constructivist, active, technology-supported, and integrative.

Traditional approaches to teaching geography emphasize didactic methods that promote isolated instruction of subject matter content. Thus, curricula focus on *teaching about* geography and rely upon static images and text-based resources. Passivity is the preferred mode of learning and content is often dry and lacks depth. Emphases are placed upon breadth of knowledge of places and locations with memorization as the key skill. In contract *teaching with* geography encourages students to engage with geographic concepts through inquiry and self-discovery. Tools for learning include technology mediated resources such as interactive and visually intuitive maps. Content is interwoven among core subjects and integrated across content areas. These constructivist pedagogical methods, technology enhanced instructional tools, and integrative content approaches change students' relationships with information and the ways in which learning takes place; redefining both content and learning processes.

PURPOSE OF TEACHING WITH GEOGRAPHY

As presented in the opening description of a secondary world history class, the transition from teaching geography to teaching with geography is an important pedagogical shift, particularly given the demands of standardized testing and state mandated curriculum standards. Teachers are faced with a barrage of external accountability measures related to students' performance on mandated tests. A student's success or failure on these tests is directly related to funding and/or sanctions. These pressures drive teachers to de-emphasize curricula that are not tested or included within the state's content standards (Kohn, 2000; Rock et al., 2006; von Zastrow & Janc, 2004). This is of grave concern as in many states geography content standards are not an integral part of the core content standards nor do they have an independent role within the curriculum (Gildersleeve, 2004; Kenney, 2004; Lewis, 2004; Morrill, 2004). Geography is often integrated within a broader social studies curriculum and is rarely taught as a standalone-subject (Sharma, 2007). The undefined role of geography, as a byproduct of the placement of geography under the umbrella the social studies, engenders an internal competition across the social studies disciplines for time in the curriculum (Howarth & Mountain, 2004). Geography finds itself jockeying for position with other social science disciplines within the social studies such as history, civics, economics, and political science.

This competition for time among social studies areas is also problematic given that social studies standards fall on the periphery of the dominate curriculum of reading, writing, mathematics, and science as defined by No Child Left Behind (Lewis, 2004; Rock et al., 2006; VanFossen, 2005). As social studies is marginalized in an era of high stakes testing, an internal battle brews among the social sciences as to what content is essential and must be maintained within a slimmed-down social studies curriculum. In many states, geography is losing this curriculum diet and is slowly vanishing from the menu of K–12 curriculum standards (Kenney, 2004; Sharma, 2007).

As geography content takes a backseat to emphasized and essential curricula, educators need to rethink the role of geography and approaches for teaching geography. In the age of high stakes accountability, a paradigm shift from teaching geography in isolation to *teaching with* geography becomes essential to ensure the survival of geography. Many curriculum areas share relevance with geography, including science and mathematics, but these courses have not been effectively integrated with geography (Howarth & Mountain, 2004). Geography can become core content to multiple disciplines rather than fighting for independent status in an already shrinking curriculum (Hinde & Ekiss, 2005).

This integration stance is supported by the Environmental Systems Research Institute, Inc., (ESRI), a private corporate that promotes geography education through an integrative model in elementary, middle, and secondary schools (1998). In many ways this integration approach is well suited for technological applications in geography. In their statement on guidelines for integrating technology in social studies, Mason et al. (2000), argued that such integration can expand and contextualize student learning of content. The next section looks specifically at this notion that technology and geography are a good fit and together enhance social studies teaching and learning.

GEOGRAPHY AND TECHNOLOGY: A GOOD FIT

Effective technology use creates learning environments that are student centered and inquiry-based and that engage students in authentic tasks that promote high order thinking (International Society for Technology in Education, 2007). This parallels ESRI's endorsement of geography as a means for weaving science and the social sciences together to explain and understand human interaction. This integration model draws from an educational paradigm which is constructivist, inquiry-based, exploratory, problem-solving, and individualized and mirrors many of the arguments for technology integration. Constructivist pedagogical principles emphasize student-centered instruction and technology fosters this through the development of learning environments which are visually appealing, interactive, self-paced, and provide self- learning feedback (Zeger et al., 2002). Merging technology and geography supports ESRI's (1998) recommended integration model and encourages the reconceptualization of geography instruction.

The use of new technologies in social studies (particularly computer-based technologies) requires new approaches to learning and new ways of understanding. Doolittle and Hicks (2003) suggest the use of technology engages students in inquiry learning and promotes high order thinking. More specifically, technology has the power to transform geography instruction from a didactic, passive experience to a more interactive, constructivist process (Kerski, 2003; Zeger et al., 2002). For example, Internet technologies enable access to a wealth of geographic content including rich images, interactive maps, and spatial data that can reshape the learning process and encourage student inquiry (Kerski et al., 2005; Krishnan, 1999). Inquiry approaches in geography contrast to traditional approaches to teaching geography that are grounded in behaviorist theory. Behaviorist instructional practices are teacher-centered and often rely on static or flat map images and textbooks for the transference of knowledge about geographic concepts. Flat paper maps are "what you see is what you get" resources and they lack the capability of digital maps to present many layers of information (ERSI, 2002, p. 1).

Learning geography within a traditional pedagogical paradigm is limited to content defined by the teacher, while new technologies can shift the focus to students' use of geography tools and content. These constructivist approaches to learning geography encourage student initiated investigations and promote problem-based learning with relevant and meaningful geographic content. A shift from traditional methods to constructivist pedagogy engenders a learning environment which capitalizes on technology's value as an educational aid and motivator of student interest (Baker, 2005, Chedid, 2005; Heafner, 2004). The constructivist pedagogical paradigm does not utilize new technology as a replacement for traditional technologies and pedagogies, but rather promotes new technology for enhancing and extending learning beyond traditional methods and resources.

Teaching with technology enables an interdisciplinary approach to geography that builds inquiry oriented, hands-on, research based, and problem-solving learning experiences (Baker, 2005; Kerski, 2003). In alignment with constructivist pedagogy, the integration of technology and internet services can promote student collaboration and communication (i.e., electronic mail, chat rooms, instant messaging, discussion boards, blogs, wikis, listservs, podcasts, and video conferencing), which effectively supports adolescent student learning (Langhorst, 2007; Martindale & Wiley, 2005; Solem, 2000). Technology applications associated with geography, such as mapping software, GIS, and internet-based mapping enable a constructivist approach to teaching and capitalize on the benefits technology for visually demonstrating geographical concepts (Baker, 2005; Shelli, Strong, & Hannon, 2007). Each of these technologies has the power to enhance student learning of geography; however, effective teaching with technology requires careful consideration of the role technology and meaningful use of technology to promote issues-based, inquiry methods in geography (Shelli et al., 2007; Solem, 2000). Teachers must purposefully select technology-based resources and effectively use these innovative tools to scaffolding student geographical understanding.

ENHANCING GEOGRAPHY WITH TECHNOLOGY

Traditional resources such as maps and globes in teaching about geography are limited in their ability to present the complexity of geographic concepts and multiple layers of geographic understanding. Concepts such as topography prove challenging when students cannot infer differences from a static map. New technologies are transforming student access to geography content and the processes they use to comprehend and interpret geographic information. Teaching geography with the aid of computer-related technologies such as GIS "fundamentally alters the manner of teaching in the classroom . . . and alters the manner of learning" (Kerski, 2003, p. 135), so as to make geography an exciting and relevant topic (ESRI 2002; Green, 2001; Kerski et al., 2005). Web-enhanced classroom geography materials can enable more resourceful use of class time through the use of repositories of images, video, sound, and real-time data to facilitate effective geography instruction (Lemke & Ritter, 2000). A significant benefit of educational technology, particularly digital resources, is the visual enhancement of these resources over print or non-digital resources, although these static images hold value in the learning process. Instructional goals in geography expect students to understand dynamic spatial concepts of patterns, relationships, and change over time. When students study these concepts with static non-digital images, they are limited in their ability to make connections, analyze multiple layers of information simultaneously, and visualize change over time. Students might see differences, but if they are unable to manipulate or layer maps, they may not recognize the relationships because images are presented individually. Reliance on static, non-digital images makes it difficult for teachers to convey complex spatial concepts. Digital geographic resources provide a more meaningful method for demonstrating dynamic geographic concepts through attractive, appealing, and engaging video and animation (Lemberg & Stoltman, 1999). With the use of multimedia-based representations, students can visualize and conceptualize dynamic spatial concepts. Digital maps allow students to link geographical and descriptive information using layers representing different themes or map features. Animation and digital video facilitate student observation of change over time as patterns emerge through of the presentation of sequentially presented images, thus, enabling students to visualize relationships.

Geography and technology are well suited as their pedagogical structures are analogous and visually based; hence, technology has the ability to effectively scaffold student learning of geographical concepts (Svingen, 1994). Geography by nature is visually based and teachers draw from illustrative resources such as data, charts, diagrams, graphics, images, maps, pictures, drawings, and photographs to explain geographical concepts and promote understanding of causality between and among dynamic concepts. As students develop spatial knowledge they will often visualize geography content including physical, human, and environmental relationships (Jain & Getis, 2003) and geography-based technologies (or geo-technologies) offer students enhanced resources for building these understandings. Geo-technologies such as Geographic Information Systems (GIS), digital video, animations, electronic atlases, geography software, and the web-based mapping resources can be used to create rich learning experiences for geography students at any level. Lemberg and Stoltman (1999) argue that "geography has become the model discipline for the application of geo-spatial software, data, and the use of models to study Earth" (p. 65).

Geographic Information Systems is a particularly important data-based geo-technology. In operation, Geographic Information Systems are collections of geographically referenced information that are visually presented and can be manipulated and layered for analysis through the use of computer hardware, software, and geographic data. GIS plays an important role in many aspects of daily life and is an essential tool in community, business, and economic decision-making (AAG, 2007b; ESRI, 2002; ERSI, 2007). Geographic Information Systems can support geography instruction and technology integration in K–12 education. When combined with other instructional approaches GIS resources can enable students to: interact with local, regional, national, and international phenomena; apply research methods; cultivate visual literacy skills; analyze various and diverse perspectives; perform metadata analysis; build spatial and relational knowledge; develop technological literacy; and learn through doing (ESRI, 1998).

Lemberg and Stoltman (1999) tout the "power of technology to deepen the teaching and learning of the discipline [geography] at the pre-college level" (p. 65). They provide four reasons why the use of technology is important to the study of geography. These include: the application to local issues, environmental problem-solving through cause-effect relationships, enhancing student motivation and interest through the study of relevant and meaningful issues, and the transference of technological knowledge and skills along with discipline specific knowledge. Technology serves multi-purposed roles in each of these four areas by enabling students to develop and improve their decision-making skills, by broadening students' awareness of diverse global, cultural, and individual perspectives through communication and collaboration, and by exposing students to new technologies that build skills pertinent to participation in the global community (Mason et al., 2000, Solem et al., 2003; Urwin & Maguire, 1990). To provide insights into the potential new technologies offer in supporting geographic understanding, a review of research on technology-mediated instruction follows.

RESEARCH ON TECHNOLOGY INTEGRATION IN GEOGRAPHY

With the expansion of geography-related technologies research is emerging that assesses the effectiveness of technology to impact K–12 student achievement and understanding of geography (Kerski, 2003; Lemke & Ritter, 2000; Linn, Kerski, & Wither, 2005). Some of this emerging research is focused on college-aged students, addressing technology's impact on academic achievement in geography. This research relies primarily on anecdotal evidence from practical applications with students and touts the benefits of technology for improving student motivation, interest, and engagement (Heafner, 2004). Although the focus of research has been on the utility of technology, other areas including cognitive limitations to using technology in geography have been recognized (Lemberg & Stoltman, 1999). For example, mapping and data analysis software such as Internet-based mapping or GIS can only display maps and provide methods for manipulating or layering data. Technology alone will neither identify a relationship, draw a conclusion, interpret data, solve a problem, resolve an issue, nor make a decision. These tasks require that students interact with maps and geographic data. Instead, learners must actively use technology for data analysis directed at making informed analytical data-based decisions through critical higher order evaluations. This level of cognition requires teacher intervention to support the learning process and student engagement with technology. To achieve these goals, teachers must structure learning experiences so that geography-related technologies match learning tasks and learners' cognitive capabilities (Solem et al., 2003).

Additional research suggests that teachers should scaffold students' work as they use complex geography-related technologies and develop higher order thinking skills. Such multifaceted learning environments enable teachers and students to utilize geography resources appropriately and effectively to maximize the potential geo-technologies offer (Lemke & Ritter, 2000; Linn et al., 2005).

A larger body of research has begun to evaluate technology's ability to enhance learning and improve learning outcomes in geography education in higher education (Brey, 2000; Feeney, 2003; Jain & Getis, 2003; Rich, Pitman, & Gosper, 2000; Rich, Robinson, & Bednarz, 2000; Ritter & Lemke, 2000; Rutherford & Lloyd, 2001; Zeger et al., 2002). Results of studies evaluating the effectiveness of technology for supporting geography instruction in higher education indicate that students are increasingly making use of communication technologies for engaging in social dialogues (Rich et al., 2000; Ritter & Lemke, 2000). Computer-related technologies such as interactive maps and GIS improved student comprehension of geographic concepts and increased content knowledge (Brey, 2000; Jain & Getis, 2003; Rutherford & Lloyd, 2001). Students enrolled in technology supported geography courses experienced a higher degree of satisfaction with labs and lessons utilizing GIS or GPS or online learning modules over traditional approaches such as lecture, textbooks, and maps (Feeney, 2003; Rich et al., 2000; Zeger et al., 2002).

Most studies at the college level on the use of geo-technologies tend to emphasize the overall educative value of technology and have not critiqued the disaggregate influence of technology on individual student learning of geography. Various student groups are impacted differently when technology-mediated instruction is provided in geography courses although direct links between student achievement and technology integration may not be evident in summative data findings (Proctor & Richardson, 1997). To explore the added value of technology in supporting geography instruction, Jain and Getis (2003) conducted a study of the impact of Internet-based instruction on student achievement in an introductory physical geography college-level course. They used an experimental design with half of the students receiving instruction through traditional methods while the other half learned the same content but through an Internet-based interactive module. The researchers evaluated the effects on student achievement of the two groups through matched paired analyses of post-test scores. Overall results indicated that there were no significant differences in achievement between the two groups; however, raw data suggested a slight tendency for scores to be higher among the group that received the Internet-based instruction. Jain and Getis (2003) recommended a more in-depth analysis of variability within and among groups to determine how technology can better support individual student knowledge and comprehension of geography. They encouraged the use of technology in geography courses, given its capability to differentiate instruction. Jain and Getis (2003) further suggested that although technology did not have a statistically significant impact on overall student achievement, it did effectively support some students.

Rutherford and Lloyd (2001) conducted a study to evaluate the role of geo-technology as an instructional strategy in a college-level world geography course. Specifically, they evaluated overall student achievement by comparing the effectiveness of technology-based instruction through online learning modules which utilized interactive mapping software with didactic and lecture-based instruction which emphasized textbook readings and map resources. They also evaluated modes of learning by identifying differences in achievement based on ethnicity and gender and at different levels of student cognitive learning. Although significant differences in overall student achievement were not revealed, there were significant differences between ethnic groups and between males and females. The use of technology reduced traditional ethnic and gender gaps in student achievement and supported geography learning within subgroups that was not evident in summative data findings. Additional analyses were performed to determine the impact of technology on cognitive learning. Variations in pedagogical approaches (traditional teacher-centered lecture-based instruction verses technology driven student-centered constructivist methods) produced statistically significant differences in student achievement in geography. Rutherford and Lloyd's (2001) findings suggested that the use of technology can improve student comprehension and is more effective than lecture. In summary, despite the lack of overall statistically significant differences in student overall achievement, a more detailed analysis of data revealed that technology does in fact improve student learning of geography and has positive impacts for marginalized student populations (Rutherford & Lloyd, 2001).

The benefits of technology in geography instruction can also be extended to students with exceptionalities. In a comparative study of the impact of technology in affecting student achievement of dyslexic college students, Feeney (2003) found that use of interactive multimedia to teach four sections of a geography lesson based on the National Geography Standards on geography improved student interest in geography as well as their content knowledge and comprehension (e.g., appreciation of content, accuracy of their knowledge, and response times for specific questions). Feeney's study compared dyslexic and non-dyslexic college students enrolled in a university geography course. Results suggest that technology enhanced instruction improved all students' odds of providing the correct answer on geography tests, with dyslexic students making larger gains than non-dyslexic students. Overall, technology produced multiple positive effects on student achievement, but was especially beneficial for improving success of dyslexic students while reducing their frustrations.

Geo-technologies, K–12 Learning, and Teacher Education

Lemberg and Stoltman (1999) conducted a review of existing research studies on K–12 student use of technology for learning geography. Their analysis revealed that there has been limited research evaluating the effectiveness of technology in impacting student learning of geography; however, their review identified the advantages of technology use in supporting real-life, collaborative, and repetitive applications of authentic content as well as students' understanding of spatial relationships and research skills. They surmised that "student learning does benefit from authentic tasks where information is applied to real problems and issues." They continued their analysis by stating that technology promotes student collaboration and discussion, while increasing "students' learning and retention levels" (p. 67). These results were affirmed by a research study of teachers' perceptions of the value of GIS in teaching and how GIS impacts student learning processes (Linn et al., 2005). According to Linn et al. (2005), geo-technologies have the power to make lessons more student-centered and promote critical thinking. Using GIS promotes "higher-order thinking skills, abstract thinking, inference, and prediction to a great degree" and students "become more critical about what they are learning" (Linn et al., 2005, p. 219).

One specific example of how technology impacts student learning can be found in Wiegand's (2003) study of 14–17-year-old students' use and understanding of choropleth maps. In particular, the study focused on the collaborative discourse of paired students as they used GIS ArcView software to design choropleth maps and then interpret these choropleth maps. Comparisons were made between paired groups of 14–15-year-old students with 16–17-year-old students as they used limited functions from the ArcView software. Wiegand (2003) found that technology was not a barrier to learning as students were able to navigate the software to accomplish their cartographic tasks from a single training session. Students' discourse demonstrated understanding of mapping strategies and the majority of the discourse was focused on making meaning of the maps students had created. Despite perceived success of the use of geo-technologies, findings did indicate potential content misunderstandings. Students struggled with directionality, numeric characteristics, and classification methods used for presenting data which led to misrepresentations of data and misinterpretations. Wiegand (2003) suggested that teacher intervention, specifically the scaffolding of cognitive processes related to constructing the misunderstood content, is essential for building student geographic knowledge and skills.

Despite the specific success stories, additional research indicates minimal use of geo-technologies to support geography education in K–12 schools. This research, in general, attributes the negligible use of geo-technologies to barriers such as: time, perceived difficulty of technology, limited knowledge of appropriate data analysis, confines of school structures, inadequate computer hardware, and lack of administrative support (Baker, 2005; Donaldson, 2000; Gatrell, 2004; Kerski, 2003; Lemberg & Stoltman, 1999). In a nationwide survey of secondary teachers who owned a GIS software package, Kerski (2003) explored instructional uses of GIS using a 33-item questionnaire addressing constructs of school access, teacher use, teacher preparation, instructional uses, technology and administrative support, and barriers to use. Kerski (2003) found that 1,900 schools or less than 5 percent of U.S. secondary schools had access to GIS software and fewer than half of the teachers owning GIS software were using it (p. 129). Only 20 percent of the teachers in the survey used GIS in more than one lesson for multiple classes. The greatest use was reported by secondary science teachers who used GIS twice as often as geography teachers. Even with limited use, 88 percent of teachers recognized the value of GIS in enhancing student learning and provided explanations of real-world relevance. Kerski (2003) attributed the lack of widespread use of GIS in secondary schools to the paradigm shift required for teaching with technology and the lack of experiential training in the applications of GIS.

In a recent review of geo-technologies, Gatrell (2004) contended that many of the problems teachers face are due to the lack of teacher training in the use of geo-technologies. Since many teacher education programs do not provide training in the use of GIS or other geographic software applications, teachers are often required to learn and master these skills on their own. This becomes problematic for teachers who are already professionally pressed for time. Professional development training in GIS often requires forty hours or more (Baker, 2005), in addition to time required to develop a comfort level using the technology to teach. Much of the professional development is geared toward learning GIS rather than modeling appropriate strategies for using GIS to promote student learning and higher order thinking (Gatrell, 2001). Gatrell (2001) has also asserted that the time expectations associated with GIS training are unreasonable and this time limitation represents the greatest barrier to K–12 teacher use of GIS. He recommended that for teachers to be adequately prepared to teach with geo-technologies such as GIS, methods for their use must be integrated into the professional education sequence. Lemberg and Stoltman (1999), ESRI (2002), and AAG (2007a) concurred with these sentiments suggesting that if teachers are to effectively use GIS in K–12 classrooms, emphasis must be given to GIS in pre-service education programs.

In addition to time, Baker (2005) has pointed out the limitations of K–12 environments, such as rigidity of school schedules, curriculum structures that isolate subject disciplines, lack of administrative support, and hardware that cannot support dynamic software. Despite existing barriers, there are significant benefits to mapping and data analysis software and these resources are essential for promoting "meaningful, problem-driven inquiries, situated in a rich context of learning with data collection, analysis, and interpretation" (Baker, 2005, p. 45). To capitalize on the benefits of technology enhanced learning while overcoming barriers to the integration of geo-technologies, Baker (2005) recommended the use of web-based GIS mapping. Although this technology does not have the full capabilities of GIS software, the functionality of Internet-based GIS mapping is better suited to the limited operations that are needed for school tasks. Baker (2005) contended that Internet-based mapping is easier to learn and use, requires less training, is more accessible, and only requires a web browser for implementation.

APPLICATIONS OF GEO-TECHNOLOGIES
IN K–12 EDUCATION

Teacher Applications

Research on the uses of technology for teaching human, physical, and environmental geography is oriented by teachers' pedagogical paradigms. Traditional teacher-centered pedagogical approaches rely on the integration of technology as a teacher tool. However, teacher applications of geo-technologies can contribute to student learning by extending access to materials beyond textbooks, atlases, and other static images (Baker & White, 2003; Lemberg & Stoltman, 1999; Rutherford & Lloyd, 2001). In many instructional settings, students are exposed to robust software applications such as GIS that are difficult for students to navigate independently. As in Wiegand's (2003) study, in such settings it is important for the teacher to provide structure and guidance to help students learn new technology skills and make sense of content. In addition, direct teacher instruction may provide a more effective method for scaffolding student understanding of complex geographic concepts (Wiegand, 2003). For example, directionality, small scale map interpretation skills, and object discrimination all might require teacher-centered heavily scaffolded instruction. Students might also misinterpret content and not recognize potential bias in data analysis or representations without structured teacher intervention and guidance (Wiegand, 2003).

Computer-related technologies provide new and innovative methods for presenting content that supports concept development and helps learners build deep understandings of content knowledge (Partnership for 21st Century Skills, 2007). Teachers can present materials such as choropleth maps, digital images and animations of concepts, statistics, graphs, charts, and other data representations all directed at higher levels of student cognition (Baker & White, 2003; Shelli et al., 2007). These resources can be used as visual aids for lectures and other teacher-centered visual interpretation exercises (Wiegand, 2003). Without these visual supports, students might not grasp spatial concepts and comprehend physical, human, and environmental relationships (Jain & Getis, 2003; Svingen, 1994). Technology can enliven traditional pedagogical approaches to interactive visual teaching and learning (Baker & White, 2003; Feeney, 2003; Langhorst, 2007). Such teaching experiences can capitalize on teacher-driven structured learning experiences; while, technology-enhanced resources serve as models for whole class inquiries, data analyses, and discussions (Shelli et al., 2007; Wiegand, 2003).

Student Applications

Several researchers have argued that geo-technologies are powerful tools that enable teachers and students to explore and analyze information in new ways by allowing students to focus on the higher order thinking skills of observation and exploration-questioning, speculation, analysis, and evolution (Kerski et al., 2005; Langhorst, 2007; Lemberg and Stoltman, 1999; Linn et al., 2005). Such student-centered approaches suggest that technology integrated should be woven into geography instruction (Baker, 2005; Kerski, 2003; Rutherford & Lloyd, 2001; Solem, 2000). Strategies for engaging students with geography through technology include: real world applications, interactive laboratories, simulations and case studies, and visual interpretation and geographic thinking (Friedman, Drakes, & Deek, 2002; Riner, Cunningham, & Johnson, 2004; Shelli et al., 2007; Solem et al., 2003).

One of the major benefits of technology integration in teaching with geography is that students are exposed to real world applications of the concepts and ideas they are learning. Real world applications allow students to work through global environmental issues while interacting with students across the globe (Bishop & Shroder, 1995; Solem et al., 2003). Students build community awareness and geographical understanding through the collaborative design of mapping software (Friedman et al., 2002; Shelli et al., 2007). Using GIS, students can explore and evaluate local health issues (Riner et al., 2004). Working with real world issues allows students opportunities to conduct critical analyses of controversial issues, determine the environmental impacts of global issues such as war or economic progress, and evaluate the benefits and negative effects of governmental policies (Bishop & Shroder, 1995; Lidstrone & Stoltman, 2004), thus, establishing the framework for global-mindedness (Merryfield et al., 2008). Methods that teachers employ to support these learning processes can include: public forum, deliberative discussion, and Socratic seminar. These student-centered strategies enhance student global understanding while developing students' research, problem-solving, communication, and collaborative skills.

Computer-related technologies such as interactive laboratories support constructivist pedagogy within geography instruction. Geo-technologies promote problem-solving techniques utilized for addressing complex human and environmental issues, such as data-driven analysis and analytical decision-making through the use of interactive mapping software like GIS (Fitzpatrick & McGuire, 2001; Lobben, 2001). Internet-based technology tools enable students to become researchers through online collaborative efforts to collect and analyze student-generated data or existing data from comprehensive databases; thus, providing real-world learning experiences that effectively scaffold student understanding of geographic concepts (Chedid, 2005; Gardner, 2003; Grant & Branch, 2005). These geo-technologies support students in data analysis by facilitating learning as students order, sort, map, and overlay data (see Annenberg Media, 2007; AAG, 2007a; ESRI, 2007; Madge & O'Connor, 2004).

Mason et al. (2000) have argued that the use of technology use in instruction with geography instruction can extend traditional instruction. Such extensions can be achieved through the use of software, websites, web-based simulations, and online case studies. These resources can provide learning experiences that promote students' cognitive skills of questioning, decision-making, and problem-solving. Working in these environments, students are presented with an issue and asked to make research-based decisions for solving conflicts like the example provided in the opening classroom vignette. Simulations afford students opportunities to test multiple decisions and evaluate possible outcomes. Case studies are similar to simulations in that they present students with a scenario and the task of making the most informed decision given the information provided. Both case studies and simulations are more effectively supported in an electronic learning environment as the complexity of the situation along with the broad scope of resources can be greatly enhanced (see Allen, 1994; Demchik, 2001; Campbell & Warner, 2004; Kneale, 1999; Kerski et al., 2005; White & Simms, 1993).

Geography and technology are a good fit due to the visual nature of both geographic concepts and technology-based resources. Methods for improving learners' geographic thinking while utilizing visualization and animation tools enable students to generate graphs, charts, maps, and other data images. GIS, Internet-based GIS Mapping, mapping software, atlas software and animations all support students in data manipulation, layering, visual representations, and data analysis (see Baker, 2005; Bishop & Shroder, 1995; Christenson; 2004; Dougherty, 1992; Johnson, 2002; Lemberg & Stoltman, 2001; Pride, 1997).

GEOGRAPHY FOR TOMORROW: UTILIZING THE POWER OF GEO-TECHNOLOGIES

Geography and geo-technologies, in particular GIS, are essential analytical tools for community and business organizations that provide services for everyday activities (ESRI, 2007). Geography and geo-technologies are consistently used to improve our quality of life and have multibillion dollar implications for businesses and governments. Geography and geo-technologies guide professionals in selecting sites for potential markets, planning developments, providing utilities and community services, responding to emergencies, and drawing voting or school districts. Examples of professions that rely on geography and geo-technologies in their business operations include: agriculture, banking, defense and intelligence, electric and gas, engineering, federal, state, and local government, forestry, human and health services, insurance, landscape architecture, law enforcement and criminal justice, marine, coast and oceans, petroleum, real estate, retail business, telecommunications, transportation, and water and wastewater (ESRI, 2002). Given that geography and geo-technologies are so prevalent in daily life, they should also be an essential focus of the K–12 curriculum.

Geography matters in K–12 education. Geography provides the knowledge, skills, and dispositions citizens need in order to be informed decision-makers who understand cultural diversity and why these differences exist, can evaluate locational and descriptive information about various places, and are aware of complexity of a global society; yet, geography remains on the periphery of core content in the K–12 curriculum. Geography's diminished value as evidenced by lack of emphasis within state curriculum standards and its secondary role within the social studies poses a disturbing trend. In an ever-changing society, there is a constant need to rethink existing practices and curriculum to determine if these are the most effective modes of preparing global citizens.

Traditional approaches to geography instruction (what I earlier called *teaching about geography*) reflect didactic approaches to teaching geography where content of place and location are emphasized. These methods fall short in promoting critical discourse. Geography instruction is more than teaching about the world, it is teaching students to better understand the world and our place within its ongoing changes. Students in a global society need learning experiences to help them understand major world events, global and economic interdependence, and global issues such as political pushes for cultural homogeneity or global warming. This type of instruction requires a pedagogical shift to teaching with geography and is supported by effective technology integration. *Teaching with geography* enables constructivist, active, and integrative experiences. In these learning environments, students interact with authentic, problem-based, relevant content in purposeful and meaningful ways. Teaching with geography involves using technology to engage students in high-order thinking and critical analysis through "interpreting data, maps, and graphs, observing patterns at multiple scales, questioning the data, looking at issues holistically, and transferring their conceptual knowledge from local to global scales" (Linn et al., 2005, p. 219).

Thoughtful instructional uses of technology can position geography at the forefront of K–12 curricula. The value of geography, as integral to multiple disciplines, essential to student cognitive growth, and useful in providing meaningful and relevant content, will be realized through the effective integration of geo-technologies in K–12 student learning. This view of geography, as core content, begins with creating an understanding of the importance of geographic perspectives and the role of geo-technologies in current decision-making practices. Geo-technologies are emerging as model methods for promoting standards-based rich contextual student learning and higher-order thinking processes representative of constructivist pedagogy (Annenberg Media, 2007; AAG, 2007a; ESRI, 2007). Internet-based mapping, mapping software, GIS, animations, modeling applications, layering, data analysis tools, and image analysis technologies can be used to promote the sort of inquiry-based, constructivist learning practices that have been envisioned by the National Council for the Social Studies (NCSS, 1994), the National Science Education Standards (NRC, 1996), National Education Technology Standards (ISTE, 2007), and National Geography Standards (GESP, 1994). By utilizing the power of geo-technologies to enhance and extend K–12 curricula, geography can be an essential component of the K–12 curriculum and promotion of 21st century knowledge, skills, and dispositions in the age of globalization.

REFERENCES

Allen, D. (1994). Technological treks. *Teaching PreK–8, 25*(2), 12–17.

AAG (Association of American Geographers). (2007a). *Teacher's guide to modern geography.* Retrieved April 1, 2007, from: Association of American Geographers Web site: http://www.aag.org/tgmg/main.cfm

AAG (Association of American Geographers). (2007b). *What is geography?* Retrieved April 1, 2007, from: Association of American Geographers Web site: http://www.aag.org/

Annenberg Media. (2007). *Teaching geography.* Retrieved April 12, 2007 from: Annenberg Media with the Harvard-Smithsonian Center for Astrophysics Web site: http://www.learner.org/channel/workshops/geography/

Baker, T. R. (2005). Internet-based GIS mapping in support of K–12 education. *The Professional Geographer, 57*(1), 44–50.

Baker, T. R., & White, S. H. (2003). The effects of G.I.S. on student's attitudes, self-efficacy, and achievement in middle school science classrooms. *Journal of Geography, 102*(6), 243–254.

Bishop, M. P., & Shroder, J. F., Jr. (1995). Integration of computer technology and interactive learning in geographic education. *Journal of Geography in Higher Education, 19*(1), 97–111.

Brey, J. A. (2000). Assessing the use of real-time DataStreme weather data in an introductory physical geography course. *Journal of Geography in Higher Education, 24*(1), 116–122.

Cambell, A., & Warner, P. (2004). Where ya at and what's happnin': Using GIS for critical thinking in the inquiry-based classroom. *Society for Information Technology and Teacher Education International Conference 2004*(1), 1694–1695. Retrieved from: http://dl.aace.rg/14564

Chedid, B. G. (2005). Energy, society, and education, with emphasis on educational technology policy for K–12. *Journal of Science Education and Technology, 14*(1), 75–85.

Christenson, M. A. (2004). Teaching multiple perspectives on environmental issues in elementary classrooms: A story of teacher inquiry. *Journal of Environmental Education, 35*(4), 3–16.

Demchik, M. J. (2001). Acid rain classroom projects. *Science Activities, 37*(3), 19–22.

Doolittle, P., & Hicks, D. (2003). Constructivism as a theoretical foundation for the use of technology in social studies. *Theory and Research in Social Education, 31*(1), 72–104.

Donaldson, D. (2000). Public high schools' ability to support GIS: An Ohio case study. *Geographic Bulletin, 41*(2), 91–102.

Dougherty, P. S. (1992). Reading the talking earth with middle school students. *Social Studies, 83*(4), 172–176.

ESRI. (2007). *Geographic Information Systems (GIS) and mapping software.* ESRI Web site: http://www.esri.com/index.html

ESRI. (2002). *Geography matters: An ESRI white paper.* Redlands, CA: Environmental System Research Institute, Inc. Retrieved from: http://www.esri.com/library/whitepapers/pdfs/geomatte.pdf

ESRI. (1998). *GIS in K–12 education: An ESRI white paper.* Redlands, CA: Environmental System Research Institute, Inc. Retrieved from: http://www.esri.com/industries/k-12/download/docs/k12educ2.pdf

Feeney, A. E. (2003). Using interactive multimedia for dyslexic students in geography education. *Journal of Geography, 102*, 21–28.

Fitzpatrick, C., & McGuire, D. (2001). GIS in schools: Infrastructure, methodology, and role. In D. Green (Ed.), *GIS: A sourcebook for schools* (pp. 62–72). London: Taylor and Francis.

Friedman, R. S., Drakes, J., & Deek, F. P. (2002). Design and implementation of mapping software: Developing technology and geography skills in two different learning communities. *Information Technology in Childhood Education Annual, 16*, 227–240.

Gardner, A. (2003). Discovering networked information in the internet age: The JISC resource guide to geography and the environment. *Journal of Geography in Higher Education, 27*(1), 103–107.

Gatrell, J. D. (2001). Structural, technical, and definitional issues: The case of geography and GIS in the K–12 classroom. *Journal of Educational Technology Systems, 29*(3), 237–249.

Gatrell, J. D. (2004). Making room: Integrating geo-technologies into teacher education. *Journal of Geography, 103*, 193–198.

Grant, M. M., & Branch, R. M. (2005). Project-based learning in a middle school: Tracing abilities through the artifacts of learning. *Journal of Research on Technology in Education, 38*(1), 65–98.

Green, T. (2001). Geographic resources on the web: Bringing the world to your classroom. *The Social Studies, 92*(6), 272–273.

Geography Education Standards Project (GESP). (1994). *Geography for life: National geography standards 1994.* Washington, DC: National Geographic Research Exploration.

Gildersleeve, C. R. (2004). Uneasy symbiosis: Nebraska's implementation of national standards in geography. *The Social Studies, 95*(6), 243–246.

Hargrove, T. Y., Jones, G. M., Jones, B. D., Hardin, B., Chapman, L, & Davis, M. (2000). Unintended consequences of high-stakes testing in North Carolina: Teacher perceptions. *ERS Spectrum, 18*(4), 21–25.

Heafner, T. L. (2004). Using technology to motivate students to learn social studies. *Contemporary Issues in Technology and Teacher Education, 4*(1).

Heafner, T. L., Lipscomb, G. B., & Rock, T. C. (2006). To test or not to test?: The role of testing in elementary social studies. *Social Studies Research and Practice 1*(2), 145–164. Retrieved from: http://www.socstrp.org/issues/showissue.cfm?volID=1&IssueID=2

Hinde, E. R., & Ekiss, G. O. (2005). No child left behind...except in geography? GeoMath in Arizona answers a need. *Social Studies and the Young Learner, 18*(2), 27–29.

Howarth, D. A., & Mountain, K. R. (2004). Geography for Life and standards-based education in the Commonwealth of Kentucky. *The Social Studies, 95*(6), 261–265.

International Society for Technology in Education (ISTE). (2007). *National educational technology standards for students: The next generation.* Retrieved from: http://www.iste.org/inhouse/nets/cnets/students/pdf/NETS_for_Students_2007.pdf

Jain, C., & Getis, A. (2003). The effectiveness of internet-based instruction: An experiment in physical geography. *Journal of Geography in Higher Education, 27*(2), 153–167.

Johnson, N. (2002). Animating geography: Multimedia and communication. *Journal of Geography in Higher Education, 26*(1), 13–18.

Kenny, M. (2004). The implementation of the national geography standards in Colorado: To everything there is a season. *The Social Studies, 95*(6), 247–249.

Kerski, J. J. (2003). The implementation and effectiveness of geographic information systems technology and methods in secondary education. *Journal of Geography, 102*, 128–137.

Kerski, J., Linn, S., & Gindele, R. (2005). Mapping standardised test scores with other variables using GIS. *International Research in Geographical and Environmental Education, 14*(3), 231–236.

Kneale, P. E. (1999). Context: Incorporating work-based case studies into the geography curriculum. *Journal of Geography in Higher Education, 23*(3), 425–439.

Kohn, A. (2000). *The case against standardized testing: Raising the scores, ruining the schools.* Portsmouth, NH: Heinemann.

Krishnan, P. (1999). The Internet's impact on geography. *World Conference on the WWW and Internet 1999*(1), 632–635. Retrieved from: http://dl.aace.org/5362

Langhorst, E. (2007). After the bell, beyond the walls. *Educational Leadership, 64*(8), 74–77.

Lemberg, D., & Stoltman, J. P. (1999). Geography teaching and the new technologies: Opportunities and challenges. *Journal of Education, 181*(3), 63–77.

Lemke, K. A., & Ritter, M. E. (2000). Virtual geographies and the use of the internet for learning and teaching geography in higher education. *Journal of Geography in Higher Education, 24*(1), 87–91.

Lewis, A. J. (2004). Geographic education in Louisiana. *The Social Studies, 95*(6), 251–254.

Lidstrone, J., & Stoltman, J. (2004). Teaching geography for a better world: Or teaching geography to better understand the world? *International Research in Geographical and Environmental Education, 13*(2), 111–113.

Linn, S., Kerski, J., & Wither, S. (2005). Development of evaluation tools for GIS: How does GIS affect student learning?. *International Research in Geographical and Environmental Education, 14*(3), 217–222.

Lintner, T. (2006). Social studies (still) on the back burner: Perceptions and practices of K–5 social studies instruction. *Journal of Social Studies Research, 30*(1), 3–8.

Lobben, A. K. (2001). Teaching with geographic information technology. *Society for Information Technology and Teacher Education International Conference 2001*(1), 1132–1137. Retrieved from: http://dl.aace.rg/3702

Madge, C., & O'Connor, H. (2004). Online methods in geography educational research. *Journal of Geography in Higher Education, 28*(1), 143–152.

Martindale, T., & Wiley, D. A. (2005). Using weblogs in scholarship and teaching. *Techtrends Linking Research and Practice to Improve Learning, 49*(2), 55–61.

Mason, C., Berson, M., Diem, R., Hicks, D., Lee, J., & Dralle, T. (2000). Guidelines for using technology to prepare social studies teachers. *Contemporary Issues in Technology and Teacher Education* [Online serial], *1*(1). Retrieved from: http://www.citejournal.org/vol1/iss1/currentissues/socialstudies/article1.htm

Merryfield, M. M., Tin Yau-Lo, J. T., Cho Po, S. C., & Kasai, M. (2008). Worldmindedness: Taking off the blinders. *Journal of Curriculum and Instruction, 2*(1), 6–20.

Morrill, R. W. (2004). The Virginia standards for learning: Where is geography for life? *The Social Studies, 95*(6), 255–260.

National Council for the Social Studies (NCSS). (1994). *Curriculum standards for the social studies: Expectations for excellence.* Washington, DC: National Council for the Social Studies.

National Research Council (NRC). (1996). *National science education standards.* Washington, DC: National Academy Press.

Neill, M., & Guisbond, L. (2005). Excluded children, lost learning: The costs of doing business with NCLB. *Social Studies and the Young Learner, 17*(4), 31–32.

Partnership for 21st Century Skills. (2007). *The intellectual and policy foundations of the 21st century skills framework.* Retrieved August 18, 2008, from: http://www.21stcenturyskills.org/

Pride, P. (1997). Using technology to enhance geography education. *Media & Methods, 33*(5), 8.

Proctor, J. D., & Richardson, A. E. (1997). Evaluating the effectiveness of multimedia computer modules as enrichment exercises for introductory human geography. *Journal of Geography in Higher Education, 21*(1), 41–54.

230 ■ T. L. HEAFNER

Rich, D. C., Pitman, A. J., & Gosper, M. V. (2000). Integrated IT-based geography teaching and learning: A Macquarie University case study. *Journal of Geography in Higher Education, 24*(1), 109–115.

Rich, D. C., Robinson, G., & Bednarz, R. S. (2000). Integrated IT-based geography teaching and learning: A Macquarie University case study. *Journal of Geography in Higher Education, 24*(2), 263–270.

Ritter, M. E., & Lemke, K. A. (2000). Addressing the 'seven principles for good practice in undergraduate education' with internet-enhanced education. *Journal of Geography in Higher Education, 24*(1), 100–108.

Riner, M. E., Cunningham, C., & Johnson, A. (2004). Public health education and practice using geographic information system technology. *Public Health Nursing, 21*(1), 57–65.

Rock, T. C., Heafner, T. L., O'Connor, K. A., Passe, J., Oldendorf, S., Good, A. J., & Byrd, S. (2006). One state closer to a national crisis: A report on elementary social studies education in North Carolina schools. *Theory and Research in Social Education, 34*(4), 455–483.

Rutherford, D., & Lloyd, W. J. (2001). Assessing a computer-aided instructional strategy in a world geography course. *Journal of Geography in Higher Education, 25*(3), 341–355.

Sharma, S. (2007). Where on Earth can you take a geography class? *Orlando Sentinel.* Retrieved from: http://www.orlandosentinel.com/feature/lifestyle/orl-geographyydummie07apr26,0,2144733.story?coll=orl-home-lifestyle

Shelli, J., Strong, J., & Hannon, J. (2007). Learning U.S. geography with the great mail race. *Social Studies and the Young Learner, 20*(2), 19–23.

Solem, M. N. (2000). The virtual geography department: Assessing an agent of change in geography education. *Journal of Geography in Higher Education, 24*(3), 353–364.

Solem, M. N., Bell, S., Fournier, E., Gillespie, C., Lewitsky, M., & Lockton, H. (2003). Using the internet to support international collaborations for global geography education. *Journal of Geography in Higher Education, 27*(3), 239–253.

Svingen, B. E. (1994). New technologies in the geography classroom. *Journal of Geography,* 180–185.

Unwin, D. J., & Maguire, D. J. (1990). Developing the effective use of information technology in teaching and learning in geography: The computers in teaching initiative centre for geography. *Journal of Geography in Higher Education, 14*(1), 77–83.

VanFossen, P. J. (2005). 'Reading and math take so much of the time...': An overview of social studies instruction in elementary classrooms in Indiana. *Theory and Research in Social Education, 33*(3), 376–403.

von Zastrow, C., & Janc, H. (2004). *Academic atrophy: The condition of the liberal arts in America's public schools.* A report from the Council for Basic Education, Carnegie Corporation of New York.

Wiegand, P. (2003). School students' understanding of choropleth maps: Evidence from collaborative mapmaking using GIS. *Journal of Geography, 102,* 234–242.

White, K. L., & Simms, M. (1993). Geographic information systems as an educational tool. *Journal of Geography,* 80–85.

Zerger, A., Bishop, I. D., Escobar, F., & Hunter, G. J. (2002). A self-learning multimedia approach for enriching GIS education. *Journal of Geography in Higher Education, 26*(1), 67–80.

CHAPTER 11

ARTIFICIAL INTELLIGENCE IN THE SOCIAL STUDIES

Daniel W. Stuckart and Michael J. Berson

ABSTRACT

In 1955, John McCarthy coined the term, *artificial intelligence* (AI), for a proposed conference at Dartmouth College, the first scientific gathering devoted to the advancement of machines with human reasoning and learning capacities. This chapter traces the antecedents of AI through the early intellectual developments and commercial and military applications. Subsequently, the authors explore the use of AI in general education as well as within the specific context of the social studies. As computer technologies continue to evolve and programmers develop increasingly sophisticated software, the realization of AI shows great promise to transform the way we teach and learn.

INTRODUCTION

The quest to create intelligent tools that mimic human activities transcends time and geography. In Ancient Greece, the myths of Hephaestus and Pygmalion conjured images of intelligent robots. The Chinese constructed animated statues powered by cascading water and steam. Later, in 15th century Europe, artisans began fashioning mechanical instruments to

Research on Technology in Social Studies Education, pages 231–251

measure time, soon followed by mechanical animals and other curiosities (Buchanan, 2002; Mazlish, 1995). However, it was not until the dawn of the computer age in the mid-20th century that artificial intelligence (AI) moved from the realm of imagination and fantasy into a new, formalized study thoroughly reflective of the modern industrial world. In 1956 a group of researchers met at Dartmouth College, and popularized the phrase, "artificial intelligence," and along with it fueled public imaginations of an existence with human-like machines, sometimes glorious and other times frightening. In the half century since its genesis, AI's integration has been uneven, and occasionally tumultuous. This chapter traces the development of AI technology from its origins in military research during World War II, to the expanded military and commercial applications in the 1950s, and subsequently to its limited adoption and promising potential in education in general and the social studies in particular.

ORIGINS OF DIGITAL COMPUTERS
AND ARTIFICIAL INTELLIGENCE

In the 1940s, scientists built the first electronic computer and AI research was in its infancy. About a decade later in the summer of 1956, the original "founders" of AI convened at Dartmouth College. The attendees arrived with established research agendas and preconceived definitions of intelligence, which would later divide the scientists into opposing camps.

Like many other useful technologies, early modern computers were a byproduct of World War II. In 1944, researchers at Harvard University developed the first electronic computer, initially called ASCC (Automatic Sequence Controlled Calculator) and later renamed Mark 1, to calculate the trajectories for naval guns and missiles. This computer measured 55 feet long by 8 feet high and contained a total of nearly 760,000 distinct parts, using a mechanical storage and counting system. The machine took between three and five seconds to solve a multiplication problem. Two years later, again with the backing of the U.S. military, scientists at the University of Pennsylvania invented ENIAC 1 (Electrical Numerical Integrator and Calculator) using vacuum tubes and resistors, which greatly enhanced the speed and complexity of computing. Like Mark 1, ENIAC 1 was a lumbering behemoth covering 1800 square feet—but unlike Mark 1 it had the ability to perform computations 1,000 times faster than any device ever invented (Bellis, 2007; O'Connor & Robertson, 1999).

In the summer of 1956, about a decade after the successful introduction of Mark 1, John McCarthy, a prominent, young, mathematician and scientist invited some of the world's leading computer experts in academia and industry to converge on Dartmouth College to formalize an AI research agenda. Although McCarthy is credited with coining the phrase, "artificial intelligence," he recalled later, "The 1955 proposal for the 1956 workshop is the first appearance of 'artificial intelligence' I or anyone else has found. On the other hand, at the time it seemed to me that I had heard the term before" (J. M. McCarthy, personal communication, January 7, 2006). The list of interested parties and attendees included brilliant scientists and mathematicians who would later become renowned masters in their fields like John Nash from Princeton University and Marvin Minsky, then a junior fellow at Harvard University. After the Dartmouth Conference, the scientists returned to their respective laboratories to focus on their areas of interest. The organizers never produced a formal record of the proceedings and "[e]veryone published their own work separately, but the conference established closer connections among researchers who already had active projects" (M. L. Minsky, personal communication, January 7, 2006). With substantial funding from the Department of Defense, AI research proceeded on multiple fronts amid optimistic public proclamations, despite the fact that scientists embraced competing assumptions well before the Dartmouth gathering.

In 1950, the British mathematician and pioneer computer scientist, Alan Turing, offered a behavioral solution to the vexing problem of how to define human intelligence. Turing asserted that if a computer could fool a knowledgeable person into believing that it was a fellow human being, then the machine behaved intelligently, a measure which became known as the Turing Test (Gams, 2001; Hawkins & Blakeslee, 2004; Saygin, Cicekli, & Akman, 2000). Turing's definition skirted the conflicting, imprecise, and varying definitions of intelligence including the ability to rapidly solve difficult problems, the capacity to achieve goals using the computing functions of the brain, and the continua of behaviors based on memory and predictive abilities (Hawkins & Blakeslee, 2004; Lewis, 2003; McCarthy, 2004a; Minsky, 1986; Norberg, 1989).

The Turing Test exposed a fissure in the AI research community between those who believed that computers were intelligent as long as the computers "acted" like human beings and others who believed that computers were only truly intelligent if they became sentient like humans. The first group became known as the proponents of "weak" AI while the latter were referred to as the "strong" camp. A third group of non-AI researchers consisted of those who believed that computers could never be intelligent, something Gams (2001) called the "mentalists." The weak AI proponents believed that computers would never be able to model all of the brain's functionalities, but instead would appear convincingly intelligent within specific domains (Shaw, 2008). By parsing intelligence into well-defined areas like natural language programming, eventually computers would develop the ability to converse like humans, even though the computers would not be "aware" of the process or the output. Likewise, they argued that the main component of intelligence was computational processing; hence eventually computers would catch up to human capabilities through technological innovation (Hall, 2005; McCarthy, 2004a; Norberg, 1989; Norberg & O'Neill, 1996). Conversely, the strong AI backers believed that brains functioned beyond symbol manipulations. According to this viewpoint, a primary component of intelligence was consciousness and metacognition. For a computer to be intelligent like humans it must be sentient and aware of its learning. An objective stated early on was "to understand these processes well enough to make a computer 'perceive, understand, and act' in ways that formerly were possible only for humans" (Norberg & O'Neill, 1996). Although in contemporary times it has become clear that the weak backers would become relatively more successful, in the early years it was the promises of the strong AI research community that captured the public's attention. The research forged a familiar path: first, the government supported military applications, second, entrepreneurs discovered commercial uses, and later, schools adopted the technologies to varying degrees as part of reform movements (Cuban, 1986). Social studies innovators were slow to adopt AI technology because it mainly supported rule-based disciplines found primarily in the economics and psychology content areas. However, in the 1990s an AI resurgence brought new and powerful learning tools.

The Interaction of Educational Psychology, Computers, and the Social Studies

In the middle of the 20th century, behaviorism usurped progressivism as the dominant learning theory. Although the first teaching machines emerged in the progressivist 1920s, schools did not adopt the technology until the 1950s with the support of behaviorist theorists who advocated programmed instruction. In the beginning, few instances of social studies programmed instruction existed because educators and cognitive scientists mainly relegated the technology to rule-based domains like mathematics and languages. At the same time, scientists achieved breakthroughs with AI technologies and computers. Eventually, computer-assisted instruction replaced programmed instruction beginning in the 1960s while cognitive theories supplanted behaviorism. As more sophisticated AI computer and software adaptations developed, new applications in the social studies emerged.

Ohio State University Educational Psychology Professor, Sydney Pressey, constructed one of the first computer-assisted instructional devices in the 1920s. It consisted of a box containing a drum that could be rotated revealing one question at a time. In a multiple-choice format, his college students would select the correct answer by pushing one of four buttons, with the correct answer triggering a latch allowing them to move onto the next question. K–12 schools did not adopt the technology until the 1950s when the dominant learning psychology shifted from pupil-centered progressivism to teacher-directed behaviorism (Skinner, 1958).

Pressey's teaching machine resurfaced in the 1950s on the crest of behaviorist learning theory. Behaviorism provided a task analysis for the establishment of objectives, the articulating of steps to achieve the objectives, evaluation, and revision. Additionally, proponents cited the advantages of efficient, personalized instruction, immediate reinforcement, and a counterbalance for poor teaching (Skinner, 1958; Teaching machines and programmed instruction, 1961). Most examples of programmed instruction were found in the "'tool' subjects in the fields of mathematics, science, and language which dealt with measurements, rules, or natural laws" (Fine, 1962, p. 120). Although some programmers created teaching machines for social studies content like economics education and psychology, the machines' technological affordances offered linear instruction based on empirical assumptions, which did not match the normative structures of most social studies content. For instance, the interpretive nature of history demanded value judgments predicated on the assimilation of overlapping disciplines such as sociology, political science, and economics. The teaching machines and programmed instruction were not able to represent the complexities (Fry, 1963). Regardless, enthusiasm for programmed instruction climaxed around 1962 and eventually dissipated in the late 1960s around the same time that computer assisted instruction (CAI) and cognitive learning theories began to take hold (Cassidy, 2004).

The first CAI programs resembled the programmed instruction found in earlier teaching machines. While programmed instruction generally referred to the use of computers in all educational settings, CAI specifically indicated drill-and-practice, tutorials, and simulations (Cotton, 1991). Researchers Richard Atkinson and Patrick Suppes at Stanford University invented the first CAI program in reading and mathematics in 1963 to offer students individualized instruction. Suppes, (1966) predicted "that in a few more years millions of schoolchildren will have access to what Philip of Macedon's son Alexander enjoyed as royal prerogative: the personal services of a tutor as well informed and responsive as Aristotle" (p. 207). The tutor was a program based on drill-and-practice and gave students immediate feedback. Within a few years, the invention of the microchip and affordable microcomputers forged the way for the proliferation of CAI software in all school domains including the social studies.

Gradually, CAI usurped traditional automated instruction, such as programmed learning machines that operated by taking a specific domain's knowledge and breaking it down into smaller pieces for students to master before moving onto the next chunk in a linear fashion. Like automated instruction, CAI also functioned as a presentation device, never deviating from the program author's sequences. What enhancement CAI did offer was a way to represent multiple disciplines in one machine, and the ability for educators to create their own unique programs using the newly invented authoring languages. In the social studies, teachers introduced CAI programs into their traditional pedagogy mainly as a means for reinforcing content knowledge. Most of these early programs were produced independently. Later, some textbook companies offered them as add-ons to textbooks and other curricular resources (Cassidy, 2004).

In the 1970s, schools began purchasing microcomputers and social studies educators began to incorporate them into instruction and practice. Computers allowed students to store and retrieve data and software provided programs for drill-and-practice, tutorial, and simulation exercises. The availability of programs expanded from psychology and economics education programmed instruction to include history content and other social studies disciplines (Adair, 1970; Klassen, 1973; Martorella & Kohn, 1970). Popular software included Discover the World, which was a simulation program involving 15th century exploration; the Carmen Sandiego series of geography programs based on a mythical ex-secret agent; and The Golden Spike: Building America's First Transcontinental Railroad, a simulation using computers, audio cassettes, and filmstrips (Bullough Sr. & LaMond, 1991). Educators readily adopted these early applications of computers because they functioned as add-ons within the existing instructional paradigms and the prevailing cognitive learning theories (Cassidy, 2004; McArthur, Lewis, & Bishay, 1993; Molnar, 1997).

Cognitive learning theories with constructivist perspectives reflected a paradigmatic shift from product-oriented behaviorist learning to a focus on learning as a process involving mental structures. To mainstream constructivists, knowledge was not transmitted; rather, it was built from action and experience. Therefore, reality was a product of the mind instead of an external reflection. Symbols became the tools for constructing knowledge; while in the traditional view, symbols were true representations of the world. According to constructivism, meaningful learning happened in a setting that was authentic, reflective, active, constructive, and cooperative. Teachers became facilitators of knowledge invoking multiple perspectives and inductive processes. Traditional teaching, on the other hand, often took a teacher-centered approach that was deductive in nature (Jonassen, Peck, & Wilson, 1999). In the social studies, old elements of behaviorism and programmed instruction persisted with certain tutorials, drill-and-practice, and simulations, but new emphases on processes also emerged. Computer databases with storage and retrieval mechanisms and interactive simulations provided students with opportunities for inquiry-based learning and problem solving often working in small groups (Berson, 1996). Different approaches to integrating technology into social studies practice mirrored the opposing approaches to AI research.

The behaviorist and cognitive learning theory camps reflected the weak and strong AI positions, which became manifested in two main research directions: The weak, supporting the validity of the Turing Test with an emphasis on computers *behaving* intelligently, embarked on pure experimental agendas or what McCarthy, (2004b) labeled, "phenomenal, based on studying and formalizing common sense facts about the world and the problems that the world presents to the achievement of goals" (para. 3). Like the traditional, behaviorism theorists, it was the output that mattered. The majority of AI researchers supported this position. The strong scientists, on the other hand, embraced experimental and theoretical agendas, a position McCarthy, (2004b) called, "biological, based on the idea that since humans are intelligent, AI should study humans and imitate their psychology or physiology" (para. 3). Representing a minority of AI investigators, the strong AI researchers advocated the examination of mental structures in creating truly intelligent machines (Gams, 2001; Lewis, 2003; McCarthy, 2004b; Norberg & O'Neill, 1996). Whether competing learning theories drove innovation or vice versa, one thing became clear: over the course of the 1960s and early 1970s, conceptualizations of educational technology shifted from traditional purveyors of knowledge where students passively received transmitted information to productivity tools that actively engaged students with the learning technology (Jonassen et al., 1999; Tyack & Cuban, 1995).

Intelligent Tutoring Systems

In many respects, CAI as a knowledge representation system offered little over traditional automated instruction and most educators shunned the rigorous process of authoring unique instructional programs (Cassidy, 2004; Elsom-Cook, 1990; Lelouche, 1998). Influenced by emergent cognitive theories, in the beginning of the 1970s investigators began to experiment with machines that interacted with students. What resulted were computer programs with varying degrees of tutoring functionalities using AI technology. Unlike CAI, these new programs did not follow preprogrammed, prescribed, linear paths. Instead, they infused some elements of AI to make the experience "generative" and "adaptive," something (Elsom-Cook, 1990) described as follows:

> By generative, I mean that the system creates teaching materials and events as
> it progresses; it is not merely storing material prepared by someone else. By

adaptive I mean that the teaching interaction is adjusted, both in content and form, to the current needs and abilities of each pupil individually. (p. 7)

Early examples of these new instructional machines include SOPHIE (a SO-PHisticated Instructional Environment), developed by John Seely Brown, and a variety of programs in mathematics and computer programming, created by John Anderson at Carnegie Mellon University. Collectively, these types of programs were referred to as intelligent CAI or ICAI. These were the first intelligent machines to be incorporated into school settings. As more sophisticated versions emerged, they became widely known as intelligence tutoring systems (ITS) (Elsom-Cook, 1990; McArthur et al., 1993; Molnar, 1997). Much like the programmed instruction of an earlier generation, ITS developers confronted some of the same difficulties in creating tutoring programs for normative social studies content. Following a similar pattern with a focus on economics education, software engineers developed an intelligent tutoring system for microeconomics called, Smithtown, which focused on the development of student inquiry and scientific skills (Raghavan & Katz, 1989; Shute, 1990).

ITS, and to a lesser extent CAI which preceded it, became fixtures in education because they were easily integrated into traditional school settings and, perhaps more important, they experimentally and significantly enhanced student achievement on standardized tests to a degree that no other technology has claimed to this day (McArthur et al., 1993; Molnar, 1997). In fact, the technology complemented the widely accepted practice of one-on-one tutoring with stated objectives and clearly defined goals. Most of the programs followed a type of drill-and-practice that fit easily into a typical school routine and required little extra effort on the part of the teacher. The AI capabilities in an ITS monitored progress and adjusted circumstances to fit the needs of the learners, but was only effective for highly structured domains such as economics in the social studies.

AI IN THE SOCIAL STUDIES

Evolving cognitive theories and new technologies contributed to new educational goals and pedagogies in all subject areas including social studies. Representing these changes, cognitive scientist Seymour Papert invented the programming language, LOGO, which brought AI technology into the math curricula of many schools. LOGO was used to create Microworlds, where in the beginning a child was able to explore mathematical concepts in physics, music, and other contexts. In the 1980s, enhanced three-dimensional graphics brought Microworlds to the social studies particularly in exploring mapping and geography as well as interdisciplinary units with math and science (Rogers & de Leeuw, 1986; Sunal & Warash, 1984; Tempel, 1985). What made this approach radically different from ITS was a stress on inquiry-based learning and the belief that higher order thinking would transfer to other tasks (Romiszowski, 1987). Moreover, the process of learning became a pedagogical focal point. Rather than just learning content, students were expected to perform like practitioners (Papert, 1971). In the 1970s, AI was mainly a component of ITS, which complemented teacher-led instruction, but with the introduction of Microworlds and similar systems AI began to focus on student skills and practice.

Another offshoot of ITS that appeared in social studies educational technology in the 1980s was the concept of expert systems (Shaw, 2008). These expert systems were initially developed by AI researchers who were working with knowledge systems. Expert systems resulted from advances in the areas of natural speech recognition, computer vision, and robotics. Many variants of the technology infiltrated military and commercial applications, including supply management for the military, diagnostic equipment for power companies, and language recognition in banking systems (Norberg & O'Neill, 1996). Some of the new expert systems also managed to permeate education (McArthur et al., 1993) including the social studies. One example from the social studies was software that allowed students to create articles much like professional journalists. The software functioned to expertly answer and pose questions to aid the students in crafting their stories (Kass, 1994). In spite of some remarkable advances in AI research and their commensurate infusion in military, commercial, and educational applications in the 1970s and early 1980s, AI research suffered major setbacks in public perceptions, and more important, in funding, causing some to refer to this period as AI's "winter" (Havenstein, 2005, p. 28; Kurzweil, 2005).

AI Winter

By the mid 1980s, AI research had proceeded under public scrutiny for about three decades, while teams of researchers at some of the most prestigious academic institutions and innovative corporations zealously pursued a "quest" to create intelligent machines. The quest led to optimistic predictions, and when the intelligent machines failed to materialize, AI's reputation deflated. Moreover, when people started to analyze the short-term objectives against the long-term one of an intelligent machine, they concluded that the objectives did not match. As a result, government funding was reduced to a trickle, even though in less apparent ways AI research was producing some revolutionary products (Havenstein, 2005; Kahn, 2002; Norberg & O'Neill, 1996).

After a period of explosive growth, ITS development slowed as researchers exposed the limits of cognitive science. Cognitive science had articulated the skills necessary to successfully negotiate a task, and the ITS developers had created representations of knowledge in expert systems to realize the goals, but when new standards began to take hold in the 1980s, cognitive science was unable to offer detailed task analyses for poorly defined objectives, often referred to as "higher order" skills (McArthur et al., 1993). For example, as part of the "Time, Continuity, and Change" standard, the National Council for the Social Studies (1994) asserted, "High school students engage in more sophisticated analysis and reconstruction of the past, examining its relationship to the present and extrapolating into the future" (para. 9). The complexity of this standard exposed the limits of task analysis in the cognitive sciences and limited AI applications. With regard to higher order cognition, the promise of AI technology did not match public expectations in education. Nonetheless, the AI winter would thaw in the early 1990s amid a new wave of technologies.

AI Redemption

Although government support and public perceptions of AI had declined because earlier researchers' promises remained unrealized, beneath the surface subtle innovations were steadily and slowly infusing AI into education. Advances in AI allowed more sophisticated ITS with better monitoring and tutoring capabilities as well as the potential for cognitive tools to facilitate collaborative learning (Kennedy, 2002; Kong, 2008). Further, new AI technologies allowed for elaborate case-based reasoning (CBR) in a process where new cases were assimilated into existing structures (Salem, 2000; Wang et al., 2003). Technological scaffolding in the learning of social studies (Brush & Saye, 2001; Saye & Brush, 1999, 2002) also began to incorporate ITS in increasingly sophisticated ways.

Potential social studies applications of Internet-based AI technologies included intelligent agents, something Salem (2000) referred to as distributed artificial intelligence, or agents that were spread across space and operated to varying degrees of autonomy and intelligence. A specific example came from Japan where programmers created a virtual museum tour guide that answered visitors' queries, updated relevant information, and detected users' interests (de Almeida & Yokoi, 2003). Social studies educators already engaged in virtual field trips (Cassady, Kozlowski, & Kommann, 2008; Holliday, 2001; Wilson et al., 2000) and intelligent agents offered the potential to provide richer learning experiences.

AI technology also contributed to more effective Internet searches related to social studies practice. Supported by the National Science Foundation (NSF), computer scientists at Carnegie Mellon University developed AI programming to improve the quality of Internet searches. Again with the backing of NSF, a Pennsylvania company adopted the technology to create a web portal commemorating the 300 years since the birth of Benjamin Franklin. The technology clustered high-quality websites, eliminating most of the spam and commercial adaptations of Franklin's name and likeness (http://ben.clusty.com/). Later, the developers created an all-purpose search engine based on the same assumptions (http://clusty.com). While the project had a computer science focus, it clearly offered benefits for social studies practice (National Science Foundation, 2006).

With the emergence of some AI applications for the social studies new questions about the role of technology in social studies came to the forefront. Newer technologies incorporating AI shifted the focus to prevailing social constructive leaning theories (Dowling, 2000), concerning others suggested that the success of AI technologies undermined traditional pedagogy and practice by placing emphases on processes rather than content (Elsom-Cook, 1990; McArthur et al., 1993; Molnar, 1997). Given research investigations reporting limited student achievement gains, some questioned technology's use in promoting the content of social studies over experiencing the process (Berson, 1996; White, 1988).

Technology, the Social Studies, and the Cultural Wars

As AI has begun to influence social studies, an existing "Culture War" of differences regarding the purposes and practices of social studies has come to shape opinions about AI and technology in general in social studies. Although cultural wars have probably been fought since the beginning of civilization, the current battle became entrenched following the release of *A Nation at Risk* (1983). Conservative calls for reform focused on a pitch for a return to core classes and core values (*A Nation at Risk*, 1983; Cheney, 1987; Hirsch, Kett, & Trefil, 1987). Although few disagreed about what constituted core classes, defining core values in a richly diverse nation presented a dilemma: What were those values and how did one transmit them? Defining the nation's beliefs about knowledge became a highly charged political affair. Hirsch et al. (1987) provided a list of everything a high school graduate should know in the history domain. Critics countered that the entire process was biased against minorities and any other group that did not subscribe to an Anglo-Saxon domination view of social studies (Nash, Crabtree, & Dunn, 1997; Symcox, 2002). The debate continued into the 1990s with the failed attempt to adopt national history standards. Conservatives scuttled the standards because they viewed the project as liberal revisionism, a distortion of facts to correct for our nation's past sins, a sort of feel-good history (Cheney,

1994; Frazee & Ayers, 2003). The logic followed that multiculturalism produced a culture of cynicism, which in the end, turned off young people to politics and civics engagement (Rochester, 2003). In this politically-charged environment, technology contributed to the acrimony.

Technology affected the cultural wars because of its ability to promote social studies learning as a process versus a focus on the content. The process approach conceptualized students using technology tools to actively construct meaning (Bates, 2008; Berson et al., 2001; Doolittle & Hicks, 2003; White & Walker, 2000). Conversely, the contrarian, conservative perspective acknowledged the importance of technology as content, but viewed its incorporation as a distraction to "get[ting] students to absorb fundamental information" (Rochester, 2003, p. 12). Advances in AI technology exacerbated the rift in the social studies because it offered greater generative opportunities. In the 1990s and 2000s, AI's redemption and infusion into multiple sectors of American society produced complex social studies education software in the form of enhanced games, which surmounted earlier limitations.

AI and Gaming in Social Studies

The redemption of AI in the public arena coincided with the advent of new and sophisticated technologies in gaming that have impacted social studies in a number of ways. The first computer games date back to the 1960s and 1970s and were mostly played in arcades. As developers saw interest in gaming increase, some started considering the potential educational benefits. Most recently the Federation of American Scientists (2006) have identified educational skills that can be taught through video games, including analytical thinking, team building, multitasking, and problem-solving under duress. For example, in the game Discover Babylon (http://fas.org/babylon) social studies students can step back in time and interact with artifacts and primary sources in a contextualized format. Games allow students in the social studies classroom to take on the identity of historic figures or key community leaders, thereby developing their situated understanding of roles, functions, and the value of risk taking, entrepreneurship, and expertise in complex interaction that emerge from the game play (Shaffer et al., 2005).

The cross between computer games and education would become known as edutainment. When games were first introduced, students were happy to have the opportunity to play games on school time, and they didn't really notice that they were being educated in the process (Navarro, 2006). These early dynamic computer environments helped to create experiences otherwise inaccessible to students, such as taking a trip back in time or visiting a distant land.

One of the first computer games to receive widespread use in the social studies was Oregon Trail, which was developed by the Minnesota Educational Computing Consortium in the 1970s. The purpose of game was to simulate a pioneer's trip in a Conestoga wagon along the trail while fighting off disease, hunting for food, and purchasing supplies. The popularity of Oregon Trail between students and its perceived educational value by teachers made it a highly requested resource for the social studies classroom (Navarro, 2006). Other social studies oriented computer games were widely distributed in the 1980s, such as the popular SimCity and Carmen Sandiego series. The detective series Carmen Sandiego, developed at Broderbund software, explored geographical and historical themes and was even turned into an award winning television show. SimCity, which was developed by Maxis and distributed by Broderbund, allowed players to design and build their own cities as well as address numerous municipal issues, social problems, and even natural disasters.

Although these early games appealed to students as an activity, in many social studies classrooms they were marginalized as rewards and not integrated through pedagogically sound approaches. These games were more than mere toys, but the limited application within the curriculum laid the foundation for a more transformative opportunity that capitalized on the dynamic power of gaming.

Initial Barriers to Early Games

While games were growing in popularity, there remained a number of issues impeding their integration into the school curriculum. Some educators were dismissive of games' educational value, viewing them as purely entertainment or critiquing the violent and misogynistic themes that pervaded games targeted to the consumer market (Shaffer et al., 2005). Constraints of the classroom time structure also provided educators with limited opportunity to transform students' learning with the technology. With limited save options and a lack of management features to foster accountability (e.g., progress reports, evaluation components), teachers also were frustrated by the design impediments of most commercial games. A small minority of highly trained and motivated teachers has persisted as visionaries, linking games with curriculum objectives, and their experience and foresight has served as a model of meaningful learning through virtual worlds.

Now that corporations, government, and the military have embraced video games as powerful learning tools, there is a call for education to follow suit and move students from basic states of knowing to evolving the capacity to engage and practice applied skills in simulated contexts. However, this transformation in education must first overcome a strong bias against video games. Several barriers inhibit the markets for education games. These include:

> Market fragmentation (e.g., 16,000 K–12 school districts), schools' unwillingness to abandon textbooks in favor of technology-based materials, limited budgets for education materials other than text books, negative attitudes about video games on the part of some parents and educators, and schools that are reluctant to purchase educational technologies that have not proven their efficacy, especially in terms of today's education standards. (Federation of American Scientists, 2006, p. 38)

Gaming and AI Today

Throughout the 1990s and into the new century digital gaming infusing AI technology has become more sophisticated and connected to educational objectives. Projects such as the Serious Games Initiative, http://www.seriousgames.org (2006) "focused on uses for games in exploring management and leadership challenges facing the public sector. Part of its overall charter is to help forge productive links between the electronic game industry and projects involving the use of games in education, training, health, and public policy" (para. 1).

Among the games that have evolved out of this new generation of educational applications is Food Force http://www.food-force.com/, a game about world hunger from the United Nations World Food program. This program was designed to educate young people about world hunger and the work of the agency. Another example includes Muzzy Lane's Making History, http://www.making-history.com/. Students take on the role of a government leader who must make decisions about policy and diplomacy in their struggling nation. The program is set in the years 1936- 1945, and students need to rely on their historical knowledge of alliances, treaties, military buildup, natural resources, trade, and population unrest to succeed in their role. Some other games related to social studies include the strategy game Political Machine, http://www.politicalmachine.com/, which simulates a presidential campaign, and PeaceMaker, http://www.peacemakergame.com/, a single-player game in which students assume the role of either the Israeli Prime Minister or the Palestinian President, and the software-based Civilization IV, http://www.2kgames.com/civ4/home.htm allows the player to build and rule a civilization.

The latest generation of games facilitates complex and emergent interaction using elements of AI technology within new social and cultural worlds. These environments help students learn by demanding integration of higher-order thinking skills, social engagement, and technology within a challenging, learner-centered instructional setting. The effort to develop games is not merely an attempt to create relevance for today's tech-savvy students, but rather it is a movement to revitalize the social studies with the tremendous educative power of technology.

> After all, the Game Boy generation is growing up. And, as they seek a deeper understanding of the word we live in, they may not turn first to the book-shelves. They may demand to play—or rather replay—the great game of history for themselves. (Ferguson, 2006)

CONCLUSION

When compared to mathematics, science, and language arts, social studies educators were relative latecomers to adopting technology for learning, mainly because of the historic lack of resources. Early computer programmers faced limitations in creating linear instruction for the varied, multidisciplinary domains that make up the social studies. These challenges were primarily attributed to problems encountered by cognitive psychologists who struggled to define the task analyses for higher-order thinking that are often interdisciplinary and normative in nature. To further exacerbate the situation, the cultural wars exposed the deep dissentions of what it meant to learn social studies and what the appropriate pedagogy should be. Despite all of these difficulties, current evidence suggests that new and sophisticated computer programs that infuse AI technology, particularly game-based applications, move closer to representations of human intelligence and may aid learner comprehension of complex subjects in the social studies content areas.

Emergent AI technologies represent a victory for the "weak" proponents. Despite public perceptions, steady advances throughout the decades have resulted in many invisible, yet critical technologies in everything from household appliances to guided missiles. AI researchers and scientists do not claim that these technologies achieve human consciousness, but rather they employ complex algorithms to mimic certain human behaviors, like fuzzy logic and natural speech recognition. The successes of these technologies in the private and military sectors have prompted educators, psychologists, and computer scientists to seek ways to integrate AI into education.

Further evidence of the recent success of AI in education can be found in the extent to which national and international organizations promote AI in education. The Association for the Advancement of Artificial Intelligence (AAAI) is a comprehensive organization that includes scientists, practitioners, financial supporters, and anyone else with an interest in AI (http://www.aaai.org). The Artificial Intelligence and Education Group (AI-ED) is

devoted to using AI to advance learning and train teachers (http://www.
dai.ed.ac.uk/groups/aied/). Moreover, there are numerous conferences
and journals as well such as the *International Journal of Artificial Intelligence
in Education* (IJAIE), which supports AI techniques and student practice
(http://aied.inf.ed.ac.uk/). While many of these endeavors continue to
disproportionately focus on mathematics, science, and language arts content areas, some research projects are increasingly multidisciplinary, encap-
sulating elements of social studies content as well.

An examination of current research projects illuminates patterns and
may inform future AI applications in the social studies (Association for
the Advancement of Artificial Intelligence, 2007). Online tutorials, video
games, and distance learning will offer highly individualized instruction
and may even monitor learners' brain waves to indicate learning (Zouaq,
Nkambou, & Frasson, 2008). Classroom applications will continue to promote collaborative learning using more challenging, realistic, and authentic situations. AI programs may even replace the laborious process of grading essays. In its current form, AI offers great promise to transform social
studies practice and pedagogy.

REFERENCES

Association for the Advancement of Artificial Intelligence. (2007). *Education.* Retrieved on June 5, 2007 from: http://www.aaai.org/AITopics/html/educa-
tion.html

A Nation at Risk. (1983). Retrieved September 18, 2003 from: http://www.ed.gov/
pubs/NatAtRisk/risk.html

Adair, C. H. (1970). *Two simulated inquiry environments: A social simulation game and
a CAI-based information retrieval system.* (ERIC Reproduction Service No. ED
045712).

Bates, A. (2008). Learning to design WebQuests: An exploration in preservice social
studies education. *Journal of Social Studies Research, 32*(1), 10–21.

Bellis, M. (2007). Inventors of the modern computer. *About.com.* Retrieved on June
5, 2007 from: http://inventors.about.com/library/weekly/aa052198.htm

Berson, M. J. (1996). Effectiveness of computer technologies in the social studies:
A review of the literature. *Journal of Research on Computing in Education, 28*(4),
486–499.

Berson, M. J., Mason, C. L., Heinecke, W. F., & Coutts, C. B. (2001). Technology innovation: An examination of beliefs and practices of social studies methods
faculty. *The International Social Studies Forum, 1*(2), 89–105.

Brush, T., & Saye, J. (2001). The use of embedded scaffolds with hypermedia-supported student-centered learning. *Journal of Educational Multimedia and Hypermedia, 10*(4), 333–357.

Buchanan, B. G. (2002). Brief history of artificial intelligence. *The American Association for Artificial Intelligence (AAAI)*. Retrieved on October 24, 2005 from: http://www.aaai.org/AITopics/bbhist.html

Bullough Sr., R. V., & LaMond, F. B. (1991). *Classroom applications of microcomputers* (2nd ed.). New York: Merrill.

Carlson, S. (2005). The net generation goes to college. *The Chronicle of Higher Education, 52*(7), A34–A36.

Cassady, J., Kozlowski, A., & Kommann, M. (2008). Electronic field trips as interactive learning events: Promoting student learning at a distance. *Journal of Interactive Learning Research, 19*(3), 439–454.

Cassidy, M. (2004). *Bookends: The changing media environment of American classrooms* Cresskill, NJ: Hampton Press.

Cheney, L. (1994, October). The end of history. *The Wall Street Journal*, p. A22.

Cheney, L. V. (1987). *American memory: A report on the humanities in the nation's public schools*. (ERIC Document Reproduction Service No. ED 283 775).

Cotton, K. (1991). Computer-assisted instruction. *NWREL: School Improvement Research Series (SIRS)*. Retrieved on October 5, 2006 from: http://www.nwrel.org/scpd/sirs/5/cu10.html

Cuban, L. (1986). *Teachers and machines: The classroom use of technology since 1920*. New York: Teachers College Press.

de Almeida, P., & Yokoi, S. (2003). Interactive character as a virtual tour guide to an online museum exhibition. *Museums and the web 2003* Retrieved November 8, 2005, from: http://www.archimuse.com/mw2003/papers/almeida/almeida.html

DeKanter, N. (2005). Gaming redefines interactivity for learning. *TechTrends, 49*(3).

Doolittle, P. E., & Hicks, D. (2003). Constructivism as a theoretical foundation for the use of technology in the social studies. *Theory and Research in Social Education, 31*(1), 72–104.

Dowling, C. (2000). *Educational agents and the social construction of knowledge: Some issues and implications*. Paper presented at the International Conference on Computers in Education/International Conference on Computer Assisted Instruction, Taipei, Taiwan. (ERIC Reproduction Service No. ED 454816).

Elsom-Cook, M. (1990). *Guided discovery tutoring: A framework for ICAI research*. London: Paul Chapman Publishing, Ltd.

Federation of American Scientists. (2006). *Harnessing the power of video games for learning. Summit on Educational Games*. Retrieved on August 12, 2009, from: http://www.fas.org/programs/ltp/policy_and_publications/summit/Summit%20on%20Educational%20Games.pdf

Ferguson, N. (2006). How to win a war. *New York Magazine*. Retrieved October 20, 2006, from: http://newyorkmetro.com/news/features/22787/index.html

Fine, B. (1962). *Teaching machines*. New York: Sterling Publishing Co.

Frazee, B., & Ayers, S. (2003). Garbage in, garbage out: Expanding environments, constructivism, and content knowledge in social studies. In J. Lemings, L. Ellington, & K. Porter (Eds.), *Where did social studies go wrong?* (pp. 111–123). Washington, DC: The Thomas B. Fordham Foundation.

Fry, E. B. (1963). *Teaching machines and programmed instruction, an introduction.* New York: McGraw-Hill.

Gams, M. (2001). *Weak intelligence: Through the principle and paradox of multiple knowledge* (Vol. 6). Hauppauge, NY: Nova Science Publishers.

Hall, J. S. (2005). *Nanofuture: What's next for nanotechnology.* Amherst, NY: Prometheus Books.

Havenstein, H. (2005). Spring comes to AI winter. *Computerworld, 39*(7), 28.

Hawkins, J., & Blakeslee, S. (2004). *On intelligence: How a new understanding of the brain will lead to the creation of truly intelligent machines.* New York: Times Books, Henry Holt and Company, LLC.

Hirsch, E. D., Kett, J., & Trefil, J. (1987). *Cultural literacy: What every American needs to know.* Boston: Houghton Mifflin.

Holliday, D. C. (2001). *Using cooperative learning in a middle school computer lab.* (ERIC Reproduction Service No. ED 452265).

Jonassen, D. H., Peck, K. L., & Wilson, B. G. (1999). *Learning with technology: A constructivist perspective.* Upper Saddle River, NJ: Merrill.

Kahn, J. (2002). It's alive! *Wired Magazine 10*(3). Retrieved January 6, 2006 from: http://www.wired.com/wired/archive/10.03/everywhere.html

Kass, A. (1994). *Using broadcast journalism to motivate hypermedia exploration.* Paper presented at the ED-MEDIA 94 World Conference on Educational Multimedia and Hypermedia, Vancouver, British Columbia, Canada. (ERIC Reproduction Service No. ED 388263).

Kennedy, K. (2002). Top 10 smart technologies for schools. *Technology & Learning 23*(4), retrieved on October 20, 2004, from: http://www.techlearning.com/db_area/archives/TL/2002/11/topten5.html

Klassen, D. L. (1973). *Computer simulation in the social sciences/social studies.* (ERIC Reproduction Service No. ED 087429).

Kong, S. C. (2008). The development of a cognitive tool for teaching and learning fractions in the mathematics classroom: A design-based study. *Computers & Education, 51*(2), 886–899.

Kurzweil, R. (2005, August 15). Long live AI. *Forbes.com.* Retrieved on January 6, 2006 from: http://www.forbes.com/home/free_forbes/2005/0815/030.html

Lelouche, R. (1998). The successive contributions of computers to education: A survey. *European Journal of Engineering Education, 23*(3), 297–309. [Retrieved October 22. 2005, from the ProQuest databases.]

Lewis, P. (2003). Overview of AI. *Current trends in information.* Retrieved on October 24, 2005, from: http://www.ecs.soton.ac.uk/~phl/ctit/ho1/node1.html

Martorella, P. H., & Kohn, D. (1970). Computer-related materials in the social studies/social sciences. *Social Education, 34*(8), 899–908.

Mazlish, B. (1995). The man-machine and artificial intelligence. In S. Franchi & G. Guzeldere (Eds.), *Stanford Humanities Review, 4*(2). Retrieved on October 24, 2005, from: http://www.stanford.edu/group/SHR/4-2/text/mazlish.html

McArthur, D., Lewis, M., & Bishay, M. (1993). *The roles of artificial intelligence in education: Current progress and future prospects.* Retrieved October 20, 2004 from: http://www.rand.org/education/mcarthur/Papers/role.html

McCarthy, J. (2004a). Basic questions. *John McCarthy's Home Page*. Retrieved on November 8, 2005, from: http://www-formal.stanford.edu/jmc/whatisai/node1.html

McCarthy, J. (2004b). More questions. *John McCarthy's Home Page*. Retrieved on November 8, 2005, from: http://www-formal.stanford.edu/jmc/whatisai/node4.html

McHale, T. (2005). Portrait of a digital native. *Technology & Learning 26*(2), 33–34. [Retrieved November 8, 2005, from the ProQuest database.]

Minsky, M. (1986). *The society of mind*. New York: Simon and Schuster.

Molnar, A. (1997). Computers in education: A brief history. *T.H.E. Journal Online*. Retrieved October 31, 2005, from: http://www.thejournal.com/magazine/vault/a1681.cfm

Nash, G. B., Crabtree, C., & Dunn, R. (1997). *History on trial: Culture wars and the teaching of the past*. New York: A.A. Knopf; distributed by Random House.

National Council for the Social Studies. (1994). Curriculum standards. *Time, continuity, and change*. Retrieved on June 5, 2007, from: http://www.socialstudies.org/standards/strands/

National Science Foundation. (2006). *Ben Franklin web portal brings the man to the masses*. Retrieved on October 28, 2006, from: http://www.nsf.gov/news/news_summ.jsp?cntn_id=105705&org=IIS

Navarro, A. (2006). The greatest games of all time. *CNET Networks*. Retrieved on October 20, 2006 from: http://www.gamespot.com/gamespot/features/all/greatestgames/p-34.html

Norberg, A. L. (1989). An interview with Marvin L. Minsky. *Charles Babbage Institute Center for the History of Information Processing, University of Minnesota, Minneapolis*. Retrieved on January 6, 2006, from: http://www.cbi.umn.edu/oh/pdf.phtml?id=201

Norberg, A. L., & O'Neill, J. E. (1996). *Transforning computer technology: Information processing for the pentagon, 1962–1986*. Baltimore, MD: The Johns Hopkins University Press.

O'Connor, J. J., & Robertson, E. F. (1999). Howard Hathaway Aiken. *School of Mathematics and Statistics University of St Andrews, Scotland*. Retrieved on January 6, 2006 from: http://www-groups.dcs.st-and.ac.uk/~history/Mathematicians/Aiken.html

Papert, S. (1971). *Teaching children to be mathematicians vs. teaching about mathematics*. Cambridge, MA: Massachusetts Institute of Technology.

Raghavan, K., & Katz, A. (1989). Smithtown: An intelligent tutoring system. *Technological Horizons in Education, 17*(1), 50–53.

Rochester, J. M. (2003). The training of idiots: Civics education in America's schools. In J. Lemings, L. Ellington, & K. Porter (Eds.), *Where did social studies go wrong?* (pp. 6–39). Washington, DC: The Thomas B. Fordham Foundation.

Rogers, L., & de Leeuw, G. (1986). Explorations in LOGO mapping with children. *History and Social Science Teacher, 22*(1), 15–18.

Romiszowski, A. (1987). Artificial intelligence and expert systems in education: Progress, promise and problems. *Australian Journal of Educational Technology, 3*(1), 6–24.

Salem, A.-B. M. (2000). *The potential role of artificial intelligence technology in education.* Paper presented at the Annual Meeting of the International Conference on Technology in Mathematics Education, Beirut, Lebanon. (ERIC Reproduction Service No. ED 477 318).

Saye, J. W., & Brush, T. (1999). Student engagement with social issues in a multimedia-supported learning environment. *Theory and Research in Social Education, 27*(4), 472–504.

Saye, J. W., & Brush, T. (2002). Scaffolding critical reasoning about history and social issues in multimedia-supported learning environments. *Educational Technology Research and Development, 50*(3), 77–96.

Saygin, A. P., Cicekli, I., & Akman, V. (2000). Turing test: 50 years later. *Minds and Machines, 10*(4). Retrieved January 6, 2006, from: http://crl.ucsd.edu/~saygin/papers/MMTT.pdf

Serious Games Initiative. Retrieved on October 18, 2006 from, http://www.seriousgames.org

Shaffer, D. W., Squire, K. R., Halverson, R., & Gee, J. P. (2005). Video games and the future of learning. *Phi Delta Kappan, 87*(2), 104–111.

Shaw, K. (2008). The application of artificial intelligence principles to teaching and training. *British Journal of Educational Technology, 39*(2), 319–323.

Shute, V. J. (1990). *Individual differences in learning from an intelligent discovery world: Smithtown.* (Report No. AFHRL-TP-89-57). Washington, DC: Office of Educational Research and Improvement. (ERIC Reproduction Service No. ED 356276).

Skelton, S. (2003). A guide to artificial intelligence in games for educators. In P. Kommers & G. Richards (Eds.), *Proceedings of World Conference on Educational Multimedia, Hypermedia and Telecommunications 2003* (pp. 1072–1075). Chesapeake, VA: AACE.

Skinner, B. F. (1958). Teaching machines. *Science, 128*(3330), 969–977.

Sunal, C. S., & Warash, B. G. (1984). *Mapping with young children.* (ERIC Reproduction Service No. ED 248163).

Suppes, P. (1966). The uses of computers in education. *Scientific American, 215*, 206–220. Retrieved on January 7, 2006, from: http://suppes-corpus.stanford.edu/articles/comped/67.pdf

Symcox, L. (2002). *Whose history? The struggle for national standards in American classrooms.* New York: Teachers College Press.

Takahashi, D. (2005). Hey mom! I got an "A" on my game: Muzzy Lane launches World War II history game for schools. *MercuryNews.com.* Retrieved on November 8, 2005, from: http://blogs.mercurynews.com/aei/2005/09/hey_mom_i_got_a.html

Teaching machines and programed instruction. (1961). *College Composition and Communication, 12*(3), 181–183.

Tempel, M. (1985). *The ECCO Logo Project: Materials for classroom teachers and teacher trainers.* (ERIC Reproduction Service No. ED 288487).

Tyack, D., & Cuban, L. (1995). *Tinkering toward utopia: a century of public school reform.* Cambridge, MA: Harvard University Press.

Wang, F.-K., Jonassen, D. H., Strobel, J., & Cernusca, D. (2003). Applications of a case library of technology. *Journal of Technology and Teacher Education, 11*(4), 529–548.

White, C., & Walker, T. (2000). Providing voice: Teacher empowerment and democratic classrooms. In C. White, (Ed.), *Issues in social studies: Voices from the classroom* (pp. 175–183). Springfield, IL: Charles C. Thomas Publisher, Ltd.

White, C. S. (1988). Computers in social studies classrooms. *ERIC Digest.* Retrieved on January 6, 2006: from, http://www.ericdigests.org/pre-929/computers.htm

Wilson, E. K., Rice, M. L., Bagley, W., & Rice, M. K. (2000). Virtual field trips and newsrooms: Integrating technology into the classroom. *Social Education, 64*(3), 152–155.

Zouaq, A., Nkambou, R., & Frasson, C. (2008). Bridging the gap between ITS and eLearning: Towards learning knowledge objects. In B. Woolf, E. Aimeur, & S. Lajoie (Eds.), *Intelligent tutoring systems: 9th international conference on intelligent tutoring systems, ITS 2008, proceedings* (pp. 448–458). New York: Springer.

CHAPTER 12

DIGITAL HISTORY

Researching, Presenting, and Teaching History in a Digital Age

Fred Koehl and John K. Lee

ABSTRACT

The emerging field of digital history is rapidly changing the shape of historical scholarship as well as school-based teaching and learning in history. Evidence of these changes is obvious in some ways given the multitude of historical primary sources available online. In other ways, changes in the field of history are more nuanced. This chapter presents an argument with supporting information from recent scholarship and research that changes in research, teaching, and learning in history are significant and long-lasting. The chapter aims to add to the emerging conceptualization of digital history as it relates to research, teaching, and learning.

INTRODUCTION

The practices of researching, teaching, and learning history are being affected by developments in technology, as have so many facets of our lives.

Research on Technology in Social Studies Education, pages 253–269

These changes are reflective of an ancillary conceptualization of histori-cal practice known as "digital history" (Ayers, 1999b). Digital history has emerged as a result of new technologies which enable the storage of exten-sive historical records in electronic form as well as remote access to these resources via the World Wide Web (Rosenzweig, 1999). Reporting on a sur-vey of professional historians Dennis Trinkle (1998) notes that there is, in his words, "an alert recognition throughout the profession that the Internet and the World Wide Web are changing, or hold the potential to change, every dimension of history—from the structures of historical knowledge to the paradigms of pedagogy" (para. 13). In their recent book on digital history, Daniel Cohen and Roy Rosenzweig (2005) echo this sentiment sug-gesting that in just the past two decades, "new media and new technologies have challenged historians to rethink the ways that they research, write, present, and teach about the past" (p. iiv).

The uniqueness and likely most important impact of digital history has come from the availability and growth of resources, both primary and secondary, and the accompanying alternatives for storing, accessing, and analyzing historical materials. The development of "digital archives" are often extensive and multifaceted such as the Library of Congress' *American Memory*, others are extensive but more highly focused, such as the *Valley of the Shadow* project, and yet others that are much more limited and highly specialized such as the online presentation of Martha Ballard's diary at Do-history.org. These resources have enabled new forms of historical research at all levels. The cumulative presence of these materials is unknowable, but without question they represent a formidable new source of authen-tic materials. Some scholars (Barlow, 1998; Burton, 2005) see revolution-ary potential in the ways technology are enabling historical scholarship, teaching, and learning suggesting that with these dramatic changes in the history profession we will experience both advances and setbacks. Others historians (Ayers, 1999a; O'Malley & Rosenzweig, 1997) are less convinced that these changes are revolutionary, but certainly see developments in digital history as significant. At minimum this tumult of change, with new forms of data being used by amateurs, students and professionals, will con-tinue to broaden the field (Rosenzweig, 2003).

In a previous review of literature, we suggested a definition of digital history as "the study of the past using a variety of electronically reproduced primary source texts, images, and artifacts as well as the constructed his-torical narratives, accounts, or presentations that result from digital his-torical inquiry" (Lee, 2002a). This conceptualization of digital history is, we think, informative, but it lacks much in way theoretical foundation. In this chapter, we attempt to add to our emerging understanding of digital history as it relates to three primary themes: (1) The impact of digital forms of history on traditional academic research, (2) The ways in which technology can be used to enrich the presentation of historical materials, and (3) The ways in which the teaching and learning of history can be transformed and enhanced.

DIGITAL FORMS OF ACADEMIC HISTORICAL RESEARCH

As more historical material is digitized and becomes accessible, some have contended that the means by which historians conduct research will change. For example, Rosenzweig (1999) suggests that "the depth of such collections as *American Memory* means that historians can now do serious scholarly research in online collections" (p. 240). Some researchers are already doing much of their work using computers and digital archives (see Sarantakes, 1999; Stephens & Thumma, 2005). In fact, Trinkle (1999) found that 93 percent of historians were using computers for some aspect of their research. One recent example illustrates the depth to which online resources have affected research in history. In 2004, Paul A. Thomsen published his research on a somewhat obscure 19th century North Carolina historical character named William Holland Thomas.[1] While very interesting and well written, Thomsen's work is otherwise typical except for a remarkable passage in the acknowledgment section of the book. Thomsen wrote "I wish to provide my gratitude toward the orchestrators of Georgia's University Digital Library of Georgia and the on-line GALILEO Project for providing this poor historian with easy access to digitized copies of hundreds of archived manuscript and papers concerning William Holland Thomas and his contemporaries' dealings with southern leadership and federal government on the behalf of the North Carolina Cherokee" (pp. 7–8).

As technological capabilities have expanded to enable more efficient storage of digital material, the amount of historical information in digital form (increasingly via the Web) has exploded. The Digital Library of Georgia, which enabled Paul Thomsen's work includes 500,000 digital objects in 90 collections. Other resources include high profile websites such as the New York Public Library's Digital Gallery, with more than 550,000 digitized primary sources and American Memory, a web resource from the Library of Congress, with more than 11 million individual primary sources available on its website. With expanded access to digital resources, students can stand side by side with professional historians and are able to generate their own interpretations about the past (Ayers, 1999b). Access to such material from remote sites continues to expand opportunities for historical analysis and interpretations (Burton, 2005; O'Malley & Rosenzweig, 1997). At the same time, some concern has been raised over the nature of the research facilitated by electronic resources, namely that resource availability might begin to drive the types of questions and problems which are being addressed (Rosenzweig, 2001).

As online content has expanded so too have alternatives for storing, accessing, and analyzing secondary historical resources. Reporting on the first five years of electronic publishing by the American Historical Association, Robert Townsend (2001) notes that electronic access has the capacity to remove some of the physical barriers between historians and the audience for their research. Although he was writing specifically about AHA publications, Townsend's comments are equally applicable to a wide range of historical materials. While not convinced that the Web is revolutionary with regard to historical work, Cohen (2004) suggests that the ability to present secondary historical information online is democratizing the profession and potentially expanding its reach and Barlow (1998) suggests that increased access to both primary and secondary historical resources has made the work of historical research less complicated or at least more straightforward. At the same time the presentation of historical materials, both primary sources and the products of analyses using primary sources have been impacted by new forms of media and design. Brown (2004) reports on new digital media and their impact on the presentation scholarship as presenting "new methods of telling stories and evaluating those stories" (p. 272).

Edward Ayers has written on the subject of how digital environments affect historical research with as much clarity as anyone. He suggests that there is a potential for a reemergent scientific history utilizing the power of analytical tools interacting with an increasingly rich set of content (Ayers, 1999b). Ayers (1999a), writing about his *Valley of the Shadow* project, comments on the benefits of these digital archives:

> The archive offers things machines offer: mass multiplicity, speed, reiteration, reflexivity, and precision. It gives us a great deal of material to think about and powerful tools to think with. It lets us take sources apart and put them together in new patterns. It suggests that even isolated and inert pieces of evidence—a list, a letter, a map, a picture—can assume new and unimagined meanings when placed in juxtaposition with other fragments. (para. 5)

Ayers (1999a) goes on to suggest that "the computer provides a powerful argument for thinking more rigorously, revealing patterns we could not see before" (para. 7).

American Studies scholar Randy Bass (n.d.) extends the notion of access and analytical capability by suggesting that online resources enlarge, in his words, "the space in which scholars and students can conduct their intellectual work. The enlarged space of interactive media enables the visualization and manipulation of objects, as well as the capacity to experiment with textual arrangements, organization, and argument" (para. 29). Specifically addressing visualization in history, David Staley (2003) posits that well organized and presented visual historical material can be a viable alternative to traditional historical prose. Staley (2003) like Brown (2003) views the visualization of the past as one of the most significant developments at the intersection of history and technology. Similarly, Lancaster and Bodenhamer (2002) detail how visualized history and geography can interact through geographic information systems, with analysis and interpretation facilitated by digital storage and powerful analytical software.

Another key impact of digital technologies to foster and support academic research arises from the development of online networks that offer asynchronous and synchronous opportunities to share professional and academic knowledge and information. Online networks, such as the H-Net family and the Center for the Study of Historical Consciousness at http://www.cshc.ubc.ca/ have been designed to create, what Barlow terms a "community of discourse" (Barlow, 1998). These electronic environments provide opportunities for scholars and students alike to share information and interact without the friction of distance. The general impact of these resources and others on the Web is affecting the spread of professional news and information (Sarantakes, 1999). Internet technology benefits the discipline by enabling connections and building bridges among scholars across the globe (Kornblith & Lasser, 2003) and increasing collaboration through this electronic access to information. Bass (n.d.) argues that these related forms of communication shift our current focus on individual "ownership" of ideas to a more community-based approach to idea ownership (para. 4) with alternatives for information sharing as facilitating a "shift from a one-to-many to a many-to-many model of communication" (para. 27). Fueling theses shifts are collaborative technologies commonly termed Web 2.0 that enabled not just information sharing but collaborative content generation using a wide range of continually evolving, primarily web-based tools (Boggs, 2007).

Benefits and challenges emerge from these digitally enhanced communities of history scholars with access to expanded bases of information. On the one hand, current and emerging information technologies make it possible to imagine new ways to study the past. Ayers (1999a) talks optimistically about these new approaches with regard to the amount of information available and with regard to the ability of people to use or manipulate information and ask questions of it, but he sees challenges as well. He suggests that historians "will be writing in an environment of plenitude, which could easily become an environment of excess without the greatest self-discipline" (Ayers, 1999a, para. 9). There is a greater possibility now for information and data overload as Ayers (1999b) notes:

> Everyone knows the past was wonderfully complex, but seeing the complexity of even a small slice of the past held in suspension before us in a digital

archive can be discomfiting. A digital archive...reminds us every time we look at it of the connections we are not making, of the complications of the past. (para. 10)

Barlow (1998) summarizes another series of challenges within the digital history environment. He is concerned about the issues of unreliability and lack of authority of electronic sources, as well as their mutability and volatility, and the significant potential for errors and dishonesty. Echoing these concerns, Lancaster and Bodenhamer (2002) cite the need for standards of information storage and documentation, without which errors can proliferate. Concerns such as these have been echoed by others, but none more powerfully than Roy Rosenzweig. Writing for the *Journal of American History*, Rosenzweig (2001) expresses concern regarding the expansion of privately funded and controlled digital repositories. He suggests that more and more of the information being converted to digital format are controlled by private organizations—which in turn has introduced some form of controlled access to the material. This control in the form of fee-based access may well inhibit the research endeavors of scholars with limited resources. But, even beyond economic considerations, the growth of separate controlled gateways to information may seriously complicate the researcher's ability to investigate all the pertinent and appropriate sources for his or her topic. Currently researchers must perform multiple searches through a range of different environments in hopes of locating all the desired material.

Additionally, Rosenzweig (2001) reminds us that even if the digitized historical content were accessible through one public gateway, the amount of historical material actually available digitally is far from comprehensive. Numerous historical sources have yet to be made available electronically—and some may never be digitized for reasons ranging from cost, control, and the sensitivity and/or physical vulnerability of the material. Rosenzweig (2001) suggests that the ease of digital access may encourage some researchers to follow the path of least resistance and only consider and use those resources that are electronically available, thus ignoring important historical sources that are currently housed in traditional archives. He asks: "Will digitization create a new historical research canon in which historians resort much more readily to works that can be found and searched easily on-line rather than sought out in more remote repositories" (p. 562)?

TECHNOLOGY ENRICHING THE PRESENTATION OF HISTORICAL MATERIALS

Current and emerging digital technologies have not only affected formal research in the discipline of history, but have also enabled historians to present their research in new and significantly different ways. Three such forms are hypertext, multimedia, and historical simulations.

Hypertext, a term coined by Theodor Nelson in 1965, can be used to reposition historical narrative and analysis as well as to expand the notion of footnotes by providing direct access to a range of related material. Given the importance of narrative in history, theory and discourse concerning hypertext and narrative is of central importance. Literary theorist and author Michael Joyce has written about the manner in which hypertext narrative decenters readers outside bounds set by traditional narrative. Joyce (1993) argues that narrative conforms to predefined modes of development built on structural requirements relating to meaning and consequentially the reader simply must consume the writer's product. In contrast, Joyce (1993) argues that hypertext is structure, as opposed to a product, and as such it invites readers to discover meaning. Within hypertexts, developers (or writers) enable emergent readings which may or may not conform to the developer's intent. Since the reader is empowered to add meaning to the document, given the way they interact with the text, the implications for historical interpretation are significant. Hypertext historical narratives may shift authority from a single interpretation and encourage multiple understandings.

The extent to which the reader is involved with the writer in constructing the text is an important ontological and epistemological issue in history. The nonlinear complexity supported by hypertext is a means to deal more effectively with the multiple sequences, voices, outcomes, and implications of historical narrative. Writers of hypertext historical narratives have the ability, through the construction of links, to creatively structure arguments within the narrative (Ayers, 1999a). Arne Solli (1998) also cites differences introduced by accessing historical materials enriched by the use of hypertext, arguing that traditional text is sequential and closed while hypertext is non-sequential and opened. These differences provide challenges as well as possibilities, but can supplement the tools available to the producers and consumers of history. Ayers (1999a) goes on to suggest that the effective use of hypertext can foster what he calls "a new kind of history, a history that can be arrayed and understood in multiple layers and sequences" (para. 8). Effective use of hypertext can provide both analytical and aesthetic benefits. According to Ayers (1999a), "it might bond analysis and evidence in rigorous ways impossible on a printed page. Or it could come to resemble high modernist fiction, glorying in complexity and connection" (para. 26).

Expanding on Ayers focus on the production of knowledge resources, Bass (n.d.) suggests that electronic information and analysis promotes a shift from linear to associative thinking for the users of digital materials (historical included) and that changes the emphasis—in both scholarship and teaching—"from knowledge as product to knowledge as process" (para. 4). These implications are echoed by Solli (1998) who references the non-sequential and nonlinear nature of much of the analysis and interpretation fostered by digital information and technology. However, while Solli (1998) recognizes the power of hypertext to allow historians to communicate in new ways by using new forms of scholarly discourse to disseminate historical knowledge, he takes care to acknowledge that hypertext is not a panacea. Such a balanced assessment of the potential of hypertext is shared by Graeme Davison (1998) in his recognition that the prospective benefits of the effective use of hypertext, in terms of its "potential for thinking about historical relationships in new configurations" (para. 1) He continues by imagining various "beginnings and endings" to hypertexts which would enable users to "exploit" links in the hypertext system in efforts to create and represent understandings (Davison, 1998, para. 1). But, Davison also counsels that hypertext can only add to, not totally transform the ways of communicating historical material. The reader/viewer still must provide his or her filter on the material. Davison (1998) continues by suggesting that hypertext might provide us with "powerful interpretive tools," but these tools are "inert" without associated education and training directed at supporting users as the construct meaning from the hypertext (para. 15). Tanka (2006) goes so far as to argue that when producing digital or nonlinear historical texts, historians need to deal with "the codes and practices that centuries of print have institutionalized in our society, especially the habits and expectations of the readers" (p. 99). In Tanka's own work on 19th century Japan, he uses the historical conventions of chronology, categories, and interpretation refashioned in an online presentation as annals, repetition, and linkages to "provide the reader with sufficiently familiar codes, despite the unfamiliarity of my conceptual structure" (Tanka, 2006, p. 99).

Digital historical narratives have seemingly been harder to produce than to theorize might suggest. Although the numbers are limited, three examples stand out as exemplars. One of the earliest efforts to publish in digital form, some historical scholarship is what Darnton (1999) imagined as a multilayered historical argument featuring six layers with the top layer being a concise version of the story or a simple narrative. The second layer is a non-narrative analytical expansion on selective themes in the top layer. The third layer includes documentary evidence possibly accompanied by interpretative essays. The fourth layer incorporates a historiographic discussion of the topic. The fifth layer is pedagogical. The sixth layer includes dialogue and commentary from readers. Darnton (2000) put his theory into practice with an article on 18th century Paris that includes extended text, discussion, and resources in support of a primary textual argument. A wider ranging online historical publication can be found in the American historical Association in partnership with Columbia University Press to publish hypertext digital versions of 21 books on a range of historical topics also published in print from 1999–2003. These online texts range in presentation from a simple collection of nodes (pages) with minimal links, to more complex presentations which include images, multiple nodes, and links. One of the most experimental digital historical texts is Thomas' and Ayers' (2003) work on the impact of slavery on the Civil War. The publication includes argumentative, analytical, and methodological sections as well as evidence, a historiography, and tools that collectively incorporate texts, primary resources, and visual presentations all focused on a central thesis.

The development and expanded use of multimedia have also opened up new opportunities for historians to organize and present less formal historical resources. Developments in multimedia allow texts to be supplemented by visuals and sound clips directed at providing a more complete view of the historical record. At first, these developments were facilitated by CD-ROM technology and, later, as bandwidth and transmission speed limitations have been increasingly addressed, through the World Wide Web. Numerous collections within *American Memory* provide examples of enriched experience with history via effective use of multimedia. The *Ease History Project*, at the University of Michigan, and *Historical Voices*, from Michigan State University, are additional examples of multimedia-based historical information available on the Web.[2] Commenting on the potential for using multimedia, oral historian Alistair Thomson (1998) notes that multimedia includes a wide array of textual, oral, visual, and video material. Thomas (1998) sees specific value in the manner, in which multimedia resources, in his words, "facilitate the simultaneous juxtaposition of diverse forms of evidence" (p. 594).

Daniel Cohen and Roy Rosenzweig (2005) developed a number of principles and suggestions for presenting multimedia historical materials in digital environments. In their book *Digital History: A Guide to Gathering, Preserving, And Presenting the Past on the Web*. Cohen and Rosenzweig argue that web-based historical materials should *"enable and inspire [one] to think about and grasp the past"* (Cohen & Rosenzweig, 2005, p. v). While they focus much attention on aesthetic and technical design issues, Cohen and Rosenzweig (2005) directly contend that the presentational attributes of digital historical resources influence the usability of these resources. Similarly, one of the authors of this chapter has presented principles for developing interpretive digital historical resources focusing on the use of (1) metaphors, symbols, images, visual aids, and textual scaffolds to frame the interpretations, (2) the presentation of resources that will invite active engagement and constructive interpretation, and (3) the presentation of resources in a nonlinear form such that they are malleable, well focused, and pertinent to the interpretation (Lee, 2002b).

With the rapid development of user-friendly technology tools and the move toward user-generated content on the Web (i.e., Web 2.0), a seemingly ever expanding number of multimedia enhanced historical interpretations are available online. These resources range from local presentations of sometimes discrete resources, to more coordinated efforts to present or interpret collections. Examples abound from Picturing American History[3] from the Center for Children and Technology to the Lakota Winter Counts[4] presentation at the Smithsonian.

Finally, there is the developing potential to use technology to conduct historical simulations to enrich both the analysis and experience of history. Ayers (1999b) strongly advocates the consideration and exploration of "new forms of participatory literature," or simulated worlds in which individuals can become immersed in an aspect of history, experiencing it in new and different ways.

> We can perhaps imagine simulated worlds that are accurate in their scale, their clothing and building styles, their language and their food. To some extent, such worlds already exist in historical reenactment. There is no reason that computers could not one day create virtual worlds that are even more satisfying in some dimensions than theses analog simulations. (Ayers, 1999b, para. 25)

What is becoming clear from the literature is that digital forms of expression and communication are expanding how history is presented and experienced. Like digital forms of access and analysis, these developments are enriching, while complicating, the expression of historical materials. While not all the advances in presentation formats are, at face value, productive, with careful preparation and contextualization, hypertext, multimedia, and simulation technologies can enhance the presentation of and engagement with historical materials.

TEACHING AND LEARNING USING DIGITAL HISTORY

Many of the advantages and issues involved with digital history for professional historians apply to the teaching and learning of history. Perhaps foremost among the advantages is the significantly greater access to primary and secondary sources (Vess, 2004). Both students and teachers can now directly access a range of material that can supplement what is traditionally available from the holdings of any one library. In documenting the extent of such access, Trinkle (1999) reported 10 years ago that almost half of college history instructors were requiring their students to use the Internet for research purposes—a number which has surely grown over the past several years. Anecdotal evidence can be found in specific reported uses of technology in university level instruction. In one such account, Stephens and Thumma, (2005) describe their experiences working with undergraduate history students in a collaborative research project aimed at creating digital historical representations related to specific stories in world history. Although they are cautious given existing cultural constraints on undergraduate research, Stephens and Thumma (2005) report success in generating a collaborative spirit around the work and in focusing their students' work within pedagogical contexts as opposed to research contexts, something they argue the flexibility of the technology enabled. The same level of pedagogical use does not appear to be evident in high school history classes. A recent national survey of high school social studies teachers found that the respondents generally accepted the need to use historical primary sources to support historical inquiry and they recognized the potential of the Web to provide access to previously difficult to access historical primary sources, but these teachers were found to be mostly infrequent users of web-based historical primary sources in their classrooms and were relatively unaware of robust history web sites such as *American Memory* (Hicks, Doolittle, & Lee, 2004). The participants in the survey expressed a need for more web-connected computers and more time in the curriculum as catalysts for increased web-based historical primary source in their classrooms (Hicks et al., 2004). The results of the survey, while illuminating the potential of the technology to support the teaching and learning of history, also supports Cantu and Wilson's (2003) assertion that: "With the growing number of technology and Internet proficient students in middle schools and high schools . . . the need for digital pedagogues in history classrooms is growing" (p. ix).

An area of more consistent pedagogical advantage with regard to using digital historical resources comes from the use of multimedia, especially through the use of visuals and sound clips to supplement traditional textual material. Newell (1997), a historian of early American history, cites the advantages of using such material to meet the learning styles of her students, who have grown up with more visual and auditory stimuli and with less skill with, and affinity for, the written word. Sarantakes (1999) further notes that "the multimedia nature of the Web also makes it an important tool for presentations. Teachers can bring sound, video, and images—be they photos, maps or drawings—into the classroom through the Web" (para. 6). Expanding on theses earlier conceptualizations of using imagery in history instruction, Ferster, Hammond, and Bull (2006) describe tools and resources which enable students at all levels to manipulate historical images for the purposes of constructing historical documentaries. Other teacher scholars (Coohill, 2006; Hoover, 2006; Robertson, 2006; Scheuerell, 2007; Taylor & Duran, 2006; Vess, 2006) have likewise highlighted the extent to which multimedia technologies are enabling a broader and more dynamic context for students to create and present historical research. Whether it be the use of audio visual materials (Taylor & Duran, 2006), podcasting (Lamb & Johnson, 2007), ipods (Vess, 2006), hypertext (Coohil, 2006), still imagery (Taylor & Duran, 2006) or digital literary materials Fitch (1997), the possibilities to expand history instruction through the use of digital technologies seems to enjoy wide spread consideration among some teachers particularly with regard to how their students create representations of their knowledge. Overall, these teacher scholars see a greater ability to deal more easily with interdisciplinary information and perspectives and a wider range of outlets for students' work using current digital technologies. Beyond just K–12 students and undergraduate students in history courses, Bolick and McGlinn (2004) describe how teachers can create content and pedagogical knowledge by taking advantage of the availability of particular digital resources that might not be available otherwise.

As these various forms for teachers and students to express their understanding of the past have emerged in the last several years, representations of teachers' and students' work have taken advantage of multimedia and all forms of digital historical media directed toward more constructivist modes of teaching and learning. Doolittle and Hicks, (2003) describe these constructivist approaches to teaching and learning social studies as capable of generating authenticity in the history classroom, allowing students to pursue ideas of personal interest while building on prior knowledge in autonomous, creative, and intellectual environments. Bass (n.d.) describes a version of constructivist learning, which he calls distributed learning, as student-centered and process-oriented, hinging on greater access to historical materials for students, especially primary sources, furthermore suggesting that students' work with these documents will significantly change the relationship of the novice learner to such materials, with attendant benefits to their own learning process.

Commenting on *Who Built America*, one of the earliest high profile multimedia digital historical teaching resources, William Friedheim (1997) noted that when used properly digital historical multimedia can position history, "as inquiry rather than . . . as received knowledge" arguing that digital historical resources can invite students "to interpret and link human experience, and to interrogate historical devices that come in many different shapes and formats" (para 6). Cohen (2004) suggests that much of these approaches to teaching history are being driven by the wide open and creative context that the Web provide for historians. For example multidimensional web-based formats for presenting historical information can allow student users to "chart their own paths, to make their own connections and interpretations, and even to question the construction of history" (Thomson, 1998, p. 594). Historian Andrea Winkler (2001) represents another example of these broadened approaches. In her work with a multimedia representation of medieval manuscripts, Winkler (2001) endorses the view that students' direct involvement with primary sources, facilitated by web-access, encourages constructivist thinking where students explore for themselves, "rather than seeing yet more static images that must be explained by a professor" (p. 202).

Although the digital environment offers a number of advantages for both teaching and learning, some challenges exist as well. The breadth of available information has a downside. Locating what you really need among all that is out there can be an enormous challenge. Secondary school history teacher Mark Newmark (2002) worries that the breadth of information and multiple forms of access can make online work "daunting and frustrating" (para. 2). Although popular search engines such as Google have significantly improved in recent years and academic search capabilities in libraries have also greatly improved, student users are still being challenged as they attempt to wade through the breadth of what they find. Without proper focus, students with less research training and sophistication can get frustrated, if not totally lost. Fitch recognizes the danger of simply "allowing students to follow multiple narratives when they have little awareness of history's linear structures" may do more harm than good (Fitch, 1997, p. 436). She like others is further concerned that allowing students to use the Web uncritically may encourage them to take the easy way out and not really develop good research skills. There is also the related and increasingly ominous potential for plagiarism. Access to so much material so easily invites the theft of intellectual property. Such concerns clearly illuminate the importance of carefully preparing students to engage in the sophisticated and systematic literacy work that is part and parcel of what it means to teach and learn the doing of history.

SUMMARY

The literature on digital history reveals that there is little debate that digital forms of history—for research, presentation, and teaching/learning—offer opportunities for extended communities interested in historical knowledge. The advantages and potential pitfalls of digital history are now better understood, much as the pros and cons of other research presentational and teaching/learning tools have been explored in the past. The discussion has generally moved beyond value judgments of whether electronic forms are good for the history profession, to a discussion of how best to utilize these expanding capabilities. Ayers, who has moved forward digital history technology as much as anyone, counsels that these new capabilities should be viewed as an extension and evolution, not a revolution, in historical scholarship. Writing of his concept of digital history, he suggests that we need "to abandon the language of displacement and substitute a language of enhancement, addition, and combination. . . . Digital history . . . need not undermine our traditional purposes and can serve as the basis for compelling narrative history of the kind that has long served our needs" (Ayers, 1999a, paras. 7 and 15). Developments in digital history have demonstrably affected the discipline, and offer the promise of continuing to do so, perhaps at increasing rates. Scholars are making extensive use of digital collections for their research. Teachers and students alike benefit from ready access to a great range of resources, in multiple forms, while traditional forms of historical materials continue to be enriched in exciting and challenging ways by developing technologies.

NOTES

1. Although an obscure topic at the time of Thomsen publication, the story of William Holland Thomas has since been popularized with the fictionally portrayal of Thomas as Will Cooper in Charles Frazier's, 2006 novel *Thirteen Moons*.
2. Ease History is available online at < http://www.easehistory.org> Historical Voices is online at < http://www.historicalvoices.org>
3. Picturing Modern America is available online at http://www.edc.org/CCT/PMA/
4. Lakota Winter Counts is available online at http://wintercounts.si.edu/

REFERENCES

Ayers, E. L. (1999a). *History in hypertext.* Retrieved September 20, 2007 from: http://jefferson.village.virginia.edu/vcdh/Ayers.OAH.html.

Ayers, E. L. (1999b). *The pasts and futures of digital history.* Retrieved September 20, 2007, from: http://jefferson.village.virginia.edu/vcdh/PastsFutures.html.

Barlow, J. (1998). Historical research and electronic evidence: Problems and practices. In D. A. Trinkle (Ed.), *Writing, teaching, and researching history in the electronic age* (pp. 194–225). Armonk, NY: M. E. Sharpe.

Bass, R. (n.d.). *The garden in the machine: The impact of American studies on new technologies.* Retrieved September 20, 2007, from: http://www.georgetown.edu/bassr/garden.html.

Boggs, J. (2007). Web 2.0 for historians: An introduction. *Journal of the Association for History and Computing, 10*(2). Retrieved September 20, 2007, from: http://mcel.pacificu.edu/jahc/jahcx2/boggs.html

Bolick, C., & McGlinn, M. M. (2004). Harriet Jacobs: Using online slave narratives in the classroom. *Social Education, 68*(3), 198–202.

Brown, J. (2004). Forum: History and the web. *Rethinking History, 8*(2), 253–275.

Burton, O. V. (2005). American digital history. *Social Science Computer Review, 23*(2), 206–220.

Cantu, D. A., & Wilson, W. J. (2002). *Teaching history in the digital classroom.* Armonk, NY: M. E. Sharpe.

Cohen, D. (2004). History and the second decade of the web. *Rethinking History,* 8(2), 293–301.

Cohen, D. J., & Rosenzweig, R. (2005). *Digital history: A guide to gathering, preserving, and presenting the past on the web.* Philadelphia: University of Pennsylvania Press.

Coohill, J. (2006). Images and the history lecture: Teaching the History Channel generation. *History Teacher, 39*(4), 455–465.

Darnton, R. (1999, March 12). A historian of books: Lost and found in cyberspace. *Chronicle of Higher Education,* B4.

Darnton, R. (2000). Presidential address: An early information society: News and the media in eighteenth-century Paris. *The American Historical Review, 105*(1). Retrieved October 31, 2007 from,: http://www.historycooperative.org/journals/ahr/105.1/ah000001.html

Davison, G. (1998). History and hypertext. *The Electronic Journal of Australian and New Zealand History.* Retrieved September 20, 2007, from: http://www.jcu.edu.au/aff/history/articles/davison.htm

Doolittle, P., & Hicks, D. (2003). Constructivism as a theoretical foundation for the use of technology in social studies. *Theory and Research in Social Education, 31*(1), 71–103.

Fitch, N. (1997). History after the web: Teaching with hypermedia. *The History Teacher, 30*(4), 427–441.

Ferster, B., Hammond, T., & Bull, G. (2006). PrimaryAccess: Creating digital documentaries in the social studies classroom. *Social Education, 70*(3), 147–150.

Friedheim, W. (1997). *Who built America? in the classroom.* Paper presented at the *American Historical Association Conference,* 1997, Retrieved September 20, 2007, from: http://www.ashp.cuny.edu/friedheim.html

Hicks, D., Doolittle, P., & Lee, J. K. (2004). History and social studies teachers' use of classroom and web-based historical primary sources. *Theory and Research in Social Education, 32*(2), 213–247.

Hoover, D. S. (2006). Popular culture in the classroom: Using audio and video clips to enhance survey classes. *History Teacher, 39*(4), 467–478.

Joyce, M. (1993). *Hypertext narrative.* Retrieved September 20, 2007, from: http://www.pd.org/topos/perforations/perf3/hypertext_narrative.html

Kornblith, G., & Lasser, C. (2003). More than bells and whistles? Using digital technology to teach American history. *Journal of American History, 89*(4), 1456–1457.

Lamb, A., & Johnson, L. (2007). Podcasting in the school library: Creating powerful Podcasts with your students. *Teacher Librarian, 34*(4), 61–64.

Lancaster, L., & Bodenhamer, D. (2002). The electronic cultural atlas initiative and the North American religion atlas. In A. K. Knowles (Ed.). *Past time, past place: GIS for history* (pp.163–78). Redlands, CA, ESRI Press.

Lee, J. K. (2002a). Digital history in the history/social studies classroom. *The History Teacher, 35*(4), 503–517.

Lee, J. K. (2002b). Principles for interpretative digital history web design. *Journal of the Association of History and Computing 5*(3). Retrieved September 20, 2007, from http://mcel.pacificu.edu/JAHC/JAHCV3/K-12/lee.html

Newmark, M. (2002). A call for a new generation of historical web sites. *Journal of the Association for History and Computing, 2*(3). Retrieved September 20, 2007, from: http://mcel.pacificu.edu/jahc/jahcII3/K12II3/Newmark.HTML

Newell, M. (1997). Subterranean digital blues; or, how a former technophobe learned to stop worrying and love multimedia. *Journal of American History, 83*(4), 1346–1352.

O'Malley, M., & Rosenzweig, R. (1997). Brave new world or blind alley? American history on the world wide web. *Journal of American History, 84*(1), 132–155.

Robertson, S. (2006). What's wrong with online readings? Text, hypertext, and the history web. *History Teacher, 39*(4), 441–454.

Rosenzweig, R. (1999). Crashing the system?: Hypertext and scholarship on American culture. *American Quarterly, 51*(2), 237–246.

Rosenzweig, R. (2001). The road to Xanadu: Public and private pathways on the history web. *The Journal of American History, 88*(2), 548–579.

Rosenzweig, R. (2003). Scarcity or abundance? Preserving the past in a digital era. *The American Historical Review, 108*(3), 735–762.

Sarantakes, N. E. (1999). So that a tree may live: What the World Wide Web can and cannot do for historians. *Perspectives: American Historical Association Newsletter, 37*(2), 21–22, 24.

Scheuerell, S. (2007). National History Day: Developing digital native historians. *History Teacher, 40*(3), 417–425.

Solli, A. (1998). Hypertext 'papers' on the web: Students confront the linear tradition. *Journal of the Association for History and Computing, 1*(2). Retrieved September 20, 2007, from: http://mcel.pacificu.edu/JAHC/Solli/Solindex.HTML.

Staley, D. (2003). *Computers, visualization, and history.* Armonk, NY: M. E. Sharpe.

Stephens, R., & Thumma, J. (2005). Faculty-undergraduate collaboration in digital history at a public research university. *History Teacher, 38*(4), 525–542.

Tanaka, S. (2006). New media and historical narrative: 1884 Japan. *Performance Research, 11*(4), 95–104.

Taylor, J., & Duran, M. (2006). Teaching social studies with technology: New research on collaborative approaches. *History Teacher, 40*(1), 9–25.

Thomsen. W. A. (2004). *Rebel chief: The motley life of colonel William Holland Thomas, C. S. A.* New York: Tom Doherty Associates.

Thomas, W. G., & Ayers, E. L. (2003). An overview: The differences slavery made: A close analysis of two American communities. *The American Historical Review, 108*(5). Retrieved October 31, 2007, from: http://www.historycooperative.org/journals/ahr/108.5/thomas.html

Thomson, A. (1998). Fifty years on: An international perspective on oral history. *Journal of American History 85*(2), 594.

Townsend, R. B. (2001). Lessons learned: Five years in cyberspace. *Perspectives.* Retrieved September 20, 2007, from: http://www.historians.org/perspectives/issues/2001/0105/0105aha1.cfm

Trinkle, D. A. (1999). History and the computer revolutions: A survey of current practices. *Journal of the Association for History and Computing, 2*(1). Retrieved September 20, 2007, from: http://mcel.pacificu.edu/jahc/jahcii1/articlesii1/trinkle/trinkleindex.html

Vess, D. (2004). History in the digital age: A study of the impact of interactive resources on student learning. *The History Teacher, 37*(3), 385–399.

Vess, D. (2006). History to go: Why iTeach with iPods. *History Teacher, 39*(4), 479–492.

Winkler, A. (2001). Digitized medieval manuscripts in the classroom. *The History Teacher, 35*(2), 201–224.

LaVergne, TN USA
19 March 2010
176607LV00002B/35/P